THE LAW MULTIPLE

In the field of socio-legal studies or law and society scholarship, it is rare to find empirically rich and conceptually sophisticated understandings of actual legal practice. This book, in contrast, connects the conceptual and the empirical, the abstract and the concrete, and in doing so shows the law to be an irreducibly social, material and temporal practice. Drawing on cutting-edge work in the social study of knowledge, it grapples with conceptual and methodological questions central to the field: how and where judgment empirically takes place; how and where facts are made; and how researchers might study these local and concrete ways of judging and knowing. Drawing on an ethnographic study of how narratives and documents, particularly case files, operate within legal practices, this book's unique and innovative approach consists of rearticulating the traditional boundaries separating judgment from knowledge, urging us to rethink the way truths are made within law.

IRENE VAN OORSCHOT is Senior Lecturer at Erasmus University College, Rotterdam. Emphasizing ethnographic research methods, her research concentrates on the situated character of practices of knowing, valuing, and decision-making. Drawing on socio-legal studies and science and technology studies, she has published on legal modes of knowledge production, the role of narrative in legal settings, the materiality and temporality of legal case files, and the construction of cases in sociological research.

CAMBRIDGE STUDIES IN LAW AND SOCIETY

Founded in 1997, Cambridge Studies in Law and Society is a hub for leading scholarship in socio-legal studies. Located at the intersection of law, the humanities, and the social sciences, it publishes empirically innovative and theoretically sophisticated work on law's manifestations in everyday life: from discourses to practices, and from institutions to cultures. The series editors have longstanding expertise in the interdisciplinary study of law, and welcome contributions that place legal phenomena in national, comparative, or international perspective. Series authors come from a range of disciplines, including anthropology, history, law, literature, political science, and sociology.

A list of books in the series can be found at the back of this book.

THE LAW MULTIPLE

Judgment and Knowledge in Practice

IRENE VAN OORSCHOT

Erasmus University Rotterdam

CAMBRIDGE
UNIVERSITY PRESS

CAMBRIDGE
UNIVERSITY PRESS

University Printing House, Cambridge CB2 8BS, United Kingdom

One Liberty Plaza, 20th Floor, New York, NY 10006, USA

477 Williamstown Road, Port Melbourne, VIC 3207, Australia

314–321, 3rd Floor, Plot 3, Splendor Forum, Jasola District Centre, New Delhi – 110025, India

79 Anson Road, #06–04/06, Singapore 079906

Cambridge University Press is part of the University of Cambridge.

It furthers the University's mission by disseminating knowledge in the pursuit of education, learning, and research at the highest international levels of excellence.

www.cambridge.org
Information on this title: www.cambridge.org/9781108494809
DOI: 10.1017/9781108859981

First published 2021

A catalogue record for this publication is available from the British Library.

Library of Congress Cataloging-in-Publication Data
Names: Oorschot, Irene van, 1986– author.
Title: The law multiple : judgment and knowledge in practice / Irene van Oorschot, Senior Lecturer, Erasmus University Rotterdam.
Description: Cambridge, United Kingdom ; New York, NY : Cambridge University Press, 2020. | Series: Cambridge studies in law and society | Includes bibliographical references and index.
Identifiers: LCCN 2020021131 (print) | LCCN 2020021132 (ebook) | ISBN 9781108494809 (hardback) | ISBN 9781108859981 (ebook)
Subjects: LCSH: Practice of law – Social aspects. | Sociological jurisprudence.
Classification: LCC K120 .O56 2020 (print) | LCC K120 (ebook) | DDC 340/.115–dc23
LC record available at https://lccn.loc.gov/2020021131
LC ebook record available at https://lccn.loc.gov/2020021132

ISBN 978-1-108-49480-9 Hardback

To my mother

CONTENTS

FIGURES

ACKNOWLEDGMENTS

I wish here to thank, first and foremost, the judges who were so kind to share their time and their thoughts, hesitations and doubts included. My gratefulness extends, too, to the clerks and administrative personnel who were so kind to take me under their wing. I cannot mention your names here, but know that I feel grateful to have learned from you.

I also wish to acknowledge the funding bodies that have enabled me to write this book: The Dutch Scientific Research Council (research project *Inequality in Sentencing Types: The Importance of Institutionalized Decision-Making*), and the European Research Council (*RaceFaceID*, principal investigator: Professor Amade M'charek).

This book has benefited from kind and critical commentary from many sources. I wish to mention here especially the participants at the Law and Science AHRC network symposium, the annual conference of the Dutch Society for the Sociology of Law (VSR), and the members of the European Sentencing and Penal Decision-Making Group (particularly Neil Hutton and Cyrus Tata). I also thank the anonymous reviewers of *Social & Legal Studies*, *Journal for Law and Society*, *Symbolic Interaction*, and Emily Grabham and Sian Beynon-Jones for their comments on the pieces that were to form the basis of Chapter 3, 4, and 5. I am also grateful to the cherished reading group Les Filles Sophies, whose unrelenting commitment to thinking ideas in relation to bodies, abstractions in relation to concrete existence, has shaped my own thinking vis-à-vis fallacious abstractionism. A special mention is in place for the Monitoring seminar crowd: Willem Schinkel, Rogier van Reekum, Sanne Boersma, Maja Hertoghs, Friso van Houdt, Anne Slootweg, Jess Bier, and Eva Gemert. Starting as a reading seminar, our monthly meetings quickly turned into so much more: A space to read, think, and experiment together – all in deep regard and friendship. I also wish to thank Lieke Wissink, Ildiko Plajas, Lisette Jong, Ryanne Bleumink, Roos Hopman, and Denitsa Gancheva for working with me on various projects throughout the final stages of writing this book, and for their friendship.

I thank, too, Angelique van Dam, for her friendship and her loving commitment to slow, ethical social science.

Peter Mascini, Don Weenink, and Romke van der Veen have also offered crucial support in the writing of this book by providing me with space to stop and start over – and stop and start over again. Amade M'charek, always challenging me to stay with the trouble, has played an important role in shaping my attention to the messy character of socio-material practices. Thank you. I thank, too, Robin van den Akker for his trust in me and for giving me the time to work on this book in its final stages. I also wish to express gratitude to Cees Boos, for his near endless patience with the editing and indexing of this book, and to Marianne Nield, for guiding me through the publication process.

My father and my two big little brothers: Thank you for being there in the worst of times and in the best of times.

Niels, my loving partner, and our newly arrived little Sep: Thank you for enriching my life.

My mother, alive for much of this book's writing, passed away before she could witness its publication. It is only upon completion of the book that I realized how much of the book's arguments have been informed by her sensibilities and temperament. From her, I learned to distrust the comfort of purified abstractions. From her, too, I learned to attend to the mundane, the messy, the concrete – in other words, learned to pay attention to the beautiful business of living, here, now, together with others. In loving memory, I dedicate this book to her.

NOTE ON THE TEXT

Chapters 3, 4, and 5 offer more or less reworked versions of arguments appearing in multiple venues. Parts of Chapter 4 have been published in Oorschot, I. van, Mascini, P. and Weenink, D. (2017), "Remorse in Context(s): A Qualitative Exploration of the Negotiation of Remorse and its Consequences" in *Social & Legal Studies* 26(3): 359–377 Copyright © 2017 (Sage). DOI: https://doi.org/10.1177/0964663916679039. Parts of Chapter 5, as well as parts of its arguments, have been published as Oorschot, I. van (2014a) "Seeing the Case Clearly: File-Work, Material Mediation and Visualizing Practices in a Dutch Criminal Court" in *Symbolic Interaction* 37(4): 439–457. Chapter 6 has appeared in slightly edited form as a chapter "Doing Truths, Doing Times: The Legal Case File as a Folded Object" in the volume *Law & Time* edited by S. Beynon-Jones and E. Grabham, Routledge.

1

Troubling Encounters

1.1 Ways of Case-Making: A Provocation

This book is a testament to a journey through social scientific and judicial case-making practices. That is, it seeks to take seriously how judges as well as social scientists make their case about the world: How, in other words, judges and social scientists draw on words, people, and things to produce an account of the way things are. The notion of case-making is used here speculatively, provocatively perhaps: Not as a way to suggest judges and social scientists may, after all, have a lot in common, but rather to propose that we take seriously the very different *practices* that go into making a case about the world, in the world. In so doing, this book commits itself to an understanding of social and legal life as practical, and occasionally messy business: always ongoing, never not concrete, irreducibly multiple.

This book concentrates, first, on the truths and facts sociologists have produced about legal practices. It is concerned with the questions of *what* these social scientific observers have seen when they cast their eyes on these practices; *how* they have seen what they have seen; and which *realities* they have enacted in their approaches. Second, this book zooms in on the ways judges, clerks, administrative personnel, and case files in a Dutch criminal court become instrumental in judicial ways of finding out "what really happened" and ways of qualifying these events legally. Drawing on an ethnography of judicial work practices, it is interested in the practicalities and technicalities of constructing, out of the very different accounts present in the file and offered in court, a serviceable, pragmatic truth to be judged. Third, it also aims to account for and reflect on the ways *this* case – the book you are holding in your hands – is made, and an attempt to work through the necessary methodological and conceptual challenges that accompany the making of such a case. Taken together, these questions produce an account of a close encounter with the ingredients of judicial case-making practices – case files, clerks, judges, courtrooms, routines, and procedures – as well as a story about sociology and the law, knowledge and judgment, more generally.

1.2 Is/Ought Conundrums

Knowledge and judgment, after all, tend to be treated as radically distinct species. On the one hand, there is knowledge, which emerges when we let the world speak for itself and adjust our expectations – our theories, our stories – accordingly. Judgment, in contrast, consists of retaining our normative expectations even when these are breached, when the world disappoints them (cf. Luhmann 2004). The distinction between knowledge and judgment is between that which passes as valid under the governing logic of facts – de facto – and that which passes as valid under the governing logic of norms – de jure. In this capacity, knowledge and judgment, de facto and de jure, are mapped quite closely onto the difference between science and law. Even though both science and law can be understood as "two institutions for making order" (Jasanoff 2007: 761), both are fundamentally at odds on their relationship with the world. If science seeks to know, law seeks to intervene. Science represents, law decides.

This demarcation between kinds of statements (is versus ought) and kinds of practices (science versus law) has some practical use, not least because it safeguards and protects these practices against each other. After all, is it not frightening to imagine a science that is blind to reality, concerned only with passing judgment? How tyrannical would such a science be! And, is it not ridiculous to require verdicts to be subjected to scientific tests of factual accuracy? We all know how scientists can never seem to agree on anything, how no scientific judgment is ever the last word . . . We wouldn't be able to make decisions! The distinction between de jure and de facto helpfully ensures the identity and distinctness of these practices – especially necessary, perhaps, given the fact that both practices draw so uneasily on a similar vocabulary of proof, validity, facts, and truth, similar rituals of verification in juries of peers, and similar-sounding appeals to the necessities of capitalized abstractions of (scientific or legal) Law and Order. The binary pairs of fact/

norm, is/ought, science/law help to manage both this potential for miscommunication and, importantly, judgment in the name of science, and truth in the name of the norm.

Yet like all binary pairs, however, these distinctions do not only *contain*, but also *create* trouble – most crucially, of course, for those people, things, or practices that do not fit wholly and neatly into either of its classificatory slots. In this capacity, such troubles are *good to think with*, as they put the self-evidence of such distinctions in doubt. Let me introduce you to one such occasion for thinking. Its principal ingredients? Three social scientific researchers; one peer-reviewed study of sentencing disparities in Dutch criminal courts; some newspapers; a political actor here and there; public shock; and most importantly: A weary, even disgruntled judiciary.

1.3 Speaking Truth to Law

It is March 2012, and my fieldwork among the files, administrative staff, clerks, and judges of a lower criminal court in the Netherlands upon which this book is based is yet to commence. Aside from some exploratory interviews with both practicing and retired judges, I have yet to gain entry to the criminal court where I hope to study judicial decision-making practices. It is in this month, too, that a brief controversy about precisely these judicial decision-making practices evolves in the pages of Dutch newspapers (see e.g., *NRC* March 14, 2012; *NRC* March 15, 2012; *Algemeen Dagblad* March 14, 2012). The immediate cause for the media attention is the publication of a social scientific study of sentencing disparities in the *Dutch Jurists' Magazine* (*Nederlands Juristenblad* or *NJB*). This study, which was developed and published by three researchers associated with Leiden University, had found that lower-court magistrate judges (Dutch: *politierechters*) tend to punish certain defendant populations more harshly than others (Wermink, de Keijser and Schuyt 2012a). These lower-court magistrate judges, the authors demonstrated, are more likely to opt for an unconditional prison sentence in cases involving foreign-looking and non-Dutch-speaking defendants than in cases involving Dutch-looking and Dutch-speaking defendants.

The study was received with puzzled shock. How could this be? Does the law not promise equality before the law? Do judges not aim to treat like cases alike? In an editorial, the politically centrist *NRC Handelsblad* for instance concluded that the "intuitive judge has been caught out" (*NRC* 2012, March 15) and that "lady Justice's blindfold" seems an "illusion, not a self-evident professional characteristic." Emphasizing that "judges are not immune to stereotypes," it suggested that further large-scale studies should be conducted, and raised the following questions: "Are criminal law judges sufficiently aware of the influence of negative stereotypes? Is there attention paid to such issues throughout their education and collegial feedback [*intervisie*]? Do people correct each other there or is this study a bolt from the blue? Are there, moreover, enough criminal law judges with a non-Dutch cultural background?" (*NRC* 2012, March 15).

In the wake of this media attention, not only did the National Minority Counsel (LOM) express their shock with the study's conclusions, members of Parliament, Recourt (PvdA, centrist Labour Party), Dibi (the Green Left), and van der Steur (VVD, the largest Liberal party) each submitted sets of formal questions to the then Minister of Security and Justice (Minister van Veiligheid en Justitie) Opstelten. These documents raised the question whether the Minister shares the researchers' conclusions "that negative stereotyping with regards to defendants with a foreign appearance play a role in their greater likelihood of receiving a harsher sentence," and queried what actions the Minister would undertake to make sure that "judges do not weigh the defendant's appearance in their sentencing decisions anymore" (Kamerstukken II 2011/12). In response, the Minister mobilized the help of the Scientific Research and Documentation Centre (WODC), whose critical appraisal of the study informed his formal reply to the Parliament. In that document, Minister Opstelten doubted the study's validity, stating that

> relevant variables that are often weighed up in the punishment stage, like having a permanent home address and a steady income, possible drug addiction, and flight risk, have not been included in the research. . . . Furthermore, variables like the severity of the case, [the defendant's] criminal record, and custody have not sufficiently been controlled for. A large measure of uncertainty surrounds the strength of the reported correlations.
>
> (Ministerie van Veiligheid en Justitie [Ministry of Security and Justice] 2012: 2)

It is for these reasons, the Minister concluded, that "the model used diverges from the practice of judgment," and that, for now, it is impossible to draw robust conclusions about the choice of punishment by police judges with regard to persons with a foreign appearance (Ministerie van Veiligheid en Justitie [Ministry of Security and Justice] 2012: 2).

1.4 Judges Speaking Back

While the controversy died a somewhat silent death in the media, its conclusions would linger on among members of the judiciary. The Council for the Judiciary (Raad voor de Rechtspraak), for instance, asked the Leiden researchers to design and execute a more methodologically sophisticated study into the judicial decision-making processes (see de Rechtspraak 2015: 6). Two practicing judges, furthermore, replied briefly to the study's findings in the same Dutch Jurists' Magazine later in 2012 (Bade and van der Nat 2012: 973). There, the two judges pointed out that it may be defendants' lack of income and lack of permanent home address, not their foreign looks, that could plausibly account for judges' choices for a prison term. Provocatively, the judges suggest that "the research seems partial," even raising the question whether the "researchers have any idea how a judge arrives at a sentencing decision?" (Bade and van der Nat 2012: 973).

In many of my later conversations with judges I would encounter similar frustrations. Many of them felt that the authors of the study did not appear to know much about judicial decision-making practices. And as a result of that lack of familiarity, it was suggested, the researchers had failed to do justice to their work. In fact, the study had rendered their own work practices alien and unrecognizable. All in all, its portrayal of their practices seemed partial at best, and distorted at worst. Judge Beech, frustrated but articulate, for instance commented that:

> At no point do I side-line the law just because I see that a defendant is from an ethnic minority. That is just ridiculous, and I resent the implication. I don't recognize what we do in what they are saying. Listen, we have our ways of dealing with cases: we have the information, we have the files. That and the law is what is important to us.

Placing knowledge of individual cases and the law in the hands of judges themselves, Judge Beech contests the researchers' credentials – what do they know anyway? – as well as the accuracy of their portrayal of judicial practices. Appealing to local knowledge – "we have the information, we have the files" – Judge Beech suggested that the study's portrayal of judicial practices is a highly specific kind of portrayal; a portrayal that distorts these practices beyond all recognition. It is as if the researchers were speaking about a different reality than that of the judges. The study and its aftermath among the members of the judiciary, then, points in the direction of a controversy over knowledge, recognition, and perhaps even respect. Perhaps the researchers merely sought to speak the truth, but their study was received as both a distorted picture and indictment of judicial decision-making practices. But – to paraphrase judicial discomfort – what do they know anyway? And by extension: Who are they to judge?

1.5 Thinking with the Trouble

The study had clearly touched a nerve. Now, it may be tempting to make sense of judges' frustrations with reference to their professional "blind spots" and their professional pride. Of course they are hurt, or anxious, or frustrated, the argument may go: After all, the study debunks a dearly held professional engagement with equality before the law. Neither is it uncommon, sociologists might add, for people to exhibit some discomfort at having been turned into objects of study, especially if the sociologist manages to lay bare some inconvenient truths, for instance that a social practice that promises equality in actual fact reproduces social inequalities. Of course, this approach to the controversy places the researchers in a privileged, epistemic position vis-à-vis the judges studied: While judges may *think* they treat like cases alike, in *actual fact* they reproduce social inequalities. And while the law may want to keep up the appearance of equal treatment, its promise is just that: an appearance beyond which social scientists find a more fundamental truth. "Forgive them, for they know not what they do": This is one way to make sense of the controversial status of the study among the practicing members of the Dutch judiciary. After all, knowledge is expressly not what the law is seeking. It merely seeks to judge, and in so doing must remain blind to the social determinants and consequences of judgment. Meanwhile, who is to blame social scientists for telling the truth? Surely their account should not be taken to be a judgment? Reading the controversy this way, we manage to reinstate the imperative that judges judge, and scientists speak the truth. In a way, this way of dealing with the controversy denies its existence, suggesting that judges may simply be sore losers who better stick to their trade – judgment – while sociological observers stick to theirs – truth telling. No category mistakes have to be made, no crossings between law and science, between knowledge and judgment, have to occur (Latour 2013).

But such crossings do in fact occur – otherwise there would be no controversy here to begin with. We might just need another way to deal with the controversy, then; a way that takes judges' objections quite seriously. For something we do not consider, if we are content to sideline these concerns as merely "hurt feelings," is that these judges might quite simply be right. That is: It might just be the case that social scientific accounts do much more than simply tell the truth about a singular world. Indeed, it might just be the case that social scientific accounts are rooted in active and specific interventions in the world, and that they shape the world about which they speak. What the judges are getting at, I think, is this performative dimension of knowledge-generating practices, that is the way knowledge-making practices shape and delineate their object in specific ways, perhaps even doing so in ways not easily commensurable with other ways of knowing the world, other "ways of world-making" (Goodman 1978). As such, the judges' discomfort points to a first conceptual trouble which is central here: the trouble presented by the fact that social scientific accounts do more than just "tell the truth" about the world. Taking this controversy seriously, then, demands that we try to understand and *account for* these *performative effects* of our knowledge practices (Haraway 1988).

Given the controversy, here is a second thing to consider: Judges may also be right to question social scientific researchers about what they think they know about judicial practices. To reiterate Bade and van der Nat's (2012) provocative question: *Do* we have any idea as to how judges arrive at a sentencing decision? That is, how do "we" – social scientific observers – tend to understand these decision-making practices, and crucially: What are we missing out on? Staying with the troubling controversy hence calls for a critical account of the work our own observations are doing in rendering judicial practices intelligible. Such an account would also, to my mind, attend to perplexities and aporias – a-poros, that which we do not manage to pass through – in our understanding of these practices. Especially provoking, in this case, is the contrast drawn between sociological understandings of judicial practices and "our own way of dealing with cases." While sociologists may have one way to "deal with cases," what are judges' ways to deal with cases? Judge Beech's comments point to concrete practices of case-making: of having "all the information, and the files," so that judges may come to a sense of what it is they must do. In that capacity, her comment also points to "epistemic practices" (Lynch 1993) within these judicial practices, that is for instance local ways of evaluating evidence, of constructing a story, of attributing plausibility to different scenarios, and of arriving at an operative sense of the truth of the matter. The controversial study missed out on precisely these local ways of finding out what happened, local ways of "seeing the case," local ways of deciding on punishment. Can we develop tools to remain sensitive to these local practices of case-making?

On a theoretical level, then, the controversy complicates a convenient mapping of judgment and knowledge onto, respectively, the law and science. There is more to social scientific accounts than just facts: They seem to be active in the making of worlds. There is, on the other hand, more to judicial practices than just judgment: There, too, an operative sense of "what really happened" must be arrived at. Scientific practices do not yield mere representation; neither are judicial practices indifferent to the facts. In a way, both are case-making practices: Ways to shape, delineate, and organize facts, and ways consequential to the realities these facts are ostensibly drawn from. These case-making practices represent the troubles and impurities that dwell at the borders of our demarcations: The fact of performativity in scientific, representational practices on the one hand, and on the other, that fact of epistemic practices within judicial practices. My efforts consist of staying with these troubles (Haraway 2016) and to see how these ways of case-making proceed in action. These efforts translate into three questions, which together make up the core of this book.

The first problematic is both specific and general, in that it wants to attend to the specifics of the aforementioned study, but also seeks to situate it vis-à-vis conceptualizations of the relationship between sociology and the law more generally. What are the limitations and productivities of sociological descriptions of the law anyway? Can the effort to define, describe, and know the law do justice to the law at all? What do these descriptions render visible and make possible – and what do they render invisible, and impossible? How, in other words, are sociological cases made about the law, and what realities are hence enacted?

The feeling, among judges, that their practices are being misrepresented of course raises the question whether there are different ways to represent these practices, grounded perhaps in different empirical engagements with judicial practices. Reading the exasperated question whether "the researchers have any idea what our practices look like," as an invitation, I aim to develop conceptual and empirical means to take seriously the everyday practices of case-making in a criminal court. How are cases dealt with, taking into account both "the law" and, to speak with Judge Beech again, "the information, the files"? In other words, how are judicial cases made in actual practices?

Questions multiply further as I allow these questions to affect my own knowledge-seeking practices. What does it take, methodologically and conceptually, to account for the case I myself am making? How do I position myself in relation to these legal practices and the dense packing of sociological descriptions around these practices? Do I need to accept a scientific role as a producer of facts, and facts only, or may I try to rearticulate just what it means to do description? How, in the midst of these case-making practices, do I make my case?

1.6 Abstract Accounts and the Concreteness of Practice

Staying with these troubles and trying to answer these three questions is, in this case, also an effort to *stay with the concrete*. In this book, I develop the argument that attempts to map knowledge onto science and judgment onto law has the unfortunate side effect of rendering the concrete practices of both "law" and "science" difficult to apprehend. For instance, once we adopt a conception of law as *really* being about judgment and science as *really* about truth, it is tempting to slide into the suggestion that law is *only* about judgment and science *only* about truth – and that other, more troubling practices are therefore out of bounds. As we will see throughout Chapter 2, "Abstractionism Revisited," this tendency to slide from the "really" to the "only" is very much with us today and exercises a strong conceptual pull on both legal positivists and social scientific observers of the law. Their attempts to radically distinguish between the normativity of the law and the factuality of science either slide into purification, in which the distinction between law and science is rigidly asserted, or else is rearticulated in the form of a problematic perspectivism, within which different conceptions of the law are argued to be rooted in the observer's location "inside" or "outside" the law. Neither of these two solutions, I argue, puts us in touch with the robust and concrete character of legal or scientific realities. Indeed, even Latour's sociology of law (2013, 2010) falls prey to this tendency towards purified abstraction, particularly so in his *An Inquiry into Modes of Existence* (2013). While he traces a trajectory through the concrete practices taking place in the highest administrative Court of France – the Conseil d'État – his sociology of law, too, is one that reinstates, after all his ambulations, the distinction between law and science, hence purifying them both of troublesome noise. Tracing the fact–norm distinction through these debates, I zoom in on a tendency William James (1909) calls "vicious abstractionism." This intellectual tendency proceeds by way of "singling out some salient or important feature" of a "concrete situation" – for instance, truth in the concrete situation that is science, judgment in the concrete situation that is the law – after which we reduce "the originally rich phenomenon to the naked suggestions of that name abstractly taken, treating it as a case of 'nothing but' that concept" (James 1909: 110). In so doing we miss out on the opportunity to do justice to concrete troubles: Truth-making in legal practices, and world-making in scientific practices. This is not to say that all abstraction is necessarily wrong: James quips, for instance, that without abstractions we merely "hop on one foot" (James 1909: 109). After all, it is only in the encounter between the abstract and the concrete that we manage to make ourselves capable of inquisitive movement: "using concepts along with the particulars, we become bipedal. We throw our concept forward, get a foothold on the consequence, hitch our line to this, and draw our precept up, travelling thus with a hop, skip, and jump over the surface of life at a vaster rapider rate" (James 1909: 109). While we need both the abstract and the concrete to move about at all, then, abstractions may also fail us in our attempts to "hop, skip, and jump." Faced with the troubling presence of performativities in social scientific accounts and truth-making within legal practices, abstracted accounts may not organize and order concrete experience satisfactorily, and as such fail to operate as "tools to think with," and think *through*, the specificity and concreteness of the practices we encounter (Stengers 2005). That is, if we accept that the law is really, and only, about judgment, we miss out on the opportunity to study and trace how, within legal practices, knowledge of the reality it seeks to judge is arrived at. To be more precise: Once we purify our conceptions of law to include only that which we call legal and exclude "the remainder of things" (Whitehead 1953: 73) we encounter in concrete experiences, we have lost the ability to do justice to these concrete, if troubling, practices. The same goes for our understanding of scientific practices. If we accept the dictum that science is really and only about faithful representation of the world out there, we have lost the ability to do justice to the performative dimensions of our knowledge practices. Dupret, Lynch, and Berard call such purification "hyper-explanations" (2015: 4): In trying to explain everything legal or scientific, such accounts actually explain very little at all.

Having discussed the limitations of abstractionism, then, this chapter also aims to give conceptual flesh and bone to a turn towards the concrete. The conceptual movement I make there is in many ways indebted to pragmatist philosophy and its sociological incarnations, that is, ethnomethodology and actor-network theory in particular. There, I show that one way out of the law–science conundrum – and with that, one way to stay with the troubles – is to rethink first what, concretely, we do when we do "description" and "representation," and second, what concretely goes on in sites, settings, or practices we point to as locations of "the law." This "pragmatic respecification," as I have come to call it, is a way of attending to the practicalities and technicalities of knowing and judging. That is, it approaches both knowing and judging as situated accomplishments. These accomplishments, furthermore, always involve practical skills, as well as concrete methods of gathering together, ordering, and classifying information, either in the form of a social scientific method, or in the form of the case file. This also means that the abstractions we fashion to understand and account for these practices of knowing and judging must, in some way or another, be able to attend to these practical and concrete realities.

Crucially, then, this chapter is not meant as a way to transcend the opposition between sociologists and legal positivists, but rather as a way to find concrete paths to follow when a reliance on the capitalized abstractions of law and science are failing us. Thinking of both science and law in concrete terms, I suggest, allows us to salvage both modest description (something social scientists are sure to welcome) and the practical robustness of legal practices (an appreciation of which is sure to matter to judicial decision-makers). Of course, this salvaging comes at a certain cost. On the one hand, it will require, on the researcher's part, an accountability (Haraway 1988) with regard to the things we do in, with, and to realities when we make knowledge. On the other hand, we will also need to include in our accounts of law those non-human things crucial to the law's practical operation, and especially of that entity which transports and transforms facts with regard to the case: The case file.

1.7 Hopping, Skipping, Jumping: One Journey, Four Interventions

With an emphasis placed on concrete legal practices and the concreteness of social scientific representation, the journeying can commence. My ambulations take off with the Leiden study once more. Equipped with a vocabulary to do justice to its performative dimensions, I will raise the question how this study enacts judicial decision-making practices in Chapter 3, "Dealing with Difference." What are the consequences of treating judicial cases as bundles of legal and social characteristics? How is the promise of "equality before the law" operationalized? How is "the law" itself reconfigured as a result of its analyses? And what kind of population (e.g., of cases, of individuals) does this analysis presuppose? Together, these questions bring us closer to zooming in on a crucial performativity of social scientific accounts of judicial practices, especially those assisted by quantitative measurement and statistical analysis. That is, my analysis shows how statistical accounts of legal practices tend to group together individual cases or aspects of individual cases as "the same" and "different" in ways that are not necessarily commensurable with the way "sameness" and "difference" are seen and produced within legal practices themselves. In so doing I show not simply that the research was, indeed, "partial" – all research is! – but precisely how this partial perspective was made and how it produces a specific and hence limited account not only of sentencing disparities, but indeed of the law itself.

Sensitized to the limitations of this statistically informed mode of approaching judicial practices, I will then take you with me into the field: a criminal court in the Netherlands. There, I traced the practices the Leiden study sought to make intelligible, that is the practices of lower court magistrate judges (*politierechters*). These judges preside over the court proceedings on their own (as opposed to judges in the "multiple chamber," which is composed of three judges), and adjudicate and sentence relatively mild offenses, punishable with up to one year in prison. Their caseloads, I would learn, are high, and their work practice is paced to match. Dealing with the vast majority of criminal court cases nationally (in 2010 for instance, magistrate judges dealt with roughly 85 percent of all criminal court cases, see Ministerie van Veiligheid en Justitie (2010), these police judges combine the role of fact- and law-finder. They are assisted by clerks who prepare their cases for them and who take notes during the court session, and draw extensively on the official *dossier* in their pretrial preparations. Indeed, entering the court is in many ways an encounter not only with human actors, but also with the nonhuman ingredients of bureaucratic practices: case files. While the Leiden study emphasizes inputs and outputs to the judicial decision, I now found myself in the middle of a specific ecology of practice (cf. Stengers 2005), a world composed of humans and nonhumans, of spoken and written words, of rather docile subjects – defendants placed before the law – and of recalcitrant objects – case files that are never quite as easily navigable and readable as one would like. Informal conversations with many of its practicing judges, clerks, and administrative personnel, observations of courtroom proceedings, careful "shadowing" of fourteen judges in their preparatory, file-based work practices and their decision-making in court, as well as a study of over 250 individual case files confronted me with entirely different ways of case-making. In this specific ecology of practice, I followed up on the Leiden study to open the "black box" of judicial decision-making and to see how judging takes place in practice.

I quickly learned, however, that there is not one way to account for such practices, not one answer to the question. Take for instance that most visible, most studied, most dramaturgically rich dimension of legal practices: the court session. There, I learned, accounts are elicited, truth and falsehood are at stake, and the "soul" (Foucault 1977) of the deviant subject becomes a matter of empirical interest: Is s/he really sorry? Is he or she remorseful? Curiously, however, while the social scientific study of remorse in legal settings has generally testified to its crucial importance to legal decision-makers, it has neglected to delve into the way it is enacted in court. How, in other words, do defendants manage to "perform remorse" in court? How do judges make sense of defendants' remorsefulness? How is it weighed and evaluated – and what are its consequences to judicial decision-making? In Chapter 4, "Situating Remorse," I delve into these questions, drawing especially on informal conversations with judges and in-court observations. With this emphasis on the morally dense texture of judicial practices, I also encounter a way of case-making that operates on the basis of narrative: Cases are, first and foremost, conceived of as stories. Or rather, as I learned, instances of recurring, "typical" stories, within which defendants' remorsefulness is made sense of, weighed, and evaluated.

This emphasis on narrative is one way to describe legal practices in a register strikingly different from that offered by the Leiden study. This is a register that recognizes that cases are made in reference to more or less typical narratives. However, this is far from a final account: After all, the everyday practice of judging is not only about stories. Moving back and forth between the court's "frontstage," that is the publicly accessible court session, and its "backstage," that is the offices of administrative staff, clerks and judges, I encountered not only moments of narrative strife, but also episodes of quiet "face-to-file" interaction (Scheffer 2005). The emphasis on verbal interaction in court and the production of narrative, then, produced a hiatus, for this emphasis on copresence and language was not easily transposed onto these quiet episodes of desk work. There, there were no defendants, no lawyers, no public prosecutor, but there were only the traces of past bureaucratic actions gathered together in the case file. This is where I found "the law" in its most materially robust sense as well: Here, central are not fleeting words, but the written report; not intangible sound, but heavy paper files and digital interfaces. It is also the setting where judges told me they try to "see the case clearly" prior to the court session. But how do they do so? Chapter 5, "Visualizing Cases," is an account of these visualization practices as they take place in relation to the file, and especially the techniques judges have developed to navigate files accurately and efficiently. Crucially, it also pays attention to the extratextual affordances of the case file. Tracing the way taken-for-granted visualizing practices were disrupted as an effect of the digitization of case files over the summer of 2013, it zooms in on the medium-specificity (Lanzara 2009) of judicial visualization practices. In doing so, it also puts in doubt suggestions that judicial work is found only in the "head of the actor" (Garfinkel 1967). Judicial thinking and seeing, I suggest, involve both "eye" and "hand." In contrast to the storytelling in court highlighted in Chapter 3, this chapter instead approaches legal practices as socio-material practices, in which judges work with the affordances and recalcitrances of paper and digital files.

Yet here we run into another aporia once again. Yes, the case file may be a recalcitrant entity in the material sense, recalcitrant in that its messiness, its incompleteness, may make it difficult for judges to "see the case clearly." However, this is not its only recalcitrance. In both judges' pretrial preparation practices and in court itself, the file also resists smooth truth- and sense-making not because it is either a paper or digital object but because it is an object with a complex history and an uncertain future. Whereas the preceding chapter has taken the case file as an object immediately present in the here-and-now of ongoing practices, Chapter 6, "Folding Times, Doing Truths" highlights the case file not as a materially, but as a *temporally* recalcitrant object. It traces the case file's procedural and institutional history, paying attention in particular to the way these histories are evoked and negotiated in court. Here, I show how the case file becomes implicated in struggles over "what really happened," and distinguish between two modes in which it does so: On the one hand, the legal case file acts as an innocent transporter of facts and truth; on the other, it becomes visible as an object that has actively transformed and delineated "the case." In the first situation, truth-production draws on the documents present in the file, treating these as neutral containers of evidence; in the second case, the documents themselves are interrogated, a process of interrogation that crucially includes the histories, routines, and decisions these documents render invisible. In so doing, this chapter offers yet another appreciation of the concreteness of the making of facts in legal settings, drawing out the ways case files variously afford and limit judicial access to "the case."

1.8 The Law Multiple

Taken together, these four empirical chapters demonstrate that "the law," that mysterious abstract being, *is* in a very real sense *something else* depending on our concrete collaborations with it. Sometimes, we learn from the Leiden study, it is an input-output mechanism distributing justice over population groups. With a sociological, cross-sectional "view" of the law we lose all sense of legality at all, even though we may be happy to see many cases at once, or at least, the "legal and extralegal factors" of which they are composed and the outputs they yield. At other times, however, the law is a morally charged practice of storytelling. In the emphasis on the processes taking place in the quintessentially legal courtroom, we encounter narratives within which the distinction between legal culpability and moral responsibility is continually at stake. Then again, it is also a practice of paper-shuffling, in which judicial visualizations of the case prove reliant upon social and material infrastructures. Lastly and yet again, these legal practices are also practices of writing and erasing histories, or of observing procedure and the facts simultaneously. How do we make sense of this multiplicity?

One way to make sense of multiplicity, Mol (2002) teaches us, is to hierarchize: To say only one of these accounts captures "the law" best, while the others are derivative, flawed, mere approximation, if not outright illusion. In a way, this is a route that retreats into purified generalities once more, suggesting that there can only be one true being to the law. This approach would solve the problem of multiplicity, but return us back to the problems that inhere in vicious abstractionism. The other, and more productive way of dealing with multiplicity, I will argue, is to hold onto it and come up with a conception of "the law" that allows researchers to make sense of this multiplicity.

In the concluding chapter, Chapter 7, "Productive Fictions for the Study of the Law," I argue that we do not need abstract hyper-explanations of presumably singular objects, but rather humble, situated accounts of *hyper-objects*. I propose to use the notion of the hyper-object as a productive fiction to make sense of the law in its multiplicity. Hyper-objects, according to Morton (2013), are objects that are tentacular, devoid of a center, and stretched out. Hyper-objects are both inter-subjective and inter-objective: not only a product of intersubjective understanding, but materially dense knottings and practices. Of course, they are slightly mysterious, not because they have a hidden center, but because of their sheer scale: They are simply too large, too stretched out across time and space, to apprehend in full. The law, to speak with Deleuze and Guattari (1986: 45), is always partially in "the office next door, or behind the door, on to infinity." This notion of the hyper-object also forces us to situate and account for our collaborations: We will never be able to claim we have apprehended the law in its totality, yet we need not sacrifice description entirely. With this conception of the law as a hyper-object we may not ignore what we do not know, we can't quite aim to purify too hastily and recklessly, we can't continue to mistake parts ("*this* legal practice," "*this* scientific practice") for wholes ("all legal practices," "scientific practices in general"). Such a conception is situated and for that reason sensitive to the fact that every inside is another outside; that it is not moving into phenomena that matters but moving through them. With hyper-objects, the point is not in arriving but in the journey itself.

2

Abstractionism, Revisited

2.1 "Before the Law": An Allegory (But Not of the Law Itself)

In this chapter, I seek to trace the outlines of a particular tendency towards purified abstraction in approaches to the law. I wish to take you through a discussion of attempts to know and describe the law, and the confusions and impasses some of such attempts result in. In the second part of this chapter, I reorient the discussion away from definitional, abstracted exercises towards a pragmatic emphasis on legal practices, as well as a pragmatic understanding of social scientific knowledge production. Offering a *pragmatic respecification*, this part of the chapter aims to offer tools, conceptual and methodological, to revisit the abstractions that inform contemporary approaches to the law and its relationship with (social) scientific description. Productive, in this regard, is Kafka's *The Trial*, and the brief story "Before the Law" offered within it.

"Before the Law" is a story about waiting, wandering, and hesitating before the law:

> Before the law sits a gatekeeper. To this gatekeeper comes a man from the country who asks to gain entry into the law. But the gatekeeper says that he cannot grant him entry at the moment. The man thinks about it and then asks if he will be allowed to come in later on. "It is possible," says the gatekeeper, "but not now." At the moment the gate to the law stands open, as always, and the gatekeeper walks to the side, so the man bends over in order to see through the gate into the inside. When the gatekeeper notices that, he laughs and says: "If it tempts you so much, try it in spite of my prohibition. But take note: I am powerful. And I am only the most lowly gatekeeper. But from room to room stand gatekeepers, each more powerful than the other. I can't endure even one glimpse of the third." The man

> from the country has not expected such difficulties: the law should always be accessible for everyone, he thinks, but as he now looks more closely at the gatekeeper in his fur coat, at his large pointed nose and his long, thin, black Tartar's beard, he decides that it would be better to wait until he gets permission to go inside. The gatekeeper gives him a stool and allows him to sit down at the side in front of the gate. There he sits for days and years. He makes many attempts to be let in, and he wears the gatekeeper out with his requests. The gatekeeper often interrogates him briefly, questioning him about his homeland and many other things, but they are indifferent questions, the kind great men put, and at the end he always tells him once more that he cannot let him inside yet. The man, who has equipped himself with many things for his journey, spends everything, no matter how valuable, to win over the gatekeeper. The latter takes it all but, as he does so, says, "I am taking this only so that you do not think you have failed to do anything." During the many years the man observes the gatekeeper almost continuously. He forgets the other gatekeepers, and this one seems to him the only obstacle for entry into the law. He curses the unlucky circumstance, in the first years thoughtlessly and out loud, later, as he grows old, he still mumbles to himself. He becomes childish and, since in the long years studying the gatekeeper he has come to know the fleas in his fur collar, he even asks the fleas to help him persuade the gatekeeper. Finally his eyesight grows weak, and he does not know whether things are really darker around him or whether his eyes are merely deceiving him. But he recognizes now in the darkness an illumination which breaks inextinguishably out of the gateway to the law. Now he no longer has much time to live. Before his death he gathers in his head all his experiences of the entire time up into one question which he has not yet put to the gatekeeper. He waves to him, since he can no longer lift up his stiffening body. The gatekeeper has to bend way down to him, for the great difference has changed things to the disadvantage of the man. "What do you still want to know, then?" asks the gatekeeper. "You are insatiable." "Everyone strives after the law," says the man, "so how is it that in these many years no one except me has requested entry?" The gatekeeper sees that the man is already dying and, in order to reach his diminishing sense of hearing, he shouts at him, "Here no one else can gain entry, since this entrance was assigned only to you. I'm going now to close it."

Much has been said about this story, which, as one commentator suggested, is precisely as impenetrable and opaque as the gated, guarded, and walled law of which it speaks (van Houtem 2010: 286; see also Derrida 1992). Aside from precisely that mystery – what lies behind those walls? – what is perhaps the most striking is *absence of action* on the part of the man from the countryside. His primary act seems to consist of the decision "to put off deciding: he decides not to decide, he delays and adjourns while he waits" (Derrida 1992: 195–196), suggesting that the man from the country never needed a key to the law's gates, then, but only: to make a decision.

This book is a testament to my decisions as I found myself in the presence of the law. Kafka's story helps to situate these decisions conceptually and assists in demonstrating the points this book will make. I will not use this story as an object to be interpreted, nor, strictly speaking, as a story that tells us something about the law. If we wish to read it as a metaphor, I suggest, it is not a metaphor for the law itself, but rather for those who seek to know it, enter it, and see it. Read this way, "Before the Law" is evocative of a descriptive desire to know and expose the law, while at the same time it demonstrates the sheer perplexities, confusions, and contradictions in which this descriptive desire has tended to result.

In this chapter, I concentrate on these perplexities, and show how these are rooted in the demarcation between norm and fact; it is this distinction, after all, that presents the law as an object of description to begin with. Tracing both sociological and legal-positivist answers to the question, what is the law?, I show how commentators' abstract, purified modes of answering this question lead to the sacrificing of either the law or scientific description. That is, while some suggest that law is indeed amenable to scientific description, something uniquely legal seems to escape their accounts. Meanwhile, those that seek to rescue some crucial and unique legality tend to insulate that specific quality against description itself. And while these two positions are extreme indeed, more moderate perspectivist solutions, in which the two conceptions of the law are understood as rooted in the observer's "perspective" or viewpoint, similarly face the choice between saving the law or rescuing description. Like the man from the countryside, commentators of the law seem to have become stuck in a state of agitated contemplation where the wish to describe and "enter the law" is met, again and again, with deferral ("not yet") that slides into negation ("not ever"). Hence, this response is largely one of awestruck contemplation animated by the will to know or to see. It is a will, too, that runs into the limitations of description itself.

Now, definitional exercises in general tend to lead to conundrums of a foundationalist or tautological character, and this foundationalism and tautology is certainly going on in the debates I am about to discuss here. Yet something else is going on here too. Or rather, two additional things are going on here: the first, an emphasis on purity – "pure" law, "pure" description or theory – and the second, an unmediated understanding of "vision" and knowledge. Taken together, these two dimensions yield accounts abstracted from both concrete legal practices and concrete practices of description and of "seeing." It is precisely therefore that these conceptual tools do not enable me to do justice to the concrete noise and troubles present in legal practices of case-making and sociological practices of case-making. For one, an emphasis on description or "vision" within scientific self-understanding hardly accounts for the performative work that social scientific accounts of the world, and of judicial practices in particular, are doing. Second, an insistence on law's normativity or legality does not help me understand legal modes of finding out the facts about "what really happened" in different cases. These troublesome presences make the foundational distinction between norms and facts, de jure and de facto, highlighted in this chapter highly problematic. The "habits of thought" I highlight, then, do little to "give to the situation the power to make us think" (Stengers 2005: 185). And as the demand that we *think* and not merely *recognize* (Stengers 2005: 185) captures quite precisely the ethnographic task, I must therefore develop and elaborate different tools for thinking. That is, if description fails in the face of the law we must scrutinize both what we mean when we speak of and study "the law" and what we do when we do "science."

I do so in the second part of this chapter, where I look for inspiration in the story that envelops "Before the Law," namely *The Trial* itself. In so doing, I will set the theoretical stage to begin asking not what the law *is*, but instead highlight the question, how, where, and when the law is *done*. Instead of relying on "looking inside," I will suggest that "inside" and "outside" are not to be taken for granted as unproblematic epistemic positions, but are mediated accomplishments in their own right; accomplishments, furthermore, that actively shape, delineate, and produce legal as well as social realities. Lastly and importantly, instead of accepting the regulatory distinction between norms and facts or law and science, I aim to stay with two realities that trouble such demarcations: on the one hand, the performativities of social scientific inquiry, and on the other, legal modes of truth production.

However, let us first return to Kafka's mysterious "Before the Law" and to the habits of thought of which it is evocative. A word of warning: the following discussion is deliberately unfaithful to disciplinary boundaries that separate the sociology of law from jurisprudential and legal thought, and it does not aim for exhaustiveness or exegesis. What concerns me is first, the habit of thought that postulates that an understanding of law should be both descriptive and move beyond appearances; second, the habit of thought that understands different conceptions of law to be due to perspective. The authors selected to exemplify these strands of thought are noteworthy not because they are representative of a consensus shared between legal scholars and sociologists of law, but precisely because they embody more extreme conceptualizations and problematizations of the law. Tracing these more extreme positions assists in highlighting the outer reaches of these debates, while at the same time they help to show how even these ostensibly opposed contributions to the debate nevertheless share some crucial presuppositions.

2.2 A Shared Commitment: What Is the Law?

The man from the countryside in Kafka's story never quite finds out what is kept inside these walls, and neither do the readers of the story. What lies at its center is a mystery, and together with Kafka's man from the countryside we are stuck contemplating the question, what is the law? This question, Hunt (2002: 16) argues, arises at the historical moment that capitalist expansion, political strife, and the colonial encounter with different customs and habits (i.e., different forms of making and sustaining social order), cast doubt on the natural or divine necessity of the law. It is in this context, too, that appeals to a positive and general understanding of the law find resonance among its commentators.

Of course, this reflex has its source and mandate in the demarcation I have briefly touched upon in the introductory chapter: the distinction between de jure and de facto, between the two different "institutions of making order" (Jasanoff 2007: 761), that postulates that law decides, and science represents. Yet the search to describe the law has quite a pedigree and, it must be emphasized, is not to be found in social scientific efforts to understand the law alone. Indeed, it is only a presentist tendency that allows for sharp distinctions to be retroactively drawn between legal and sociological description of the law. The law and the social, after all, posed similar ontological and epistemological puzzles to their eighteenth and nineteenth century observers. Once severed from a necessary grounding in natural or divine order, or, for that matter, from the will of the sovereign (Hunt 2002), both the social and the law confronted observers with an entity that is neither natural nor a product of individual acts of will or consciousness alone: a thing that behaves and acts seemingly "on its own" even though it does not "belong to the world of atoms and molecules, of gravity, electricity, or magnetism" (Rudzinski 1976: 111). The puzzle presented by this thing that behaves on its own and seems to have a sui generis existence irreducible to God, individual volition, or the laws of nature should alert sociologists to the heritage they share with legal scholars. In a way, both "the social" and "the law" are answers to a similar problem, that is: how to understand, account for, and explain the presumed fact of order. How is "order in the plenum" (cf. Garfinkel 2002) achieved? Where and how is it sustained? These are crucial questions for the social sciences, and different disciplines may emphasize different dimensions of the question and privilege different kinds of explananda, for example, society, the state, culture, markets. Within legal thought, too, there has long been a strong current that aims to avoid the trappings of normative or metaphysical contemplation and instead aims to similarly ground its appeal in the realm of positive facts: legal positivism. Despite the large differences between self-designated legal positivists, legal positivism can be understood as the attempt to arrive at an evaluatively neutral, general description of those things which are necessarily true of the law (Priel 2013).

Foundational in this regard is Bentham's (1988 [1776]) introduction within legal thought of two differentiated roles: that of the censor and that of the expositor. Drawing on Hume's distinction between the realm of the *is* and that of the *ought*, Bentham insisted upon the necessity for legal scholars to divorce themselves from the normative impulse of natural law theories. Natural law theories, it was argued, have both descriptive and prescriptive intent: they must simultaneously function as descriptions of the laws of nature and in so doing be capable of guiding decision-makers. In that capacity they combine the role of the censor, who makes normative judgments, with that of the expositor, who seeks to expose the law as it is. In combining the two roles they confuse the realm of the (legal) ought with that of the (empirical) is. It is precisely this confusion, the utilitarian Bentham argued, that is corrosive to the very legal order such natural law theories seek to understand and protect (indeed, there is some sense in calling this a normative argument in favor of non-normative legal positivism, cf. Waldron 1996). This disconnect between is and (moral) ought "haunts" (Hart 1958) legal thought: it appears in Austin's dictum that "the existence of the law is one thing; its merit or demerit another" (Austin 1995 [1832]: 157); we see it reflected in Kelsen's emphasis on non-normative, "pure" theory of the law (1960, 1981); and legal philosopher H. L. A. Hart's concern with the "separation of law and morals" (see 1958, 1961), whose account emphasizes the both "general" and "descriptive" nature of his own interventions (Hart 1994 [1961]: 239). Legal positivism is far from uncontroversial and is not an internally homogenous set of thought; however, it does tend to draw on this Benthiam, descriptive mandate. It is that descriptive desire they share with sociologists, and it is on that descriptive promise I am taking them up now.

2.3 The Appearance of Law: Genetic and Documentary Understandings of the Law

A non-normative, descriptive impetus coupled with wonder about this strange object of the law may be understood as a shared commitment among sociologists and legal positivists, but upon a closer look these similarities give way to crucial differences. That is, while both legal scholars and sociologists seek the law, what they have tended to find bears little resemblance. While both treat law essentially not as linked to divine will or natural order, but as a "construction" (cf. Hunt 2002: 16), *who* or *what* is doing the constructing is disputed. At its most extreme, the first line of response answers that what law is can only be properly defined and understood by law itself, as law is crucially a legal construction. The second line of reasoning suggests, in contrast, that law is a manifestation of something else, particularly of political economy, power, or the social; here, law is conceived of as a social, not legal, construction. The following discussion in which I unfold these approaches is not exhaustive, but rather concentrates on a few particularly extreme exemplifications of these strands of thought in order to fully trace the conceptual terrain upon which we find ourselves.

2.3.1 Law All the Way Down: Kelsen

An obligatory passage point in this discussion is, first and foremost, Kelsen's highly influential "pure theory" of law. It is first of all, like legal positivist theories more generally, a response to natural law theories which postulate that law is and ultimately should be grounded in the law of nature or in divine law. Kelsen (1960, 1981) roundly rejects such normative, natural law, and insists that his own "pure theory" merely aims to describe the law. He further makes a distinction between the world of facts and the world of norms, within which the first is the site of "nature" (and hence the object of science), while only the latter is the true province of the law. Coupling these two moves leads Kelsen to insist that, descriptively, law is a system of norms that express "objective oughts": normative statements that postulate acts to be, or not to be, performed (Kelsen 1960; see also Spaak 2005). In so doing Kelsen diverges from accounts that highlight commands (e.g., Austin 1995 [1832], see Vinx 2012), and we will see later on in this chapter that this conception of the law contrasts with Hart's emphasis on rules (1994 [1961]). These objective oughts, crucially, form a consistent whole, a *Stufenbau*, as each of these norms is, in the end, supported and grounded in a basic norm: the *Grundnorm*. This is the norm that ensures the legal validity of all other legal norms: "The basic norm represents, as it were, a blank check, while the task of prescribing the content of the legal norms is the province of the act giving rise to the constitution and of the law-positing acts that ensue in conformity to the constitution" (Kelsen 1981: 185). Kelsen's pure theory of the law postulates, then, that the only arbiter on what law "is" (and what it is not) is law itself; and that it does so with reference to a legal basic norm or *Grundnorm*. The tautology of this line of argument is precisely the point: law is, for Kelsen, a tautological being. Founding his "pure" conception of law upon law itself, Kelsen suggests that his theory is therefore "nonmetaphysical" (Kelsen 1981: 185), and excludes grounds upon which the basic norm itself can be evaluated, questioned, or understood:

> A norm of a positive legal order cannot be denied validity on the ground that it prescribes behavior incompatible with a norm not belonging to this legal order, and in particular not on the ground that its content can for one reason or another be judged unjust. A legal norm is valid, it belongs to a valid legal order, not because it is just but because it was created in accordance with the procedures specified in the constitution.
>
> (Kelsen 1981: 185)

This *Grundnorm* is not grounded in anything other than itself: it only and merely "presupposes the existence of an authority that could not possibly exist" (Spaak 2005: 204).

This "pure" understanding of law, then, insists that all explanation must come to an end with law's basic norm. As such this conception is weary of further reduction of the law to moral, political, or natural realities. Priel (2013) likens the legal positivist in this regard with the botanical taxonomist, who "seeks to identify the central features of law and this way distinguish it from other phenomena" (Priel 2013: 2). In so doing, this botanist must assume that *despite differences in appearance*, members of a genus or species share with each other a crucial and determinative morsel of genetic *code* that makes them what they are. It is only through the "removal of all features found on comparison to vary from species to species" that it becomes possible to speak of the "natural character of the genus" (Stearn 1959: 37 cited in Priel 2013). Kelsen's understanding of the law is, in precisely this sense, genetic: Kelsen's legal positivism promises us that beyond all individual manifestation lies a constitutive, if necessarily fictional, legal norm that ensures law's identity (and therefore distinction).

2.3.2 *Storming the Bastille: Marx and Black*

Now if, for the (extreme) legal positivist, law holds itself suspended above the mire of political, moral, and cultural concerns it is precisely these concerns that dominate a second response to the question raised, and never answered, in Kafka's story-within-a-story. The man from the countryside came to seek the law where it promised it would present itself to him: behind its gates. There are no guarantees, however, that law is what it promises to be. A second line of response, then, seeks behind the law something else: a something else the law either manifests or conceals. These kinds of arguments, it must be said, predate Kelsen's positivism developed in the early twentieth century: Kelsen was writing precisely against efforts that sought to "illustrate the primacy of the social over the legal" (Banakar 2002: 34). Again, I will sketch the outlines of these arguments only impressionistically; what concerns me is the basic mechanisms of their explanation. What they share is an unease with the way legal positivist descriptions of the law "assume its [law's] own completeness and its unassailable integrity," and their tendency to "close off inquiry because within its sphere answers are already known" (Cotterrell 1996: 11).

It is quite impossible to tell this story, first, without reference to Marx. While not explicitly trying to account for law, his vocabulary of structural base and ideological superstructure has had important repercussions for contemporary understandings of how law operates in society. Even though Marxist understandings of power have been modified and critiqued, Marxists' understanding of the law have informed important strands of thought both within the sociology of law, as well as critical legal scholarship. Very broadly, Marx's (dispersed and fragmentary) comments on law suggest that "beneath sanctified juridical categories" such as right and liberty lie concealed "real social antagonisms" (Fine 2002: 102) so that his contribution lies in uncovering how "social relations [are] expressed, mediated and obscured" (Fine 2002: 102) in and by these same legal categories. The law's deceptive trick, to Marx, consists of introducing the formal equality and freedom that form the legal preconditions, under capitalist relations of production, for labor power to be freely bought and sold. In doing so, however, it merely masks the substantive inequalities between those who are "doubly free" to sell their labor and those who buy it. Of course, this line of critique pivots on the central promise of (liberal, modern) law: that of individual liberty, which, according to Marx, quickly falls apart once it is established how formal liberties are leveraged in the production and reproduction of substantive, social inequalities. These arise as a result "not from a violation, but, on the contrary, from the application of these laws" (Marx 1887: 413). Hence:

> The relation of exchange subsisting between capitalist and labourer becomes a mere *semblance* appertaining to the process of circulation, a *mere form*, foreign to the *real* nature of the transaction, and only *mystifying* it. The ever repeated purchase and sale of labour-power is now the *mere form*; what really takes place is this – the capitalist again and again appropriates, without equivalent, a portion of the previously materialised labour of others, and exchanges it for a greater quantity of living labour.
>
> (Marx 1887: 412, emphases added)

The italicized words in this fragment from the first volume of *Capital* are particularly suggestive of the kind of response I am highlighting here: that of approaching law as both an expression and concealment of the real and structural violence that comes with a notion of "right" and "liberty" to buy and sell labor power: "the illusion of a free and equal relationship is dissolved once we explore the content of the exchange" (Fine 2002: 104). Its norms are empty form, mere mystifying gloss on the substance of actual fact of exploitation.

Although it does not place absolute primacy on relations of production as the realest real, another mode of response that structurally resembles this mode of thinking is Black's sociology of law. If Kelsen promised us to purify law and extract it from the contingent "remainder of things" (Whitehead 1953: 73), then Black is aiming to offer us, in symmetrical fashion, a "pure sociology" that is "more Durkheimian than Durkheim" (Abramowitz and Black 2010: 39). Like Kelsen, Black insists that law is a normative practice, and that "the core problems of legal policy-making are problems of values." These value-considerations set law apart from science: they are "as irrelevant to a sociology of law as they are to any other scientific theory of the empirical world" (Black 1976: 1087). While this reads, at least on the surface, as a mode to respect the law's normative integrity, we will see that Black's strict behaviorism effectuates a similar reduction as that of Marx. For upon what is the law in all its normativity based?

In *The Behavior of Law*, Black (1976) sets out to understand law in strictly behavioral terms. Target of his criticism is in particular a sociology that engages itself with individual motivations and subjectivities; all this "psychology" must be purged from sociology if it is to become an actual science. Enter his strict behaviorism: only behavior, and in particular, amounts and intensities of behavior can be the object of sociology. Behavior, according to Black, takes place within a "social space," the shape of which is defined along several structural axes, for instance (vertical) stratification, (horizontal) differentiation and organization, and a realm of "morphology" or culture. One of these axes is social control. Law, within this framework, is defined as "governmental social control" (Black 1976). Governmental social control displays variation in two ways: quantitatively and qualitatively, that is in the kind of sanctioning it results in. Black emphasizes this quantitative dimension of law, showing how the amount of law mobilized in specific situations depends on the respective social locations the two parties involved inhabit in the geometry of social space (e.g., a lower-class defendant charged with petty theft faces harsh punishment, while those accused of white-collar fraud can settle their way out of a criminal prosecution).

Black's promise to leave the law in all its normativity untouched proves, however, an illusion. Precisely because he evacuates from his "pure sociological" account considerations of meaning, of evaluation, and of subjectivity, his sociology of law is unable to account for the normativity of law it claimed to protect. Hunt suggests, then, that Black "must disallow any conception of 'legality' or 'illegality'; he can say nothing beyond that which governments act against or rewards is law" (Hunt 1983: 26). In his interest in purifying sociology, Black seems stuck with a sociology without law and its normativity at all. Again, law is reduced; not, this time, to capitalist relations of production, but that other beast: to "social behavior." In a way, Black takes Marx's reduction a step further, even: Marx at least attributes to law a capacity for action in that it is capable of concealment and mystification, while no such agency exists for Black at all; all is determined by the shape of social space.

The Bastille of the law is, much like the historical Bastille, in fact empty: form, gloss, mere semblance. If the legal positivist can be likened to the taxonomist who carefully distinguishes noise from a shared "genetic" signal across legal practices, then, the kind of explanation offered here is rather that of the commentator who treats appearances as a sign of an underlying reality. Garfinkel understands such a reading as a "documentary" mode of interpretation: "the method consists of treating actual appearance as 'the document of', as 'pointing to', as 'standing on behalf of' a presupposed underlying pattern" (Garfinkel 1967: 78). In more scathing terms, Nietzsche compares this scientific practice to that of the astrologer, who is similarly motivated by an almost libidinal "thirst, a hunger, and a taste for hidden and forbidden powers" (Nietzsche 1974 [1882]: 170) of which actual reality is merely a surface manifestation. Latour, in similarly dismissive terms, locates this thirst at the heart of sociology more generally when he suggests that reliance on "the social" as a final explanans constitutes a "magical invocation" (Latour 2005: 65), that testifies, more than anything, to a "mythical belief in another world behind the real world" (Latour 2005: 67). In any case, the differences with a Kelsenian understanding of law are now becoming clear: while one seeks for a shared, original signal, the other treats the law as a sign of something else.

2.4 Jurisdictional Troubles and the Two Provinces

My discussion so far has concentrated on the more extreme positions advanced in these disputes about the law. These descriptions of the law are both concerned with teasing out a general truth about the law, yet proceed along different paths: the first a genetic mode of interpretation looking for a shared constitutive signal across legal practices (exemplified by Kelsen), the second a documentary mode of interpretation seeking that of which the law is merely a sign (exemplified by Marx and Black). In so doing these contributions also imbue the law with varying levels of autonomy or dependence. The suggestion that law is what it says it is makes law impenetrable to moral, political, or cultural concerns and portrays it as independent of the social: a walled fortress. The suggestion that law is merely politics or the social by other means leaves it wide-open to sociological inquiry, even though by these accounts the law is in fact an empty space. In Kafka's story, this tension between accounts that posit law's closure and autonomy on the one hand and those that treat it as "open" to social determination on the other is captured quite precisely in law's status as both walled and open.

Empirically and historically speaking, there can be little doubt that both positions are indeed reconcilable. Weber suggests as much when he locates the unicity and autonomy of legal practices in the historical rise of formal rationality (1978 [1922]). This formal, as opposed to substantial, rationality is the law's kernel, but this kernel itself emerges from social and historical contingencies. Luhmann (2004) similarly treats the legal subsystem's autonomy as a product of historical processes of differentiation. Hunt argues, then, that: "these [two] views of the law are not antithetical; the rise of law as autonomous system increasingly separated from the political sphere is consistent with a view of law as dependent on society, in the sense of being a historical achievement" (Hunt 2002: 17). And of course, the two different positions share a few things as well. Logically speaking, neither of the positions fully escapes tautology, for reducing law to the social and then proceeding to explain the social with reference to the social leads the sociologist into yet another tautological puzzle. Bourdieu grasps the irony when he suggests that: "stare decisis, the rule which decrees the authority of prior legal decisions for any current actions, stands in relation to juridical thought as Durkheim's precept, 'explain the social by the social' does to sociological thought" (Bourdieu 1987: 823). Crucially, stare decisis is "but another way of asserting the autonomy and specificity of legal reasoning and legal judgments," Bourdieu argues (Bourdieu 1987: 823). Tautology burgeons at yet higher levels of abstraction as well. Ask a jurist what ensures social order and the answer is likely to be, "the law"; ask a sociologist what shapes the law and one is directed to "the social." The social explains the law and the law, the social. At the same time, both approaches may have to end up drawing the similar conclusion in that they both, to speak with Gertrude Stein (1937), suggest that "there is no *there* there": for Kelsen's genetic reading must presuppose a fictional signal that shapes actually existing law and legal practices, while Marx's and Black's documentary readings instead treat the empty formalism of the law as a sign of a realer social real.

As something that requires explanation itself, the distinction between law's tautology and law's social determinants, between "law as autonomous" and "law as dependent on society," continues to haunt commentators. The dispute is, in this sense, jurisdictional, in that it operates on the basis of an almost territorial understanding of the object of study: is the law a separate jurisdiction? Or is it merely an administrative province in and of that much larger territory of which it must obey the laws, that is, the territory of the social? Both positions have large consequences for the distribution of authority over both legal and nonlegal commentators: who gets to authoritatively speak about the law? And who gets the decisive last word?

In a sense, we are dealing here with a territorial dispute, and territorial disputes tend to concentrate on the question of borders: borders to distinguish those inside from those outside, those with claims to a right to speak, and those without. It is here that a vocabulary of "perspective" and of "seeing" makes its entrance. That is, the distinction between law-as-autonomous and law-as-social-being is rearticulated as a distinction between internal and external points of view (Hunt 2002: 17; cf. Hart 1994 [1961]), or distinctions between the legal, professional "vision" and that of laypeople. This approach *accepts* the difference between the accounts and their portrayal of the law, and seeks to understand such differences with recourse to a vocabulary of perspective. Law is whatever it is, and what one understands it to be is a function of one's perspective.

2.5 Inside/Outside Visions

As exemplifications of this perspectivism I will use, first, Bourdieu's most specific account of the law: *The Force of Law: A Sociology of the Juridical Field* (1987), and second, the aforementioned Hart's *The Concept of Law* (1994 [1961]). Both authors have a central and authoritative position within their respective disciplines; both take issue with the more extreme accounts of the law their disciplines have offered (exemplified here by Kelsen, Black, and Marx) and both try to come to a settlement somewhere in the middle ground between tautology and reduction, between conceiving of law as a hermetically sealed off space and law as mere chimera. Importantly, both authors mobilize visual metaphors and draw borders in order to settle the dispute: Bourdieu speaks of vulgar versus professional vision, while Hart zooms in on the distinction between internal and external points of view. Their work, then, is an exercise in the drawing of borders between law and non-law, between law's inside and its outside, so that accounts of it may be situated either internally or externally.

2.5.1 Bourdieusian Perspectivism

As is suggested by the title of Bourdieu's piece, *The Force of Law: A Sociology of the Juridical Field* is first and foremost an attempt to elaborate on law as a social field. Noting the necessity of moving beyond tautological "formalism" and reductive "instrumentalism" – positions we can roughly recognize in Kelsen's and Marx's accounts – Hart suggests that the juridical field is primarily a site of competition. In this case, competition takes place over the "monopoly of the right to determine law" (Bourdieu 1987: 817). Professionals in the legal field vie with each other for the right to "determine law," and it is through such struggles that professionals dictate law's "practical content" (Bourdieu 1987: 827) The law's content is "product of a symbolic struggle between professionals possessing unequal technical skills and social influence" (Bourdieu 1987: 827) This implies that "the juridical effect of the rule – its real meaning – can be discovered in the specific power relationship between the professionals" (Bourdieu 1987: 827). Note, here, how Bourdieu locates the meaning of legal rules in their effect; that is, in their enactment or use as it is shaped by struggles over power between legal professionals. "Control of the legal text," Bourdieu states, "is the prize to be won in interpretative struggles" (Bourdieu 1987: 818)

It is here that Bourdieu explicitly distinguishes the "vision" that is produced within the juridical field from those outside of it. Those competing with each other for the right to determine law have, he states, a "professional vision" that contrasts with those outside, whose vision upon the law Bourdieu calls "vulgar." These two visions can be mapped onto two wholly different mental spaces: that of the person engaged in the struggle over the right to determine the law and those without the juridical, technical skill to do so (Bourdieu 1987: 828). The difference between these two modalities of vision, Bourdieu argues,

> is far from accidental. Rather, it is essential to a power relation upon which two systems of presuppositions, two systems of expressive intention – two world-views – are grounded. The difference, which is the basis for excluding the nonspecialist, results from the establishment of a system of injunctions through the structure of the field and of the system of principles of vision and of division which are written into its fundamental law, into its constitution.
>
> (Bourdieu 1987: 828–829)

Bourdieu hence maps different kinds of vision upon the distinction between member and nonmember, specialist and nonspecialist, those trained, educated, and habitually cultivated within the juridical field and those who are not. Of course, such a conception helps to understand (arguably frequent) misunderstandings between legal professionals and lay participants in legal proceedings. Crucially, however, such an understanding also allows Bourdieu to characterize this professional vision as a kind of miscognition:

> within this field occurs a confrontation among actors possessing a technical competence which is inevitably social and which consists essentially in the socially recognized capacity to interpret a corpus of texts sanctifying a correct or legitimized vision of the social world. It is essential to recognize this in order to take account both of the relative autonomy of the law and of the properly symbolic effect of "miscognition" that results from the illusion of the law's absolute autonomy in relation to external pressures.
>
> (Bourdieu 1987: 817)

For all Bourdieu's emphasis on dynamics internal to the juridical field, then, it is this internally and socially produced vision that does not, more generally, have epistemic value except perhaps as a manifestation of miscognition. Of course, this conceptualization of the juridical field itself and possible perspectives upon it leads us right back to where we started, that is, with the sociologist who seeks behind the surface of the law a deeper reality of social processes. This reality, is, again, concealed by the law, to which concealment the law's participants must remain blind.

This point assumes importance if we pay some attention to Bourdieu's own vision upon the juridical field. If not "professional" or "vulgar," how is Bourdieu's own vision upon the juridical field (and by extension, that of the sociological commentator) to be understood? It seems neither inside nor outside. On the one hand, it distances itself perpetually from the "illusion" and "miscognition" that constitutes juridical vision. On the other, it desires to offer a more incisive, altogether more knowledgeable vision of the law than laypeople's vulgar vision can provide. Bourdieu's vision is not itself, then, subject to this regulatory distinction between outside or inside perspectives. In fact it is elevated beyond the distinction: a perspective upon perspectives, a meta-perspective (Schinkel 2015). It is only that outside vision, or that vision from above, that has descriptive value; those on law's inside may have something to say, but it is mere miscognition.

It is almost needless to say, then, that Bourdieu reproduces in many ways Marx's understanding of the law. But it is crucial to see how a Bourdieusian conception of the law incorporates, and tries to account for, the tautology of law. It does so by suggesting that this tautological insistence upon law's autonomy is in actual fact a perspective produced within the law. At the same time, this internal perspective is fatally flawed, at least by Bourdieu's standards of sociological description: it cannot truly transcend its own limitations and come to inhabit sociology's meta-perspective (cf. Schinkel 2015).

2.5.2 *Hart's Internal Point of View*

A second, influential form of perspectivism is that offered by Hart. Much like earlier efforts in analytical jurisprudence, Hart considers his work to be an exercise in description, suggesting that his work "may be of use to those whose chief interests are in ... sociology, rather than law" (Hart 1994 [1961]: v). In doing so he does not run counter to the positivist aspirations of earlier analytic jurisprudence; in fact, Hart seeks for a more empirically accurate portrayal of the law, and in particular law as it is experienced, used, and oriented to by those who accept the law as guides for conduct.

A first step to come to a more accurate understanding of the law, Hart argues, is to rid ourselves of sanction-based accounts of the law and in so doing, come to an understanding of "law's social being" (Hart 1994 [1961], see also Fitzpatrick 1992: 6). Empirically, Hart argues, a sanction-based understanding does little to help us understand those cases in which actors do in fact exhibit rule-following behavior but are not, or not primarily, guided by the threat of force (Hart 1994 [1961]: 40) but rather by a sense of obligation. What is necessary to understand law, he argues, is a conception that is sensitive to its broader appeal to those acting according to its dictates. Importantly, this is where Hart seeks guidance in the realm of social, and not strictly legal, rules.

Human societies, Hart suggests, hang together by virtue of social rules. These may not be unambiguously accepted or at all times followed, but they nevertheless constitute the texture of social life. People follow them and accept them not simply because they fear sanction if they do not (although such a motivation may, of course, be present); they also follow them out of a sense of obligation. But what if there is a contradiction between these primary rules? How to decide, then, which rule should take precedence? In the bustle of social life, doubts are surely to arise about the correct and appropriate application of these first order rules, and it is at that moment that: "there will be no procedure for settling this doubt, either by reference to an authoritative text or to an official whose declaration on this point are authoritative" (Hart 1994 [1961]: 90). Second-order legal rules, then, are rules "concerned with the primary rules themselves" in that they specify how, when, and by whom these primary rules should be taken into account. Governing the use and mobilization of these second-order rules, however, are not further third-order rules. Rather, here the 'rule of recognition' makes it entry, which is the rule that governs precisely the questions who, when and under what conditions certain rules are to be understood as legally valid. With this understanding of the rule of recognition as a convention, we find ourselves miles away from a Kelsenian, tautological insistence upon the basic norm.

At the same time – and this is where I think Hart's legal thought closes off law again – he introduces the "internal point of view" that resists any description or understanding. To understand this it is necessary to further specify Hart's answer to the question: How do people come to follow rules at all? What is the affective texture of these relations of obligation? To Hart, sheer habit, that is, people follow social rules because they are used to doing so, is not an adequate answer to this question, because it mistakes regularities in behavior for the mechanism through which such patterns in behavior are established. What is needed instead is an account of various orientations towards rules. This is where Hart introduces the distinction between internal and external aspects of rules. In a crucial passage, Hart speaks of the distinction as follows:

> The following contrast . . . in terms of the "internal" and "external" aspect of rules may serve to mark what gives this distinction its great importance for the understanding not only of law but of the structure of any society. . . . [I]t is possible to be concerned with the rules, either merely as an observer who does not himself accept them, or as a member of the group which accepts and uses them as guides to conduct. We may call these respectively the "external" and the "internal points of view."
>
> (Hart 1994 [1961]: 88–89)

Taking an external point of view, then, is to be a nonmember, "merely an observer who does not himself accept them," while the internal point of view is reserved to "a member of the group which accepts and uses them as guides to conduct." Tamanaha (2006) points out that hence effectuated is a mapping between being a nonmember, being an observer, and not accepting a rule, and between being a member and accepting a rule.[1] But this mapping proves untenable, Hart realizes very well. On the one hand, external observers may be content to describe regularities and patterns in the members' actions without reference at all to the rule (Hart 1994 [1961]: 89). On the other hand, there are surely instances in which participants in rule-following do not accept the rule but merely follow it "because they judge that unpleasant consequences are likely to follow violation" (Hart 1994 [1961]: 90). Describing rule-following can be done without recourse to the rule at all; while being a member does not guarantee any acceptance of the legitimacy or morality of the rule (see also Tamanaha 2006).

In order for a point of view to be truly internal, then, rules must both be *oriented to* and *accepted*. This does not mean one cannot "go against" the rule: the rule must to some extent be internalized as obliging to allow people to go against it; it is only theoretical (as opposed to practical) non-acceptance that marks the external perspective. Shapiro points out that Hart's "internal point of view" is more adequately grasped, then, as an "internalized point of view," that is the view of "a specific kind of normative attitude held by certain insiders, namely, those who accept the legitimacy of the rules" (Shapiro 2006: 1159); it is furthermore a view that refers to "the *practical* attitude of rule acceptance" (Shapiro 2006: 1159, emphasis added).

This emphasis on the practical attitude of rule-acceptance as constitutive of the internal point of view represents an acute challenge to descriptive efforts (Shapiro 2006). This is so because each description of the internal point of view will necessarily be external: the internal point of view can only be inhabited, not described in "internal" terms. Now this impossibility is not necessarily a problem: just like sociologists seek to take seriously, as objects of empirical attention, all kinds of moral, religious, and aesthetic evaluations, judgments, and justifications without facing the need to "adopt the point of view" of the actor (see for such exercises in particular Becker 1982; Bourdieu 1979; Boltanksi and Thevenot 2006), they may similarly continue to describe what legal rule-following looks like. Hart suggests as much when he states that one may still seek to describe this kind of internal perspective: after all description "may still be description, even when what is described is an evaluation" (Hart 1994 [1961]: 244). Crucially, however, what is in fact *not* permitted, according to this schema, is to mistake that external point of view with that of the internal rule-follower.

Precisely, then, by nodding to social rules and in advancing a rather sociological thesis that relies on forms of recognition, Hart's legal thought at first reads as a diplomatic exercise: it grants sociologists their due. Yes, legal rules depend on the social rule of recognition; only that confers legal validity. At the same time this very gesture erects an epistemic border between internal and external, but behind the border is something that actively resists efforts at representation. Again, what is truly internal resists description. Again, our descriptive impulses have been thwarted; precisely as we attempt to move inside law's gates, we find ourselves outside, barred by yet another formidable obstacle: the limitations of description itself.

2.6 What About the Concrete?

Working through recurring answers to the ever-present question, what is the law?, and working through several perspectival solutions to the contradictions and tensions between various answers to this question has led us to return once again to the crucial ordering principle within these discussions. Taken to their logical extremes, neither Kelsen nor Marx nor Black allow us much leeway to understand concrete instances of doing, using, mobilizing, challenging, thwarting, resisting, or even ignoring law. With Bourdieu and Hart, our choice between tautology and reduction is now rearticulated to become a choice between trying to inhabit the impossible, Archimedean, all-seeing location of the Bourdieusian sociologist or assume the position of the practical rule-follower whose perspective on the rule is itself something that cannot be described. Either we see much, but not much legally; or else we act legally, but do not see. Either we're out, or we're in.

The priest's story, then, evokes and simultaneously disavows certain habits of thought that seem to govern our thinking in the presence of the law. These habits of thought find their source and mandate in the demarcation between fact and norm, science and law, but simultaneously find their nadir in description itself. It couples description with the demand for purity, which coupling leads to diametrically opposed conclusions with regard to the law. Tellingly, both of these positions remain haunted by the sense that there is no substance to law, only fiction, mere form.

It is against this background that I wish to introduce a last approach to the question, what is the law? This approach is provided by Bruno Latour. Concentrating on his sociology of law (Latour 2010) and positioning it within his broader engagement with different "modes of existence" (Latour 2013), I show how Latour offers us a glimpse of a different way of approaching and answering this question, but ultimately falls prey, again, to the habit of purification I highlighted in the preceding pages. That is, while he restores at first to both science and the law a concrete existence lacking in the more abstract understandings put forward by the preceding authors, his sociology of law similarly falls prey to the temptations of purification. Drawing on a specific notation system for these different modes of existence, Latour again emphasizes the crucial differences between mode of existence [LAW] and that of science, [REF]. Latour's argument is rather complex, but working through it will provide us with a sense of the tenacity of the distinction in descriptions of the law, and, importantly, the academic work of purification that sustains it.

Latour casts his sociology of law within two different problematics. The first is by now familiar: he seeks to account for law in a way that does not fall back on sociology's "magical invocation" of "the social" while it at the same time does not want to uncritically adopt law's tautological self-understanding (Latour 2005, 2010). The crucial step he makes is to focus, in a more empirical manner, on the actual practices that go into the "winding of reasoning itself" (Latour 2010: 143) that takes place within the French Conseil d'État. The Conseil d'État is the highest appellate and advisory administrative court in France, and through an ethnographic study of the practices of its members as well as its various clerical assistants and its files Latour sets out to construct an account of these practices that does not fall prey to either tautology or reduction. On the one hand, these practices show how there is no simple translation of violence, power, or interests into legal decisions: for that, the members of the Conseil d'État are far too legalistic, far too detached, far too recalcitrant, even in the face of government (which after all they are supposed to keep in check). On the other hand, these practices show the existence of hesitations, of interruptions, of little experiments in reasoning, of doubts and of debate, which "winding of legal reasoning" is glossed over in legal self-descriptions that put center stage the self-evidence of rules and their intuitive grasping.

The focus on actual practices here operates in much the same way as it has in Latour's previous work. There, scientific practices are similarly understood to be irreducible to academic power-play or bourgeois knowledge production, and as invariably more complex and rich than suggested by the impoverished epistemologies that have to serve double duty as both their description and legitimation (see e.g., Latour and Woolgar 1979; Latour 1999). Ever the realist, Latour treats these descriptions as the purified abstractions they are and have always been, paying attention instead to the concrete practices of scientists in their labs. In many ways, Latour pursues this agenda, too, in the Conseil d'État.

Bracketing both sociological and legal description of legal practices, Latour starts instead with the legal practices *themselves*. This emphasis on practices is highly laudable, and indeed a powerful corrective to excessively abstracted and purified accounts of the law. As such, this sociology of law has the capacity to function as direly needed "therapy" (cf. Wittgenstein 2001 [1958]) against the confusion that ensues once we start to understand the *teloi* of practices as their guiding, omnipresent logic. Indeed, this emphasis on practices is part and parcel of what I will introduce as a pragmatic respecification in the second half of this chapter. But here Latour and I will start to diverge quite radically. The reasons for this divergence are found in the second problematic Latour addresses in his sociology of law, in particular in relation to his recently elaborated *Inquiry Into Modes of Existence* (2013). It is in this second problematic that the categorical distinction between legal and scientific practices rears its head once again.

2.6.1 Diplomatic Purifications

The second problematic within which Latour situates his sociology of law is both more general and more specific than the first. It is more general, as it aims to account for not only the legal mode of existence but a variety of other modes of existence as well. In doing so Latour aims to formulate a vocabulary to talk not only about the law, but also about science, art, or politics. At the same time the problem is highly specific to what Latour considers the weakness of actor-network theoretical approaches as they have been developed over the last few decades. Helped along to no insignificant degree by his own previous work on scientific practices, actor-network theoretical approaches have done important work by showing how there is no straightforward "social." Rather, the "social world" (or rather: worlds) hangs together by virtue of highly specific but heterogeneous entanglements, practices, or networks, composed of very different parts (technical, scientific, economic, political, etc.) all of which are irreducible to "the social." To Latour, this is both its greatest strength and its Achilles heel. This actor-network theoretical focus on "the network" (or networks) has remained largely oblivious, he states, to *that which passes along these networks*. In so doing it runs the risk of becoming unable to differentiate between specific "modes of existence" and in so doing opens up room for reduction: not to "the social," but rather to "the network." This possibility of reduction is dangerous both theoretically and politically: on the one hand, we run the theoretical risk of becoming unable to distinguish between very different kinds of "being," confusing for instance a religious invocation with a scientific fact or a legal verdict. Politically, we run the risk of glossing over the unicity of these beings and in doing so treat them disrespectfully and violently, for instance when we ask of religion to justify itself upon epistemic grounds. These kinds of question constitute "category mistakes": we ask questions within a register of "felicity conditions" – for instance, true or false, or legally sound or unsound – which the mode of existence in question does not share. It is in this sense that Latour casts his *Inquiry Into Modes of Existence* as an exercise in diplomacy: the diplomat aims to respect the highly different beings it has brought to one table, and to not ask them to meet demands they are unable to meet.

The beings Latour speaks of are not simply different substances or essences. Modes of existence differ not because they are made of different substances, but differ because of the different ways they deal with the inevitable fact of *discontinuity*. Between states of being lie hiatuses, and it is the modality according to which these hiatuses are bridged that defines the specific mode of existence. For instance, [REF] is a mode of existence associated with scientific practices: there, information has to travel along chains of reference tying together, say, a patch of soil in an Amazonian forest, through samples, through tables and calculations upon paper, to its publication in a peer-reviewed journal. The hiatuses are bridged *referentially*: each of the links in the chain of reference retain information by referring back to the link preceding it. [LAW], crucially, is different.

Latour argues that the legal mode of existence [LAW] is characterized by a different kind of movement or circulation than those characterizing scientific practices. The passage at stake in his portrayal of these legal practices is the movement between the text of the file and the text of the law. Latour traces this passage as the work of the members of the Conseil d'État unfolds around the hefty case files accompanying the cases it seeks to judge. This work consists of a series of sequentially distributed note-taking operations through which the members will try to "extract, like diamonds from the ore" (Latour 2013: 201), the precise legal issue at stake. They have to "extract the means from the confused pile which constitutes the file," the means here being his translation of the French *moyen*, in legal practice meaning both legal ground and argument or the precise legal issue at stake in this or that case. This moyen is the

> connection, the coming-and-going between two types of writing: on the one hand, the ad hoc documents of both parties which are produced for and

> through the occasion, such as statements and various productions, and, on the other hand, the printed, authorized, voted upon and connected texts which are carefully arranged on the shelves of the library [written law].
>
> (Latour 2010: 86)

The moyen is a particular bridge that has to span a hiatus, a gap, between two kinds of texts; and this movement is what Latour calls the "passage of law" (2010) which characterizes mode of existence [LAW]. In so distinguishing between [REF] and [LAW], the mode of existence that organizes reference to the world and the mode of existence that emerges in the bridging of the text of the file with the text of the law, Latour bifurcates between legal and scientific practices. Of course, Latour recognizes that judges, like scientists, are sometimes concerned with the question of reference, that is, with "superimposing layer upon layer of documents and tracings, which are very different in terms of their materiality (photographs, graphs, documents and plans)" (Latour 2010: 226). Yet this activity, according to Latour, is nothing legal: "to be sure, it is possible to retrieve numerous traces of this very particular kind of activity that one finds in laboratories in judicial files, but far from defining the nature of judicial activity, it merely organizes a few of its segments, the remainder being characterized by activities that are more properly legal" (Latour 2010: 226). This is the movement – circulation – of reference, that is [REF], and is as such radically distinct from the legal passage. While recognizing, then, that the law does need "facts" to do its work, Latour nevertheless delegates these to the mode of existence [REF] and expulses them from [LAW]. "The making of law" is fundamentally unlike – and independent of – the production of facts and (referential) truths.

In its interest in the legal moyen and in its delegation of factual questions to mode of existence [REF], Latour's sociology of law reproduces, then, the same distinction that structures law's self-understandings. While he warns against hasty purification, his account nevertheless again purifies the law in a way that is by now familiar. On the one hand, faced with the "hesitations, the winding paths, the meanders of reflexivity" in the deliberative practices of the members of the Conseil d'État, he suggests that "we should not be too hasty to *purify* this movement" (Latour 2010: 151, emphasis added). At the end of his ethnography, however, Latour is quite comfortable abstracting a specific movement – the moyen – from these practices as quintessentially legal. In sharply distinguishing between quintessentially legal movement [LAW] from the characteristic movement of scientific practices [REF], Latour's sociology of law is itself an exercise in purification.

Only in recognizing the difference between [LAW] and [REF] can we, according to Latour, remain diplomatic in our dealing with these different modes of existence. But what, I wonder, is diplomatic about an effacing of large swaths of judicial work, that is, fact- and truth-making in legal settings? And while it may be helpful to keep the differences between [LAW] and [REF] in clear sight, what are we to do, conceptually and empirically, with concrete practices of truth-telling in legal settings and with the performativities of social scientific accounts of the world?

What started quite innocently as a search for the law has now become a self-perpetuating circle of thought. With our expository mandate we run into the limitations of description itself. Kelsen, Marx, Black, Bourdieu, Hart, and finally, Latour: we have traced the work that the distinction between norm and fact, law and science, judgment and knowledge is doing in the fraught debates about the character of the law, and, for that matter, the character of description itself. While Latour is the odd duck in that we find ourselves, with him, in the middle of concrete practices, we run into a similar tendency towards purification. There, too, the distinction between law and science is reinstated: each are governed by wholly different felicity conditions, wholly different tonalities (Latour 2013). It is at that point that law's expositors have to admit that whatever they say will not quite approach the tonality of the law itself. Running the risk of striking such a disharmonious chord, it is better, perhaps, to remain silent. But how, then, to proceed? Perhaps more unforgivably, we have purified and abstracted both law and science in such a way as to divorce their presupposed purity from their practical, particular, and concrete existence. Tracing this conceptual looping has led us not, then, to the capacity to inquisitively "hop, skip and jump" (James 1909: 109) through the many concrete practices we encounter, but to confusion, contradiction, and in the end, silence, the tools for our thinking lying quite uselessly at our feet.

A similar weariness with interpretation, with description, and even understanding itself descends on Joseph K., who becomes "too tired to think about all the ramifications of the story." The story, related to him by the priest, has led him into all sorts of thoughts, thoughts "not familiar to him, unrealistic things" (Kafka 1924: 263). "The simple story" Kafka (1924: 263) writes, "had lost its shape, he wanted to shake it off, . . ."

So do I. The following is an attempt.

2.7 Shaking it Off: Lessons from Joseph K.

If Kafka's "Before the Law" is suggestive of several habits of thought surrounding the description of the enigma of the law, the book from which it is taken, *The Trial*, offers a bewildering sense of what it is not to contemplate the law or to try to steal a glance inside, but to find oneself already enveloped by it.

At first glance, this interpretation is not immediately obvious. Think of the tragedy of Joseph K. frantic searching: Does he not, in the end, fail to find the elusive magistrate judge capable of finding him innocent? While Joseph K. may find himself inside various rooms and offices where the law is done, he never finds what he presumes to be law itself. In this, he is at least superficially quite like the man from the countryside, who fails to find what he was searching for all along. The suspicion running through both stories is at first sight quite similar: it is the suspicion that there is no magistrate, that there is no center to this power . . . Indeed, both stories raise the suspicion that there is no *there* there. "Seeking a being, an essence offered to [their] mediations, something meaningful to command [their] respect" (Hegel cited in Derrida 1992: 208), both the man from the countryside and Joseph K. seem to find nothing at all: law itself remains "ungesehen und ungefühlt," unseen and unfelt (Hegel cited in Derrida 1992: 208)

However, this interpretation relies on the assumption that "Before the Law" is supposed to function as a metaphor for the law itself. Only then do the parallels between the two stories become so obvious. However, there is also the possibility that "Before the Law" captures not the law, but one of our delusions in the face of the law. Indeed, the priest warns Joseph K. that he is "deluding himself about the court," and that "that delusion is described thus," after which the priest relates to him the infamous "Before the Law." Let's zoom in, then, on the *differences* between the two stories. Before Joseph K. is to meet the priest-cum -prison chaplain, Joseph K. finds himself at one of the entrances to a large, officious building. There, he had been informed, a first hearing with regard to his case would be held: a chance for him to plead his innocence. The building is large, but, like many of Kafka's buildings, not spacious. Searching various hallways for the room in which he is expected to make his appearance, Joseph K. makes some inquiries. Ashamed for his legal troubles, he invents for himself an alibi. Going around knocking on doors and asking for Lanz, the joiner, he is surprised to be pointed in the direction of one room in particular. Entering it,

> K. thought he had stepped into a meeting. A medium sized, two-windowed room was filled with the most diverse crowd of people – nobody paid any attention to the person who had just entered. Close under its ceiling it was surrounded by a gallery which was also fully occupied and where the people could only stand bent down with their heads and their backs touching the ceiling. K., who found the air too stuffy, stepped out again and said to the young woman, who had probably misunderstood what he had said, "I asked for a joiner, someone by the name of Lanz." "Yes," said the woman, "please go on in." K. would probably not have followed her if the woman had not gone up to him, taken hold of the door handle and said, "I'll have to close the door after you, no-one else will be allowed in." "Very sensible," said K., "but it's too full already." (Kafka 1924: 46)

The resemblance between the woman's words – "I'll have to close the door after you, no-one else will be allowed in" – and that of the Tartar-bearded guard in "Before the Law" – "here no one else can gain entry, since this entry was assigned only to you. I'm going now to close it" – is uncanny. Both guard and woman are mysterious representatives of the law; but where the guard keeps the man from the countryside out of the law, the law now swallows, envelops Joseph K. Even if he does not find that final judge, that final office, he is nevertheless caught in its machinations, forced to move about. The law, whatever it is, behaves differently in the two stories: in "Before the Law," it rests and only asks for waiting; in *The Trial*, its tentacles force Joseph K. from room to room.

Indeed, that movement is a second salient difference between the man from the countryside and *The Trial*'s Joseph K. Both the man from the countryside and Joseph K. may share the same delusion – the delusion that there is a *there* there – yet the first remains stuck in static contemplation, while the second is continually wandering from room to room, from office to office, negotiating and pleading. Deleuze and Guattari highlight the contrast when they suggest that Joseph K., more than anything, is a *figure in movement*: "he [Joseph K.] will find justice only by moving, by going from room to room, … He will take control of the machine of expression: he will take over the investigation, he will write without stop, he will demand a leave of absence so that he can totally devote himself to this 'virtually interminable' work" (Deleuze and Guattari 1986: 50–51). Envelopment and journeying: these are the two dimensions upon which the crucial difference rests. In *The Trial*, the law is not some mysteriously gated, bounded entity but rather a concrete, even networked, many-faced thing. It makes itself known, to Joseph K., not in the guise of a solitary guard but is made present in many different placeholders ("lieutenants"): from mysterious men who show up in Joseph K.'s apartment, to voices on the telephone, and from lowliest chambermaid, to artist, to investigating judge and his notebook. All, to Joseph K., appear to have something to do with the law, but neither are its pure embodiment. Of course, Joseph K. keeps searching, but the final and decisive magistrate judge is never seen or felt. Meanwhile his journey is shaped by concrete conversations and collaborations that always lead him into yet another room, yet another office.

This, then, is *The Trial*'s comedy: it consists in Joseph K.'s delusions, coupled with his unwillingness to trust his own eyes. Deluded by abstracted metaphors for the law, escaping him is the possibility that his own searching, pleading, and wandering, his own journeying from room to room, representative to representative, may as such just provide for a more productive understanding of the law than the priest's story. That he might be helped in his journeying not by revealing parable nor "intellectualist philosophies," but that he is helped along by the "surprises and cruelties," the "wildness" (James 1995 [1907]: 9) of these experiences. *The Trial* suggests that the facts of encountering, of cajoling, of collaborating, of finding yet another passage or room are *themselves* the space of the law.

This is why Joseph K.'s fraught attempts to find the law are far more interesting than that of the man from the countryside: while the latter assumes knowledge of the law to come to him through waiting, Joseph K.'s seeks concrete ways to deal, to collaborate, to convince, to mobilize. That he does not find what he expected to find – capital-L Law – is an indictment of his presumptions, not of his methods of inquiry. After all, it is precisely through these concrete, if fraught, practices of collaboration that the reader comes to appreciate the viscose and the opaque, as well as the smooth and the seamless, of the world in which Joseph K. is thrown. Indeed, *what is the law?* has been the wrong question to ask. With Joseph K., we wonder instead where it takes place, whom and what it envelops, how it is done, and how we might move about in its elusive presence.

In this part of the chapter, I will make a turn similar to the one effectuated by my juxtaposition of the man from the countryside and Joseph K. This is a turn that emphasizes concrete legal practices and concrete practices of description and "vision"; it is also a movement towards an appreciation of the concrete beings that populate these practices, for example methods of inquiry, instruments of measurement, and case files. Last, it is also a movement that puts center stage movement itself, especially where it pertains to my own inquiries and investigations. The following is an elaboration.

2.8 Abstraction and the Remainder of Things

Description fails in the face of the law: it must, at some point, throw up its hands and accept the fact it has merely circumvented, rather than penetrated, the law. Far from a theoretical problem only, this defeatism is a challenge, too, for the practices I seek to understand. Relying on a purified conception of both law and scientific description, these tools do not enable me to do justice to sociological modes of enacting worlds and legal modes of finding out "what really happened." In so doing, both the abstraction "law" and the abstraction "science" fail to operate as good abstractions should: as tools to think with, and think through, the specificity and concreteness of practices (Stengers 2005). Hence the necessity to scrutinize both what we mean to refer to when we speak of "the law," and what we do when we seek to describe it and to see it at all.

The answer to these questions lies in the relationship between the abstract and the concrete. That is, it lies in understanding the descriptions proffered by commentators in the preceding pages as the outcome of exercises in abstraction. In working through several answers to the question of the law, we have seen descriptions of a particular kind. Not just any description will do, it has been suggested; description must be separated from normative evaluation, the ought, so that description and description alone must do the trick. Descriptions, secondly, must not only themselves be purely descriptive, but must also index and isolate an essential or necessary feature of the phenomenon described. This is the function of appeals to descriptive purity: proper descriptions of the phenomenon law do not include the inessential, the accidental, or the contingent. Description of the kind offered in the preceding chapter, then, relies upon abstraction: on the teasing out of something general, something determinative, about the phenomenon in question. By distinguishing figure from ground, signal or sign from noise, abstraction proceeds by way of flight away from the concrete. In so doing, the operation of abstraction always and necessarily produces its own exclusion: not everything can be included in one's abstraction. Abstraction always generates its own "remainder of things" (Whitehead 1953: 73).

Of course, that things are excluded from description after the process of abstraction is not in and of itself a problem. Indeed, abstractions are eminently useful in the same way good theories are: conceived as "tools for thinking" (Stengers 2005), they help focus attention, draw distinctions between figure and ground, are the precondition for agreement and shape the possibilities for dissensus. They are operationally valuable, too, when they mediate between different observations, ideas, prior knowledges and programs of action in fruitful ways: when, as ideas, they "help us get into satisfactory relation with other parts of our experience" (James 1995 [1907]: 21). But abstractions may also be mobilized to *sever* the link between themselves and "the remainder of things." It is at that point a return towards the concrete may come to present acute problems. In the conceptions of "the law" presented in the preceding chapter this is evident in their drive towards purification. In asking what is *necessarily true* of the law concrete legal practices are either understood as constituted by a determinative signal or sign of the underlying, substantive "social." In doing so these accounts risk prioritize abstraction itself over the concrete practices to which they aim to refer.

Dupret et al. (2015) speak of this process when they coin the kinds of accounts I have highlighted in the preceding chapter "hyper-explanation." Wanting to account for the operation of law, commentators put forth accounts that "deploy abstract concepts that have (arguable) relevance to any and all social situations and social actions" (Dupret et al. 2015: 4). Their own examples of such hyper-explanations include the notion of bureaucracy, modernization theory, and general theories of power and domination. It is instructive, here, to add to this brief and non-exhaustive list of examples of hyper-explanations the kind of descriptions proffered by Kelsen or by Marx. In their own ways, these descriptions reduce the many varieties of legal practices to zoom in on the code they share or on the societal interests, purposes, or structures they serve. Aside from obvious differences in opinion and foreseeable breakdowns in communication between (the admittedly rare) pure Kelsenian jurists and Marxist sociologists of law, such hyper-explanations suggest that legal practices can adequately be explained with reference to their preferred abstraction.

However, the irony here is that we may look for concrete occurrences of capitalized "Law" only to find nothing at all. Precisely this chasm between abstract and the concrete is written into Kafka's *The Trial.* "This is where the Law is done," proclaims the Court. Yet instead of that elusive law, embodied in the absent magistrate judge, Judge Joseph

K. finds offices, rooms, lawyers, examining judges, notebooks, pleadings, and proceedings. Compare this with my own experiences: instead of hidden interests or the logic of the *Grundnorm*, I was, upon entry to the court under study, confronted with documentary practices, with e-mails, faxes, and telephone calls, and with episodes of quiet work punctualized by the occasional court session or shared lunch. I saw offices, computers, files, and filing cabinets, hurried judges whose ritualistic dress failed to conceal the fact they are only humans. I found, in other words, "the remainder of things" (Whitehead 1953: 73): the things we have not included in our abstractions but that nevertheless stubbornly persist in experience. Here, our attempts at abstraction runs into troubles accompanying their own "craving for generality" (Lynch 1997; cf. Wittgenstein 2001 [1958]: 18) when we are faced with the concreteness and specificity of legal practices.

Of course, we can choose to stay at the level of abstraction and disregard practices altogether, yet we have seen this does not necessarily lead to conceptual clarity, nor does it help us to say something about *these specific cases*, these being: social scientific performativities as well as concrete legal practices of truth making. Another option is to retain abstraction and to approach legal practices as manifestations of their preferred, hyper-explanans. Of course, one might say, I don't "see" the *Grundnorm*: it is after all a fiction! And of course, I don't "see" powerful interests at work; law precisely conceals their operation, so that the fact that I do not notice them is a sign of their efficacy (cf. Valverde 2008). Notice, however, how this objection proceeds: it saves these specific abstractions, yes, but it can only do so by downgrading the concrete facts of experience. Both "focus on another reality, one that is invisible to the actors themselves but which is supposed to explain their behavior: either the true reality of society and social violence or the true reality of the rule [or norm] and its immanent logic" (Latour 2010: 142). This gesture is one of saving abstract concepts by treating them as more real than the stubborn facts of experience. Whitehead calls this the "fallacy of misplaced concreteness": of attributing to abstractions a realer, more concrete existence than experience itself (1953: 73). In doing so, it looks suspiciously like "throwing out the baby and leaving the bathwater for analysis" (Wilkens cited in Dupret et al. 2015: 4). Of course, there is nothing wrong with a study of bathwater per se – except, of course, when you were interested in the baby.

One way out of these both conceptual and practical conundrums is by asking *where and how our abstractions are concretely done.* Within sociology, this gesture can be traced most directly to Garfinkel's ethnomethodological studies (1967, 2002). Think, by way of an example, of the problem of social order – a quintessentially sociological conundrum. How can we explain social order? How does it arise? What are its consequences? Garfinkel suggests that precisely this question has suffered from sociological tendencies towards abstracted hyper-explanation. Not disputing the "objective reality" of social order, Garfinkel draws a contrast between two orientations to the question of social order. The first, he suggests, implicitly assumes that sociologists derive their mandate from the way they distill and isolate "order in the plenum." Often, they are assisted by what Garfinkel calls a "technology of formal analysis" (2002), within which the concreteness of life is reconfigured. Faced with the "concreteness of social facts of ordinary activities," social scientists have sought to measure and specify these activities so that they may be "displayed in details of orderliness in formal analytic and generic representational theories" (Garfinkel 2002: 65). The implicit assumption made, Garfinkel argues, is that there is "no order in the plenum" and that sociologists are privileged in their access to the objective reality of social facts in a way the actors themselves are not. Yet theoretical problems begin to burgeon as soon as these sociological abstractions are imbued with a concrete existence out there: How precisely do these objective social orders steer social action, concretely, "on the ground"? Lost in this process of abstraction, Garfinkel suggests, are two important things: first, an appreciation of the ways social order is concretely done and enacted as a matter of ongoing, practical action; second, an understanding of sociological hyper-explanation as just that – a practice of abstraction assisted by a specific technology.

While we may not agree with this portrayal of contemporary sociology (of course it is partial!), it is nevertheless worthwhile to stay with Garfinkel's programmatic remarks here. Note how Garfinkel does not deny the objective reality of social facts and of social order, but that he suggests these must be respecified: that is, brought into touch with concrete practices of doing social order and, where necessary, modified. The focus is not on the social fact as a *principle of inquiry* but on its status as a *phenomenon*, in other words, something that is concretely achieved. Garfinkel's novelty lies in translating this more general problematic of abstractions and their relationship with the concrete into a program for investigative action. With Garfinkel, we find ways to stay with the concrete for a while and to inquire into how abstractions are locally enacted. Latour's sociology of Law is precisely in this sense important: it refuses to treat legal practices in the Conseil d'État as exemplars or manifestations of an invisible governing norm or social logic; instead, he is interested in "the winding path of practice" (Latour 2010: 142).

It is with this respecification in mind that I will turn to the two abstractions that, in the preceding chapter, were continually played out against each other. On the one hand, I want to replace overtly abstract speech of "the law" with an appreciation of, even care for, concrete legal practices. On the other hand, I want to move away from conceiving of representation in the abstract towards an understanding of how "representation" and "vision" is done. Together, these gestures constitute a pragmatic respecification of the law–science conundrum. Emphasizing concrete practices of description and vision as well as concrete legal practices, this pragmatic respecification opens up room to stay with the conceptual troubles within the practices that we call "law" or "science." In the following, I concentrate on a series of salient dimensions – the courtroom, the legal rule, the file, methods of scientific inquiry – of concrete legal and scientific practices to give flesh and bone to this pragmatic respecification.

2.9 Legal Practices: The Courtroom and the Archive

A pragmatic respecification of the enigma of law returns to the concrete practices in and through which the law is done and enacted. It does not seek for pure law embodied but locates it in its concrete operations, most notably those taking place in self-designated legal practices. Of course, legal practices are never tied only to a specific site nor tied to a specific professional group; laypeople may orient their actions towards legal standards (Garfinkel 1967), and the law is done at borders, in policymaking, in trade and commerce, in the fabrication and legal qualification of "people and things" (Mundy and Pottage 2004). Yet courts, precisely by promising the unity of place, time, and act – "this is where the law is done" – offer themselves up as the legal setting par excellence. What better way to situate our abstractions than to start with the concrete practices that make us this promise?

2.9.1 The Courtroom

Joseph K. is partially right to go on searching for the law in courtrooms: they are the site of interrogation, of narrative strife, and of interaction between copresent participants (Atkinson and Drew 1979; Conley and O'Barr 1990, 1997; Matoesian 1993; Dingwall 2000). In the specifically

Dutch context studied here – the practices of magistrate judges, or *politierechters* – they are also sites of judicial inquiry and decision. In a sense, courtrooms dramatize precisely the (abstract) encounter of subject and law deferred in both *The Trial* and "Before the Law": that of the subject thrown before the punishing gaze of the judge. Yet treating judgment as a practical, ongoing achievement, the pragmatic task is to inquire into how judgment is achieved over the course of the interaction between defendant and judge. Pointed to as sites of "degradation ceremonies" (Goffman 1956), courtrooms are pregnant with both legal and moral possibility. Not only the defendants' legal culpability, but also her morality is in question: courtrooms are among the sites where the "soul" of the defendant (cf. Foucault 1977) and particularly his/her remorsefulness (Weisman 2004, 2014) is an empirical question for decision-makers. While studies of the role of remorse in these decision-making practices have generally demonstrated its importance, precisely how, on a local level, remorse is communicated, negotiated, and challenged remains a question ill-attended to (Bandes 2015). This lacuna in studies of the role of remorse in legal settings raises questions about the "practical grammar" (Dupret 2011) of remorse; in other words, how "remorse" is interactively and narratively established. How, then, do judges make sense of the defendants' remorsefulness in court? How is such sensemaking mediated by the stories told by the defendant him/herself? How do judges weigh, prioritize, and evaluate these narratives?

Courtrooms are ethnographically rich settings: they dramatize, in their infrastructural layout and procedural demands, the encounter between the subject and the law that is often elevated to the level of general truth. Yet settings like these are far from the only venue where the law is enacted in the broader sense. That is: although they may be the site of face-to-face interaction, as well as the performative utterance par excellence – the "you are guilty" (Austin 1955: 59) – these courtroom dramas depend on protracted episodes of quiet "face-to-file interaction" (Scheffer 2005: 75) taking place in the court's "backstage" (Goffman 1959), as well as professional familiarity with legal rules and statutes. It is to these dimensions of legal practices I now turn.

2.9.2 The Archive

If the aforementioned face-to-face interactions are fruitfully studied as practices of doing law and doing remorse, a crucial difference between social and legal orders starts to emerge when we take into account two further specificities of legal practices. The first difference pivots on the distinction between "social rules" and legal rules; the second emphasizes the specificities of bureaucratic action in its concern with the legal case file. More concretely, first I am referring to the body of legal rules stored and transmitted in black letter law; second, I am pointing to the information storage, transmission, and retrieval technique of the case file. Both concerns – the rule and the file – are intimately connected with the materiality and the temporality of the legal archive. That is the way legal practices mobilize, produce, and process materials explicitly aimed to outlast their moments of mobilization, production, or processing. Both are two sides of the archival coin:[2] the first pertains to commandment – to rules, to obligations, to "the place from which order is given" – while the second pertains to commencement, the site "where things commence" (Derrida 1995: 9) with the original filing of a document. Both are salient dimensions of legal practices. Indeed, with Latour (2010) we might understand these legal practices as engaged in the making of a connection between these two dimensions of legal practices: from file to law book. Of course, the empirical, pragmatic question is how, precisely, this connection is made.

2.9.3 *A Body of Laws*

Think, first, of legal rules: the written constitution and the stored and transmitted decisions that make up legal precedent. In legal practices, we are not solely dealing with a purely sociological abstraction – "social order" – which then must be treated as an ongoing and practical accomplishment, but rather with a kind of practice ingredients of which clearly exist prior to these practices. That is, legal practices can emphatically not invent standards of legality each time anew in a way similar to the ongoing, practical accomplishment of social order with each and every interaction. Specific to legal practices is precisely their stability over time: with the exception of a constitution, typical legal practices do not invent law anew each time but are oriented to a body of rules and statutes. In short: legal practices are enacted with reference to an archive of rules and precedent that envelops the locality and temporality of specific work practices. But that does not mean that legal rules can be understood to unproblematically guide and steer legal activities. Hawkins (1992) suggests that there is significant fact-finding and fact-defining discretion involved in the choice for a certain legal rule over another. In this sense legal rules are not a fixed "legal context" to legal practice, but part and parcel of these practices. Within a pragmatic understanding of practices, legal and procedural "context becomes a moving horizon" (Scheffer 2010: 45) made relevant to the here-and-now by en-folding, im-plication: that is, when these rules are oriented to, included, and enfolded in the here-and-now of practical activity. The normative "theory" or "model" of decision-making, written down in black letter law, does not stand apart from the practice to guide it. How and when legal actors draw on what rules in practice is then a crucial question to attend to, but it is also, according to Dupret et al. 2015: 4–6), a glaring "missing-what" in much sociolegal scholarship (see also Garfinkel 2002: 99, Dupret 2011, Travers 1997). A pragmatic respecification of "the law," asking where and how law is done, must remain sensitive to this difference between legal rules and the "social rules" sociologists speak of and inquire into the ways legal rules become oriented to and implicated in practical action.

2.9.4 "Fallen Writing": The Case File

This understanding of the interrelationship of legal rules and legal action – that is, the point that they constitute legal practices together – also offers a way into the specificity of these concrete practices, that is those taking place within a Dutch, inquisitorial, lower criminal court. The specificities of this setting lead me to a second permutation of the legal archive: that is, the legal case file. This object has received rather little attention in sociological accounts of the law's workings (Scheffer 2005, 2007; a problem these share moreover with historical studies, see Vismann 2008). Perhaps this has to do with our tendency to treat documents as mirrors onto the world instead of objects of interest in and of themselves (see Prior 2008) or with a more Anglo-Saxon focus in the study of legal practices, which jurisdictions tend to rely to a far smaller extent on the "administrative technology" of the legal case file (Vismann 2008). While Anglo-Saxon courtrooms are in general more "phonocentric" (Derrida 1967) in that they privilege oral testimony and may dismiss written evidence as hearsay, Dutch criminal law in contrast makes far more procedural allowances for (formal) written materials: not "voice" but the "fallen writing" (cf. Messick 1989) of administrative forms, process-verbals, expert reports, and witness statements found in the legal case file play an important role in Dutch criminal law. In contrast with black letter law, these legal case files are more humble "pragmatic writings" (Luhmann 2004: 237) that may not be made to last forever but must nevertheless allow for decisions in the here-and-now about the there-and-then. Procedural demands, as well as the practicalities of face-to-face interactions between different actors shape not only what is retained, but also in what specific form it may be retained for future use (see especially Komter 2019). Indeed, recent advances in the study of documents alert us to their absolute centrality not only in organizing state power (Hull 2003), but also in producing, retaining, and channeling various forms of formal and informal knowledges (Riles 2008). Legal practices are also archival practices, then, in the informational sense of the word: they draw on case files to collect, store, and transport materials that allow a decision in the here-and-now of the courtroom about the there-and-then of the offense in question. After all, judges say, "we were not there when [the offense] actually happened," which observation raises the question how the case file becomes instrumental in rendering absent events present in the here-and-now. Omnipresent, but strangely invisible, case files and the documents within them require an approach to practice that takes seriously the way they variously resist and afford certain practices. Again, the empirical question is hence how, over the course of practical work, case files come to be implicated in the unfolding of everyday judicial activities, and how they allow the production of a spatiotemporal bridge between the here-and-now of the decision, and the there-and-then of the (alleged) offense in question. Legal practices may hence fruitfully be studied as practical, archival work concerned with the bringing into a mutual relation "deposits, traces, signs or clues" (Osborne 1999: 58).

2.9.5 Time-Space Matterings

In this sense this pragmatic respecification builds upon Latour's sociology of law (2010, 2013) in that it takes seriously the practices that go into making a connection between the text of the file and the text of the law. Both rule and information, or more concretely, law book and case file, are implicated in legal practices. Both legal rule and case file are things we need to contend with if we seek a pragmatic respecification of the thin and ephemeral abstractions that have proven unproductive as tools for thinking. Yet the conception I am seeking diverges from Latour's conceptualization in that it directs more attention to both the materiality and the temporality of the archive. One, Latour has a tendency to treat case files solely as containers of texts of which the decision-makers try to make sense (see also van Oorschot 2014a, van Oorschot and Schinkel 2015). In portraying juridical practices in this light it is tempting to forget that the case file has a material existence: that it is made of heavy carton folders collecting written and photographic evidence, or of digital files that can be accessed using personal computers. A second difference pertains to its temporalities, that is the fact that the "bridge" between case file and law book in question requires a temporal folding as well. The building of this bridge, involves, in other words, the making of a relation between the here-and-now of the decision and the there-and-then of the offense in question. Just how the legal case files mediate this temporal folding is another question that assumes importance in my efforts to restore to legal practices their practical robustness (see Chapters 5 and 6 respectively for my empirical discussion of these issues).

2.10 Knowing the Law: How Vision Happens

Part of our task is now respecified: it consists not of seeking abstract law above or behind the concrete, but starts with the concrete itself and devises abstractions that may do productive work in organizing experience satisfactorily. However, with a pragmatic understanding of abstractions comes not only the question of the concrete practices they wish to help navigate, but also the question about the making of abstractions itself. In other words, how are these activities situated? In the preceding chapter, we see that such exercises in abstraction have either adopted a language of representational description – speaking in the realm of the "is," within which a word comes to stand for a world – or, when meeting the challenge of incommensurable understandings of the law, have shifted in focus to adopt a language of perspective. Yet this perspectivism similarly runs into the limitations of description of the law: either we are returned, via Bourdieu, to the unmasking expositor already embodied in Marx; or, via Hart, to the viewpoint-that-is-no-viewpoint of the internal rule-follower. The problem with these understandings of description and of perspective, I argue here, lies in its disregard for the concrete, situated activities of knowing that precede and inform both vision and description. In this sense, both representational description and vision may be convenient catch-all ways of speaking about (knowing) practices, yet both miss out on the concrete "in-between" (James 1995 [1907]): that which lies between the knowing subject and the known object.

2.10.1 The Mediated In-Between

The implicit model of knowing that informs both mandate to representational description and the emphasis on vision and perspective can be understood as the "spectator theory of knowledge" (Dewey 1929). It postulates a crucial distinction between, on the one hand, the perceiving mind (the metaphorical "eye") and on the other, the world which extends before it. Within this model, knowledge can be arrived at in either of two ways: it passes from the world into the perceiving mind; or else the eye surveys the world. The postulated direction of the arrow, either from world to mind or from mind to world, is suggestive of "empiricist" or "rationalist" understandings of knowledge respectively; yet what they share is the distinction between eye and world.

For Dewey such a conception of knowledge must, from the start, exclude an appreciation of knowing as a matter of practical activity (Dewey 1929: 22). We do not simply "know" the world because we survey it or because it impresses itself mercilessly upon our passive senses. Instead knowledge is the outcome of various ways to experiment, collaborate, and grapple with the world's recalcitrances and affordances (Gibson 1979). Think, for instance, of trying to find out where the light switch is in a strange and darkened hotel room. Our eyes may not help us, but our sense of touch, coupled with our guesses as to typical locations for light switches, do. Our body and our expectations mediate the encounter. It is only in retrospect that these activities become the "in-between," or rather, the "before" of metaphorical (and in this case, literal) illumination. In contrast with approaches that treat knowledge or vision as unproblematic and radically separate the observer from the observed, a more pragmatist understanding emphasizes, instead, this neglected in-between. The empirical question facing us, then, is how this "in-between" takes place concretely. Or, formulated differently, it raises questions about the situatedness of knowledge: how, in other words, our capacities for "sight" and "vision" are mediated and distributed.[3] In order to tease out these concerns I turn to Donna Haraway (1988).

2.10.2 *Situated Visions*

Like Dewey, Haraway (1988) draws out the metaphorical connection between knowledge and "vision" when she suggests that visual metaphors – vision, E/enlightenment, insight – have proven productive in glossing over the active work that constitutes knowing. Yet she seeks to retain the metaphor of vision by mutating our conception of the "eye." She does so by translating it from either an all-seeing force or a passive recipient of data into an active and situated perceptual system. The metaphorical eye is assisted by "prosthetic devices": instruments that amplify and mutate our "seeing" capacities: "the 'eyes' made available in modern technological sciences shatter any idea of passive vision; these prosthetic devices show us that all eyes, including our own organic ones, are active perceptual systems, building on translations and specific ways of seeing, that is, ways of life" (Haraway 1988: 583). With its emphasis on prosthesis – literally, that which is "put before" but better conceived of as that which is "plugged in" – this conception of vision understands knowledge to be mediated. That is, the "in-between" that constitutes subject and object is made out of many parts that help us "see": for example experimental set-ups that help us stabilize and isolate a phenomenon of interest; measurement techniques such as the survey, eliciting responses on pre-coded categories; or data analysis techniques that help us order and reorder into patterns suggestive of correlations. Our "ways of seeing" depend on this mediated in-between and are shaped by it; after all, there is only so much one can "see" with a particle accelerator, an experiment, a survey, or for that matter an interview. This mediated in-between is a material-semiotic assemblage populated by things of many kinds: cultural codes and categories play their part, sure, but the in-between is also populated by things, *pragmata*. This conception of knowing calls for attention to the material-semiotic mediations and distributions of knowing practices: "there is no unmediated photograph or passive camera obscura in scientific accounts of bodies and machines; there are only highly specific visual possibilities, each with a wonderfully detailed, active, partial ways of organizing worlds" (Haraway 1988: 583). Now, such an understanding of knowing clearly disallows any appeal to absolute, capital-T Truth. There is no "view from nowhere": no all-seeing eye that, unmediated and detached, observes the world as it is. Claiming this Archimedean position constitutes, for Haraway, a "God trick" (1988): it glosses over or positively ignores the many mediations that allowed vision to occur at all. In a way, Bourdieu's sociology of law falls prey to this specific "God trick." Note how Bourdieu (1987) situated both laypeople's and legal professionals' specific "visions." But what about his own perspective on these issues? Where is that perspective located, and how is it mediated? We have seen that his perspective leads us back to the role of the unmasking expositor who sees things as they really are behind the legal façade. Here, Bourdieu aims to "represent while escaping representation" (Haraway 1988: 581). Of course, such a move is impossible: there is no Archimedean point of view. Nor does this emphasis on situated knowledge amount to relativism in which every perspective is as valid as any other: truth does not "vary with the subject" but rather speaks to the "condition in which an eventual subject apprehends a variation" (Deleuze 1993: 21). Condition, situation: both speak to the constitutive implication of the observer in "detailed, active, partial ways of organizing worlds" (Haraway 1988: 583).

2.10.3 *Visions and Worlds: On Enactment*

Haraway's insistence on the "organization of worlds" is crucial here. If the subject only emerges as a result of observation, then the object to which the perspective refers is similarly an effect of observation. The relation is one between ways of seeing and ways of world-making (the formulations here are, respectively, Berger's (1972) and Goodman's (1978: 7)). Within the study of knowledge practices, this dimension of knowing activity is often referred to as performativity (Butler 1990), or enactment (Mol 2002). Mol's (2002) study of the concrete ways through which the disease atherosclerosis is done and enacted is especially helpful in this regard. Much like Butler (1990), Mol is not content to understand (in this case biological) matter as a passive substratum of knowing activities. The distinction between biological sex and social gender, between physical disease and socially constructed illness, is one that continues to uphold a sense of a world from which we are quite radically cut off. This world is conceived to be unitary, prior to, and independent of our actions. Yet precisely because knowing is always an activity not just "about" the world, but *in* and *with* specific worlds, the distinction necessarily collapses. Within the hospital practices she studies, Mol (2002) notes that the disease atherosclerosis is not "constructed" or "thought of" in different ways, but rather that its reality is enacted in different ways.[4] We do not simply "know" objects; we "enact reality in practice" (Mol 2002: 50). In that sense, there is a real and nontrivial sense in which there is not one world at all; only multiple worlds that may, or may not, be unified under the banner of the one. Precisely this recognition – that we make different worlds as soon as we start any kind of collaboration with specific worlds, and that these worlds are not necessarily compatible with each other – opens up room for us to become able to assume responsibilities for the worlds we make. For Haraway, this kind of responsibility is the ability to give an account: an account-ability that consists in the willingness to "become answerable for what we learn how to see" (Haraway 1988: 583).

2.11 Making Room: Three Ways of Case-Making

Slowly but surely we are arriving at the possibility to make room for the troubles I highlighted in the introductory chapter of this book. The law has been de-purified and restored to its practical and concrete robustness; description and vision have similarly been shown to be situated in concrete and highly variable, highly specific ways of knowing and enacting the world. It is with this vocabulary that we can start to do justice to both sociological and judicial "ways of case-making."

2.11.1 Enacting Worlds: Social Scientific Case-Making

First, if abstraction always generates a "remainder of things," and making knowledge is rooted in specific engagements and collaborations with reality, room is opened up to start inquiry into the *reality effects* of sociological accounts of legal practices.

Raising this question allows me to inquire into the specific reality effects produced by sociologists who, much like me, have sought to study legal practices. For instance, it allows me to ask just what it was about the Leiden study that rendered legal practices so alien to judges. With a conception of knowing as a situated and mediated practice comes the possibility to unpack the mediations crucial to the production of the Leiden study's account. On the one hand, it is worth inquiring how the Leiden study has enacted its object – judicial decision-making – but we may also ask what other realities, perhaps "collateral" (cf. Law 2009) to that central object, are being made. In so doing this approach also moves away from understanding legal professional's self-understandings as "miscognition" (cf. Bourdieu 1987) and instead aims to treat their perceptions as at least partially correct in that the "view" granted by the Leiden study is but one, and far from the only, mode of enacting legal practices. Inquiring just how this reality is made allows us to take seriously the rather significant levels of discomfort judges expressed in relation to the Leiden study, and question how "their practice" was made and remade in the researchers' attempts to know it.

But this recognition of the relationship between knowledge-making and world-making also raises questions with regard to the situatedness of other kinds of accounts of legal practices. For instance, we find more interpretatively oriented sociologists criticizing statistical accounts of legal (sentencing) practices because these would tend to neglect actual, unfolding instances of legal decision-making. Often, a concentration on narrative and spoken language is perceived as capable of counterbalancing this emphasis on offender and offense "factors" (Mears 1998). For example we find Tata suggesting that these "factors" only emerge over the course of narrative typification practices on the part of decision-makers: "Far from being discrete, immutable and irreducible elements, in the routine decision process 'factors' are inextricable and inseparable from the meaning of the constructed and reconstructed typified whole-case narrative" (Tata 2007: 435; see also Tata 2020). Often, the courtroom is pointed to as a particularly salient site of storytelling and of narrative strife (Jackson 1988, 1990, 1996). This emphasis on narrative typification and its situatedness in courtrooms is important to follow up on, yet the question – again – is how and where such a mode of enacting legal realities is situated, and whether accounts like these do not themselves neglect other important facets of legal practices. As we will see, these narrative-centered accounts have the tendency to enact legal practices as a kind of dematerialized struggle over the meaning of words and the sense of stories, hence neglecting a crucial, if recalcitrant object in and of legal practices. I am referring here of course to that transporter of evidence, clerks' and judges' access to "what really happened," object of struggle in and of itself: the legal case file.

2.11.2 Truth As a Legal Epistopic: Judicial Case-Making

The legal case file assumes particular importance in relation to local ways of finding out "what really happened." As I have bracketed the constitutive distinction between norm and fact, law and science, the presence of truth making practices within legal practices represents not a conceptual problem but an object of study in and of itself. Opened up is the question how various "epistopics," that is, topics of epistemological concern like truth, method, and observation, are done as a matter of unfolding activity in the sites we study (Lynch 1993). How, in other words, does observation take place? How are facts made? How is truth established? This is not to suggest that the truths made in legal settings will pass scientific tests of accuracy, but merely to insist on local ways of "seeing" and enacting specific realities. In other words, where legal practices promise some kind of access to "what really happened" these instances are helpfully addressed using a distributed, mediated, and practical conception of observation. Particularly the case file, allowing the transportation of evidentiary materials and the translation of an event into a punishable offense, is a salient ingredient of these epistemic practices: without it, there is no "case" to be made.

An insistence on the specificity and materiality of mediation (Haraway 1988), coupled with a concern with enactment (Mol 2002), all in all allows for a more fine-grained understanding of knowing practices – wherever they practically occur. It proceeds on the basis of the suggestions that "observation" of the world is never a disembodied, dematerialized practice of detached surveying but a situated and mediated practice (Haraway 1988). Indeed, treating the question as to "what really happened" as a mediated practice also means opening up room to study its distribution over a variety of actors. Among these actors are human actors, particularly court clerks, or defendants, but also nonhuman ones, specifically of course the transporters and transformers of written evidence: the legal case files. But this activity is also distributed over various sites: on the one hand, the veridictional site of the courtroom; on the other, the relatively quieter backstage offices and file-rooms. This approach, then, brackets juristic understandings of the judge as the all-determining actor within such local "epistemic practices" (Lynch 1993) and instead distributes knowing activity over both human and nonhuman actors. If we wish to cast this discussion in perspectivist terms at all, the question is not who "has" the internal point of view, but rather one that wonders how, where, and when perspectives upon the case practically take place.

2.11.3 Situated Ambulations: This Case

The emphasis on activities of seeing, description, and abstraction raise a question as to the "case" I will be making throughout this book. In other words, what does the "in-between" of my own collaborations with realities look like? How is this case situated?

Of course, the first thing to emphasize here is how this case is the product of speaking with and working alongside a total of fourteen lower court magistrate judges in a Dutch court, of acquainting myself with the many other actors populating this ecology of practice (especially clerks and case files!), and of following cases from file room, to judicial desk, to the courtroom. Taking place over a period between March 2013 and November 2015, this fieldwork consisted of trying to understand the goings-on within the court's administrative offices, its dealings with files, and judges' pre- and post-trial appraisals of the individual cases. Drawing on a technique of "shadowing," my observations of judges' work practices mostly took place right at their desk and right in the courtroom, where after some months I was allowed to take place, properly attired in robe and bib, at the judicial desk. I "shadowed" fourteen judges this way. I studied "their" files prior to their preparatory work practices as well, so that I became familiar with about 250 individual cases (this number excludes the case files studied during my own preparatory study of files), the vast majority of which were decided on by the judges I shadowed (some cases were suspended). Informal talk and conversations with judges and clerks over lunch and throughout the ethnographically infamous hallways further helped me along, as well as the opportunity I was granted to participate, in the Fall of 2013, in a three-day educational course for beginning police judges. Throughout this book, or rather case, I will refer to the fourteen crucial judges using a pseudonym, while other judges I spoke with on a more informal basis will be referred to simply as "a judge." Similarly, defendants whose individual case I have observed (and about which I have spoken with judges) are referred to by a (fictional) name, while more generalizing statements, either mine or those made by judges, will simply refer to "defendants."

Now, the preceding notes are only a bare outline of the activities of which my collaborations with this practice consisted, and as such are only a beginning of an answer to the question how this case is situated. Indeed, this question is difficult to answer in such broad strokes, as each of the following chapters is rooted in different kinds of collaborations. One is based on a close reading of the Leiden study and aims to reconstruct, from the text as well as from correspondence with one of its authors, a sense of the specific choices made and methods used. Another chapter focuses on verbal interactions in court and is rooted in informal conversations with judges and observations of court proceedings. Yet another takes as its object clerks' and judges' file-based preparation practices, and is largely rooted in observations of their face-to-file interaction (Scheffer 2005). The last empirical chapter, in turn, combines various sources of data, that is conversations as well as observations of court proceedings. Taken together, these modes of collaboration combine a critical approach to social scientific approaches surrounding judicial decision-making practices with a *praxiographic* concern (Mol 2002) with the practical work that constitutes "judging."

This praxiographic concern is itself less a well-defined method than a sensitivity to the vagaries of actual practices. Indeed, what exactly constitutes praxiography is in and of itself difficult to say; it all depends on the way it is exercised in relation to specific problems, specific settings, and specific objects. In lieu of a neatly packaged definition of praxiography, then, I prefer to think of it as an active mode of paying attention to actual practices, and, with James (1995 [1907]: 9) especially to their "surprises and wildness." Given my emphasis, too, on the case file as a salient ingredient of these practices, this praxiographic sensibility contrasts productively, for my purposes, with ethnography as it is commonly understood: that is, with ethnography as a mode of researching and writing that takes as its object human actors and their culture. Praxiography's objects of concern are not any predetermined human collectives (the "ethnoi") or their culture, but rather ongoing and unfolding practice. Last, and much like ethnography, it places emphasis on writing and rewriting (graphein) over the extraction, from practices, their guiding logos (as in: praxe-ology, see also Schatzki, Cetina and Savigny 2001).

To me, praxiography's definitional openness is immensely productive, precisely because there are no preexisting habits that can dictate how one should go about "doing" or "using" praxiography. Indeed, the very notion forces us to think about how we conceive of practices and how we might write about them. Praxiography is precisely therefore a "tool for thinking" (Stengers 2005), that is an attempt give "to the situation [itself] the power to make us think" (Stengers 2005: 185). It also raises direct questions with regard to its own "toolness," that is, its own non-innocence in mediating our inquiries. It is not immediately ready-to-hand to us, but mere contemplation upon its capacities and limitations will not do either. It must be taken up so that we can work through its affordances, and there is no guarantee such efforts will yield the desired results. In other words: it produces itself the risk the researcher will have to be willing to take (cf. Stengers 2005). Taking it up is each and every time a new and particular gesture (Stengers 2005: 185). Its "application," or rather its exercise, is intimately connected with the specificities of the object of study, whether this is a peer-reviewed article, narratives in court, or various "doings with documents" (Harper 1998) in legal practices. It is for that reason that I will not isolate these concerns in a separate methodological chapter, but comment on the way this praxiographic sensibility takes shape in relation to specific sites and objects of study throughout the separate chapters in more detail than I can provide here.

2.11.4 "Knowing As One Goes"

Together the following chapters demonstrate not only an attentiveness to the situatedness of knowledge, but also to the value of *movement* between various perspectives. Each of the following chapters takes up a hiatus produced, a reality unmade, in the preceding chapter by moving from one standpoint to the next. From a study of the "factorial approach" to legal practices evident in the Leiden study, I move to the unfolding of decision-making in relation to narrative typification practices taking place in court (Tata 2007), specifically as they pertain to the mutual elaboration of questions of guilt and remorse. From the court, I move "backstage" (Goffman 1959), where clerks, judges, and files are all implicated in extracting from the paper or digital file a condensed "image of the case" (van Oorschot 2014a). From an understanding of the file as a materially recalcitrant object, I move to an appreciation of its temporalities, so that I find myself always in relation to the file, but also, both "here" in court, and "there," at the time and place of the offense in question.

This ambulatory and praxiographic mode of paying attention, then, is not necessarily rooted in one place in particular, although it is always situated. It takes seriously the pragmatic dictum that in order to arrive at truth, we'll have to set ourselves in motion: after all, methodology – *meta-hodoi* – is always a matter of travelling roads. The roads travelled between these epistemic situations are written into this book as part and parcel of the "case" I am making. In a sense, I practice a metaphorical praxiography "on foot" (Ingold and Vergunst 2008), as my position is not tied down to one static perspective but instead seeks to travel between situations. This kind of travelling cannot forget or gloss over the fact that the roads travelled may be bumpy and the terrain treacherous. In contrast to a conception of knowing that forgets this rocky in-between – a floating eye that "barely skims the surface of the world, leaving no trace . . . or even any recollection of the journey" (Ingold 2006: 25) – I will attempt to retrace my steps and reconstruct the building of a perspective as well as my lines of escape towards differently situated perspectives. These trajectories are shaped in relation to the physical, digital, legal environment; they are also shaped in relation to disciplinary problematizations, theoretical blind alleys and conceptual lines of flight. Both the "mechanics of movement" and "formation of knowledge" (Ingold 2007: 50) are always implicated in each other; my task is to show you how, where, and with what effects. With Joseph K., I will stay on the move – without hope of finding that elusive magistrate judge, perhaps, but in anticipation of encounters with the unexpected.

3

Dealing with Difference

Doing Criminal Law and Social Order

3.1 Guilt and Denial?

Intellectual work takes patience, practice, and, of course sheer serendipity. Serendipity would have it that the start of this research project was marked by a controversy that went directly to the heart of the issues I am discussing here: the relation between legal practices on the one hand and their social-scientific description on the other. I am referring here to the study of sentencing disparities in Dutch criminal law titled "Differences in Sentencing in Similar Cases: A Quantitative Study into the Role of Specific Defendant Characteristics," authored by Wermink et al. (2012a), and published in the Dutch Jurists' Magazine [*Nederlands Juristenblad*]. On the basis of observational data and statistical analyses, the study concluded that defendants with foreign looks, particularly when they did not speak Dutch, were more likely to receive a prison term than defendants who both look and speak Dutch.

As I have shown in the Introduction to this book, judges were not pleased with this study. They raised questions about the "partiality" of the research and about the qualifications of the researchers themselves – do they have "any idea how a judge arrives at a sentencing decision?" (Bade and van der Nat 2012: 973). Judges who I was to meet later during my fieldwork had not forgotten about the study, and would assert in no uncertain terms that they were not happy with the study's implications. The implications being, of course, that judges systematically disadvantage people with certain legally irrelevant characteristics, specifically those with foreign looks and those unable to speak Dutch. Of course, there is a (very much disputed) word for making such illegitimate differences: racism.

Given this implication, it is particularly tempting, perhaps, to understand judges' responses to the study as variations on the psychological mechanism of denial: "I know very well I am guilty, but I will pretend not to be (even to myself if need be)." Or, it is possible to understand, with Bourdieu (1987) perhaps, these reactions as rooted in a blind spot that would accompany judges' professional pride: surely discriminating people on the basis of their looks would go against the very thing in which service they are working, that is the law and its promise of equal treatment. Or, yet more generally, it is also possible to explain these reactions as a broadly Dutch kind of racism in and of itself: a racism that, more collectively than individually, thrives upon its own denial of guilt in a claim to either "Dutch" or "white innocence" (cf. Wekker 2016). All such readings fundamentally find the root of judges' reactions to the study in pride and self-deception. Crucially, all such readings also attribute to the sociological observer epistemic privilege: the social-scientific researcher simply knows best. Now, I am the last to dispute the political import of diagnosing and addressing racism, especially when it takes on complex and opaque psychological, structural, and cultural forms. Yet in this specific instance I think these interpretations of the judges' reactions to the Leiden study are both theoretically reductive and actively harmful in their appeal to the epistemic privilege of the social-scientific observer. Let's zoom in on three problematic consequences in particular.

3.1.1 Situating Expert Knowledges, Establishing Rapport

For one, such readings are reductive in that they gloss over the ways judges may have been on to something when they spoke of "partiality." In attributing judges' responses to a psychological or cultural mechanism of denial, in other words, we miss out on the opportunity to take their concerns seriously and to inquire into the differences between this specific account of their practices and local ways of making cases and doing justice. That is, even if we agree that illegitimate forms of making differences can and should be studied using social-scientific methods and standards of inquiry (which I do), we may still want to understand just how specific combinations of subject matter, methodological apparatuses, research questions, and implicit assumptions shape and enact realities that may, or may not, be commensurable with local ways of judging. After all, social-scientific interventions do "category work" as well (Krebbeckx, Spronk and M'charek 2016; Yanow 2003). Differences, to speak with Krebbeckx et al. (2016: 3), are always "in the making." Lumping and splitting individuals or cases, the researchers may just categorize and classify in ways that do not necessarily resonate with local ways of "seeing" and making differences between cases or individuals.

This emphasis on the realities enacted in and through this study is all the more important, secondly, considering the politics of undisputed claims to social-scientific privilege and the singular reality these claims tend to presume. Indeed, if there are valid indications that the all-knowing subject of knowledge or science has historically hidden its own situatedness at the center of Western, imperial, and male power (e.g., Chakrabarty 2000; Haraway 1988; Spivak 1988) is it not crucial to political struggle itself to question the self-evidence of the "view from nowhere" (Haraway 1988) of the social-scientific expert? Does such a project not require us to put into doubt the possibility or the desirability of absolute, unmarked, unmediated vision and the mighty subject it presumes? Against an understanding of politics as driven by facts about a singular world, I would point out that the precondition of political struggle – including that of anti-racism activists – is precisely multiplicity in *perception* (of realities) and *conception* (of alternatives).

Last, I doubt that relegating judicial responses to a variation on the psychological mechanism of denial has the capacity to establish *rapport* between social-scientific observers and practicing jurists, that is, the possibility of first, understanding, and second, independently valuing, the specificity of both social-scientific research practices and legal practices. Precisely this kind of rapport seemed very much missing throughout this controversy. Like Bade and van der Nat (2012) in their written reply to the Leiden study, many of the judges I met felt that the Leiden study suffered from a similar ailment: the researchers did not seem to know "what judging looks like." Doubtlessly making this epistemic controversy particularly tenacious is the charge of discrimination, which is in essence a discussion about what differences – between cases, between individual defendants – should, and should not, be allowed to make a difference to judicial decisions. With commentators "talking past each other" this way, it is my aim not to adjudicate between these two positions at epistemic war, but rather to trace what realities the Leiden study enacts.

3.2 Journeying and Points of Passage

In tracing the specific performativities of the Leiden study, this chapter is an account of the kinds of methods social scientists have employed in the study of judicial practices and the kinds of realities enacted in doing so. It is a reflection on a set of common-sensical assumptions made about the objects of sociological attention, and a commentary on the frictions that emerge when such assumptions are coupled with an unproblematic appeal to social-scientific jurisdiction. At that moment, not only is there little room to establish rapport with the practices and people hence judged, but also conceptually difficult to find ways to do justice to local, practical, and unfolding ways of "doing justice."

Yet this chapter is also an effort to incorporate the fact of journeying into this narrative, and to retain a sense of the roads travelled in my account. That is, journeying is not only a question of navigating physical boundaries (although it is that, too), but also of encountering densely packed and entangled knowledges, claims, and truths surrounding one's object of study. Often, we encounter these at the stages of exploratory literature review, and incorporate the insights these offer about the object of study into our own questions, methods, and choices for topics of inquiry. In doing so we use these accounts as a lens, sharpening (or perhaps dulling) our preliminary insight into the object of study. We look *through* these accounts, directly to the (presumably singular) reality to which they refer, trying to combine and contrast insights just to know more about the object of study. Yet the Leiden study and the brief controversy it sparked precisely seem to disallow such exercise in "looking through" accounts of "our" object of study: it is a moment where the people studied spoke back and (re)claimed jurisdiction, raising the question how social scientific knowledges about this object – judicial practice – are active in the making of that very object. As an entanglement of professional, epistemic, and methodological claims, then, it proffers itself as an object to be *looked at* in its own right.

This is all the more so as the Leiden study places itself within an established tradition of statistical research into sentencing disparities (see e.g., Zatz 1987; Spohn 2000). This tradition proffers itself as crucial to not just (epistemic) understanding of legal practices but also aims to mobilize interest by pointing out the difference between "law on the books" and "law in action" (see Pound 1910), the promise of equal treatment on the one hand, and different outcomes on the other. As part and parcel of the various modes of research into judicial practices, this kind of research approach is in many respects an "obligatory passage point" (Callon 1986) for those seeking to understand judicial practices. All the more reason, then, to look at, rather than look through, this kind of approach to sentencing practices. What happens when we journey using this obligatory passage point? How is criminal law constituted?

As such, this attention to the obligatory passage point of the Leiden study contrasts, too, with more classically ethnographic modes of writing that emphasize arrival in the "field". Captured most famously in Malinowski's "Brief Outline of the Ethnographer's Tribulations," the arrival trope is mobilized when he asks the reader to imagine "yourself suddenly set down surrounded by your own gear, alone on a tropical beach close to a native village while the launch or dinghy which has brought you sails away out of sight" (Malinowski 1922: 4). Of course, this ethnographic arrival scene is a narrative artifact (Pratt 1986) and tends to write away the fact that arrival was made possible by capitalist and colonialist expansion to begin with – something Malinowski laments and later, Levi-Strauss comments on with significant tristesse (1961). This narrative gesture is present not only in such more classically ethnographic writings, however; in the social study of knowledge practices, it is perhaps most interestingly drawn on by Latour and Woolgar (1979), whose first chapter in *Laboratory Life* similarly starts with a plunge into the deep end, the laboratory under study. While there are excellent reasons to start, pragmatically, "in the middle of things" (after all, that is where we always already are), this does not always mean we must start our narratives as if we are suddenly set down in the field. Writing as if we were "suddenly set down" in the middle of things glosses over our explorations, our detours, our stumbling about in the face of objects of study both familiar and strange. Moreover, arrival scenes isolate both "the field" and "the researcher": the field from many specific (research) practices and networks within which it is taken up, even if only as an "object of study"; the researcher from a community of scholars and from the conceptual pull of disciplinary borders, problematizations, and obligatory passage points. Yet these all shape one's travels, and should be accounted for. Starting, then, not with arriving in the field but with the beginning to journeying, this chapter is both a study of the Leiden study's performativities and an account of the passages I sought.

In the following, I will first briefly introduce the Leiden study in more detail, taking care to introduce its theoretical concerns, the methodology it employed, and the conclusions it draws. After this brief discussion, I turn to a discussion of its performativities, distinguishing between its enactment of decision-making, of (criminal) law, of the individual defendant and, in relation to the individual defendant, the naturally occurring population its enacts.

3.3 The Specifics of the Leiden Study

The three researchers of the study published in the peer-reviewed section of the Dutch Jurists' Magazine, studied, in brief, what defendant characteristics exert influence on judges' decisions to unconditionally imprison defendants or opt for another (conditional or unconditional) sentence type, for example a community service or fine. That is, it is interested in finding out what factors play a role in judges' decision between sentence types. Theoretically, the researchers draw on what in the Anglo-Saxon literature is called the "focal concerns theory" (see e.g., Steffensmeier, Ulmer and Kramer 1998). Originally "focal concerns theory" was constructed to account for the cultural dimensions of lower-class gang life (see Millers 1958), yet later generations of sociologists have come to apply it to members of the judiciary to account for the concerns they incorporate into their sentencing decision. Focal concerns theory suggests that judicial decision-makers incorporate three focal concerns into their sentencing decisions (see Millers 1958; Wermink et al. 2012a: 727):

1. the offender's culpability,
2. the offender's (perceived) dangerousness to society, and
3. the practical consequences of the decision for the offender, as well as the organization itself.

Each of these three focal concerns are expected to have some explanatory power; yet as concepts, they are in dire need of operationalization. That is, they have to be translated into a set of concrete variables. Here, sociodemographic factors make an entrance in their operationalization.

The authors identify the first focal concern, the offender's culpability, as plausibly connected with an offender's criminal past, as "that kind of past would suggest greater culpability for the current offense" (Wermink et al. 2012a: 727). In addition, the authors state that a criminal past is also plausible to increase perceptions of offenders' "dangerousness," the second focal concern. But offenders' criminal past, they note, together with the legally relevant factors of offense type and severity, does not appear to explain all variation in sentence types. Previous research also suggests that "socio-demographic characteristics, like the offender's ethnicity and gender" (Wermink et al. 2012a: 727) similarly seem to play a role. Here, too, focal concerns theory, and in particular focal concern number two, the perceived dangerousness of the offender, helps the authors to justify their hypothesis with regard to these sociodemographic factors: "allochthons or defendants with a foreign appearance could be deemed more dangerous through stereotyping by judges, for example because of [allochthons' and foreign-looking defendants'] disproportionate participation in criminal activities and overrepresentation in the prison population in comparison with the Dutch [population]" (Wermink et al. 2012a: 728). Both the offender's criminal history and various sociodemographic factors, particularly whether he or she is allochthon or has a foreign appearance, are hence included with reference to focal concern one (the offender's culpability) and focal concern two (the offender's perceived dangerousness to society).

Positing, furthermore, a slightly different causal mechanism, as well as a causal mechanism exacerbating the influence of stereotyping, the researchers also suggest that the language the offender uses in court is likely to matter as well: first, miscommunication between judge and offender is more likely, and second, because those who do not speak Dutch and appear foreign are likely to have an ever higher chance of being stereotyped than those who look foreign, but speak Dutch. The authors also touch upon the last of the three focal concerns – the practical consequences of a sentence for the offender or the organization itself – when they suggest that practical considerations make those who do not speak Dutch even more likely to receive a prison term, as their incapacity to speak Dutch will likely pose problems when a community service must be executed.

The researchers also incorporate a set of control variables such as the location of the court, the type of offense, the defendant's age category, and a series of binary variables detailing whether or not the defendant has spent time in pre-trial custody, whether or not the defendant has a criminal record, and whether or not the defendant perpetrated the offense alone or in association. Importantly, the dependent variable details whether or not the defendant receives an unconditional prison sentence and is hence dichotomous. A distinction is made between unconditional prison sentences on the one hand, and on the other, all other sentence types, such as a fine, an unconditional community service, or conditional prison sentence (all of varying gravity). Crucially, as this dependent variable is dichotomous, the authors cannot use measures of correlation but instead turn to a binomial logistic regression analysis. Without detailing much about this particular kind of analysis – which contrasts with more traditional forms of regression analyses of variation on (presumed to be) continuous variables – the authors go on to present their descriptive statistics (Wermink et al. 2012a: 730) and then their analysis (Wermink et al. 2012a: 731).

Going on to review their findings, the authors state that their expectations with regard to the role of "foreign appearance" and "speaking Dutch" have been confirmed: controlling for all relevant variables, they find that defendants who look and speak Dutch have the smallest chance of being sent to prison, while those who do speak Dutch but have a foreign appearance are five times more likely to be sent to prison than not being sent to prison in comparison with that group. Those who do not speak or look Dutch are twenty times more likely to be sent to prison than being not sent to prison in comparison with the Dutch-looking and Dutch-speaking reference category, so that this category of defendants qualifies as the "most severely punished" (Wermink et al. 2012a: 732).[1]

Now, I have alluded to the fact that this study, upon publication, sparked a brief controversy in the media. Following the publication of the study, the NRC Handelsblad paid attention to its findings in a brief newspaper article, summarizing the researchers as having found that judges

> punish defendants with a "foreign appearance" more severely than they do the Dutch, in particular when the defendants do not speak Dutch. . . . The researchers have judged by the defendant's appearance whether he or she is possibly from abroad. Whether the defendant is in actual fact a foreigner was checked with help of the defendant's country of birth, which is always mentioned in court.
>
> (NRC 2012, March 14)

In the next day's editorial, the NRC concluded that the "intuitive judge has been caught out" (NRC 2012, March 15) and that lady Justice's blindfold "seems an illusion, not a self-evident professional characteristic." Emphasizing that judges are not immune to stereotypes, it suggested that further large-scale studies should be conducted. Indeed, while it emphasizes that "solid conclusions about the possible lack of sentencing parity between allochthons and autochthons cannot be drawn from one study," it nevertheless raised the following questions: "Are criminal law judges sufficiently aware of the influence of negative stereotypes? Is there attention paid to such issues throughout their education and in collegial feedback [*intervisie*]? Do people correct each other there or is this study a bolt from the blue? Are there, moreover, enough criminal law judges with a non-Dutch cultural background?" (NRC 2012, March 15). Other actors similarly extracted, from the article, the suggestion that the Dutch judiciary is facing significant problems in dealing with difference.

Members of Parliament Recourt (PvdA, centrist Labour Party), Dibi (the Green left) and van der Steur (VVD, the largest Liberal party) each submitted sets of formal questions to the Minister of Security and Justice Opstelten. These questions roughly concentrated on whether the Minister shares the researcher's conclusions "that negative stereotyping with regard to defendants with a foreign appearance play a role in their greater likelihood of receiving a harsher sentence," and the actions the Minister would undertake to make sure that "judges do not weigh the defendant's appearance in their sentencing decisions anymore" (Kamerstukken II 2011/12). In response, the Minister asked the Scientific Research and Documentation Centre (WODC) to critically appraise the study and used this to inform his own reply to the request of the members of Parliament (Ministerie van Veiligheid en Justitie 2012). A more detailed reply written by two WODC researchers was later published in the same Dutch Jurists' Magazine (Weijters and Leeuw 2012), together with a reply of the three authors of the study (Wermink, de Keijser and Schuyt 2012b) and a reply by two judges (Bade and van der Nat 2012). These assorted documents, together with personal correspondence with one of the study's authors, make up the core materials upon which this analysis is based.

3.4 Seeing Decision-Making, Making Differences

Let's turn, now, to the central questions addressed in this piece. How is the Leiden study's "perspective" upon judicial practices made? And what realities are enacted in the building of this perspective?

3.4.1 Oligopticism-in-Action and the Black-Boxing of Decision-Making

While Hartian sociolegal scholars may be quick to understand the Leiden study to embody an "external point of view" (Hart 1994 [1961]), it is nevertheless instructive to be a bit more specific about how this perspective is built and how it is situated. First of all, what strikes any reader is the rather large N of the study. While a sample size of 333 cases may not seem much in comparison with other, larger databases, this number of cases nevertheless effectuates itself what Latour (2005: 181) calls a kind of oligopticism. This sociological oligopticism allows the researchers to "see" many cases at once. However, this is a qualified kind of oligopticism: it is far from an effort to see "everything," but rather to "see" cross-sectionally in order to gauge differences between groups of individuals. In so doing its ambition is revelatory: it tries to see many cases at once and to reveal consistencies and patterns one might not see "up close."

It must do so, crucially, by cutting up cases into dependent and independent variables. In this case, there is only one dependent variable: whether or not the defendant was sentenced to an unconditional prison sentence. There are more independent variables, for example the presence of a criminal record. Now, the making of these variables is inevitably a practice of lumping and splitting: of making differences, as well as grouping together, phenomena of a certain kind. This is, incidentally, where the study attracted most criticism. For instance, the objection to this study that the researchers had opted for a binary variable detailing only *whether* the defendant did or did not have a criminal record in their measure of the defendant's criminal history, is one such criticism. The question is not whether a defendant does or does not have a criminal record, it was argued, but also precisely how "long" it is, and whether it details "relevant" recidivism (i.e., whether the current offense is of a similar type as the one the defendant was previously convicted for). Neither did the study adequately control for the severity of cases lumped together, it was argued: dealing in large quantities of heroine is arguably a wholly different offense than the possession of a small amount of party drugs, for instance (see also Ministerie van Veiligheid en Justitie 2012; Weijters and Leeuw 2012). In the social study of legal practices, much has been said about the particular reduction such a "perspective" effectuates. Case-specific characteristics of relevance to decision-makers may not be measured at all (if only to function as control variables in the final analysis), or, distinctions of local relevance may be glossed over and grouped together as constituting a single variable. Lumping and splitting, then, are never neutral operations. And as we will see later on, the "category work" the study did in lumping and splitting defendants' in their social characteristics will prove somewhat controversial as well.

However, let's first look at its object of study: the outcomes of judicial decision-making. The charge that statistical research inevitably runs into difficulties accounting for the causal mechanisms at the heart of its analyses applies here to some extent as well. Analyzing the effect of "input" on the decision's "output," judicial decision-making itself is "black-boxed" (Latour 1999). That is, enacting judicial decision-making as an input and output system – values on the independent variables go in, values on the dependent variable come out – the statistical analysis has the tendency to seal off the complexities of such decision-making itself.[2] This, of course, is not necessarily a problem: black-boxing decision-making in favor of a more cross-sectional perspective is instructive. Yet the theoretical addition that the observed differences in output are plausibly explained with reference to focal concerns theory adds, in turn, another black-box at the heart of the postulated causal mechanism, that is: the "head of the actor" (Garfinkel 1967) him/herself. The suggestion is hence that the observed differences are due to cognitive processes: "focal concerns." And there, too, yet another black-box makes its appearance, as the authors distinguish between a transparent part of that "head of the actor" – the conscious – and the opacity of the unconscious, where bias resides.

For sociologists, these remarks on the performativity of the Leiden study are doubtlessly exemplary of a broader criticism of statistical methods. They have a history: for instance, Becker suggests that statistical analysis, although having some use, is of limited value precisely because it reduces the richness of life-as-lived: "it's only *your analysis* that produces the abstract and discrete variables which *then have to be put back together*" (Becker 1996: 56, emphasis added). What the fieldworker in contrast "sees is not variables or factors that need to be 'related' but people doing things in ways that are manifestly connected" (Becker 1996: 56). In so doing this specific argument has the tendency to separate the vagaries of everyday life from the "premature quantification" (Thomas and Thomas 1928: 567) associated with statistical methods. The argument so made is more or less explicitly naturalist, erecting a distinction between the richness of everyday social life and the cold formalisms of statistical analysis. While there is some merit in an emphasis on the limits of statistical analyses, this argument does little justice to the fact that statistical analysis is *itself* a productive and concrete practice – that, I repeat, can and should be studied in its own right. In other words, as soon as statistical analysis is contrasted with the "actually occurring," lost from view is the fact that statistical analysis is itself "actually occurring." Indeed, while such objections are cast in a register of lack and failure (to measure, to adequately grasp), statistical accounts, it must be remembered, do productive work as well. As a consequence of lumping and splitting and black-boxing, several "collateral realities" (Law 2009) are enacted into being (Mol 2002). These "collateral realities" are best conceived of as realities that may not be the delineated object of study – the outcomes of judicial decision-making in this case – but realities that are made as a side effect of investigative work.

That is, they are a kind of ontological fall-out to the ways knowledge is made. So what does the study's emphasis on aggregates do in the production of a specific conception of criminal law? And who or what, secondly, are its subjects?

3.4.2 *Distributing Justice, Sorting Population Groups*

One of the Leiden's performativities is the way it approaches criminal justice as, essentially, a distribution and sorting machine. It distributes justice in the form of punishment, and it sorts people by attributing them differential statuses. Indeed, the conception of criminal law enacted here has affinities with Hasenfeld's conception of organizations more generally as "people-processing organizations" which are defined as organizations "attempting to achieve changes in their clients not by altering basic personal attributes, but by conferring on them a public status and relocating them in a new set of social circumstances" (Hasenfeld 1972: 256). Importantly, it is precisely this approach that renders criminal law, at least conceptually, comparable to other "people processing organizations," for example to medical practices or to educational practices. This is a significant advantage, as it then becomes possible to look for differences in the performance both within these machines (between, for instance, individual courts) and between them, for instance when one is interested what role is played by different institutions or organizations in the reproduction, exacerbation, or mitigation of social inequalities. Yet this same advantage translates into what Hart would call the "external point of view" (1994 [1961]) that has little to say about what distinguishes criminal law from other distributing and sorting machines. What, in other words, sets criminal law apart from other institutions that similarly operate to distribute collective goods (and bads) and similarly sort people? The very problematization of criminal justice as a "sorting machine" ensures that little legal is said about the exercise of law. There is, to be precise, only one place where "the legal" can be said to play a role, that is in the distinction between case characteristics deemed legally relevant and those deemed legally irrelevant. Crucially, however, those factors deemed legally relevant – in particular the kind and severity of the individual case – are precisely delegated the status of a *control* variable, so that the "legal" is enacted as a context to the actual substance of "social" distributing and sorting processes.

3.4.3 *Social Order: Factors, Population Groups, Nature and Nationality*

Now, if this study enacts the criminal justice process as a distribution and sorting machine, then who are the object of such sorting and distributing work? The short answer is: naturally occurring, always already there, groups within society. That is, the object of sorting and distributing work are population groups [*bevolkingsgroepen*] of which individual defendants are understood to be a member. This operation is evident in the way the study disaggregates, and assembles anew, individual court cases. Enacted in the Leiden study is the case as a collection of factors, some of which pertain to the offense in question, some of which pertain to the offender in question. In this distinction, it echoes the judicial distinction between the offense and the "personal circumstances" (or "person of the defendant") characteristic of offender focused jurisdictions like the Dutch, but it is also typical of studies in the sociology of sentencing more generally (Mears 1998; Tata 2007). At the same time, the "person of the defendant" figures not as a judicial category but incarnates sociologically. That is, the "person of the defendant" is the location of a set of imputed, arguably "social" qualities. Gender is one of these presumed qualities in the Leiden study, but perhaps more interesting is the strange and slippery way it enacts differences tied to defendants' degree of "Dutchness."

That "Dutchness" is of prime importance to the authors' analysis goes without saying: drawing on a binomial logistic regression analysis, the authors need a reference category against which to measure other groups of people. Of course, the choice for what category constitutes the reference category is statistically arbitrary, and the authors – as is often the case, see Boersma and Schinkel (2015) – have elected to use "Dutch-looking and Dutch-speaking" as the reference category against which variation is measured. The interesting question here is how precisely this category is made; that is, how presumed differences in the population are made consequential to their measurement of "social factors." While the authors variously refer to "ethnicity" or the distinction between "allochthons" and "autochthons" (e.g., Boersma and Schinkel 2015: 728), something a little more complex is happening in the Leiden study. Remember that the study does not draw on officially registered data on the ethnicity or allochthon status of defendants appearing in court (indeed, that information is, in the Netherlands, not registered at all either by courts or other actors, even though there are efforts to categorize those registered as suspects using several databases, see e.g., Blom et al. 2005).

Instead the Leiden study relies on student assistants' observations in court. However, the article itself is curiously silent about how these observers make differences between defendants according to their "foreignness" or "Dutchness," and does not elaborate on how such foreignness and Dutchness is to be operationalized. So what do these student assistants observe, precisely?

According to the official publication in the Dutch Jurists' Magazine, the students have observed whether or not the defendant (1) speaks Dutch and (2) has a "foreign" or "Dutch appearance." The second measure of "Dutchness" is particularly interesting: it seems to enact Dutchness and foreignness as something completely and commonsensically evident, visible at first glance to the eye of student observers. In that sense, it enacts Dutchness and foreignness as a "superficial," immediately legible difference of the body and the face. Indeed, in a fact-checking blog of April 17, 2012, Schuyt tells us that with regard to this measure of difference, "one could think of having a moustache, black hair and brown eyes" (FHJ Factcheck, 2012, April 17).

This collection of differences awkwardly combines the cultural (a preference for moustaches most commonly associated with foreign men) and the biological (hair and eye color), congealing into *phenotypical mode* of doing difference (van Oorschot 2020). The individual's body, there, is a collection of biological and cultural signs. Interestingly, Schuyt here makes no mention of that marker most commonly associated with difference, that is, skin color. This hesitancy speaks perhaps to the "absent-presentness" of biological race in contemporary, Western-European speech about difference (M'charek, Schramm and Skinner 2014; M'charek and Skinner 2014; van Oorschot 2020; M'charek and van Oorschot 2019); that is, the way explicit reference to biological race, particularly so skin color, has to be suppressed and denied. At the same time, difference remains something legible on and of the body: mobilized are moustaches, hair, and eye colors as markers of difference.

However, complexities continue to multiply. Whether or not a defendant had a "foreign" or "Dutch" look, the authors tell the NRC, "was checked in the context of the hearing with reference to the defendant's birth country and the defendant's [migration] history" (NRC 2012, March 14). Here, the plot thickens: birth country and "the defendant's history" have also played a role in the categorization of defendants. Does this mean that the in-court observers have "checked" their own observation of the defendant against what is now presumed to be his or her *actual* foreignness, a foreignness which is here tied to defendants' birth place and migration history? Now, the article or other sources do not detail how such "checking" took place and how observers have prioritized different "measures" of foreignness: for instance, what if their observation was wrong and the person was, indeed, born in the Netherlands? Which "measurement" of foreignness would they have prioritized?

Replying to precisely this question raised by Weijters and Leeuw (2012), the authors explain that the distinction between Dutch and foreign was based particularly on the defendants' birth country (which is always mentioned in court) (Wermink et al. 2012b). However, as one of the study's authors further explained, this measure of "foreign-ness" was complemented by a second: "The students received instructions for that variable to code people born abroad as foreign, and to code people who were born in the Netherlands but look foreign as also 'foreign'" (Wermink 2016, 27 June). The study's author suggests that this procedure ensured that "2nd and 3rd generation allochthons could also fall into the category 'foreign'." Here, then, a *third* mode of doing difference enters the picture: the distinction between allochthons and autochthons. This is a distinction quite particular to the Dutch context (but see Geschiere 2009 for its use in African settings). The category allochthon, introduced as a way of speaking about immigrants in 1971 by Verwey-Jonker and formalized, in part, by the Central Bureau for Statistics (CBS), refers to people with either one or two parents of a foreign nationality.

Thus we encounter a third mode of doing category work: the distinction between autochthons and allochthons, a recurring one in the Dutch context. In this one measure of difference, in other words, three different ways of making population groups are at work: first, there is reference to nationality; second, there is reference to phenotypical looks, self-evidently present on the surface of the body; third, both are drawn on to categorize people into the categories of allochthony and autochthony. These are registers of difference that pivot on different markers: the first, birth place; the second on phenotype, while the third, allo- and autochthony, combines a logic of soil – where one is born – with descent – where one's parents come from (see Geschiere and Jackson 2006).

And indeed, the form the students were required to use during their in-court observations speaks not of looks, nor of birth country, but directly aims to register the defendants' "background" [*afkomst*]. It provides the following three categories:

1. Autochthon
2. Allochthon, namely: European / Non-European / Unknown
3. Don't know

The nation, the body: this is how the Leiden study enacts differences between individual defendants, who are from now on either slotted as allochthons or autochthons. This enactment of difference, then, is spectral, drawing on phenotype, soil, and blood simultaneously. If law is enacted as a sorting machine, the operation of sorting assumes and enacts a self-evident difference within the population; a difference, furthermore, at once administrative and phenotypical. At play is a very particular enactment of difference, and it must be said it is one not entirely disconnected from racial imaginaries of biological difference that, within that imaginary, map race onto geography and territory. "Face," "race," and "place" are here tied up with each other, and if they are not aligned – in case someone is born in the Netherlands but "has" a foreign look – it is "face" that is the deciding factor in this politics of belonging (cf. Geschiere 2009).

Now, it is well-known that variations and differences within populations have historically emerged as prime objects for both knowledge-production and government (Foucault 2004); it is also well-known that the history of statistical analysis and its concern with the population is deeply intertwined with the advent of nineteenth-century evolutionary biology and, of course, eugenics (Desrosières 1998). Yet it is equally important to note that explicitly racial modes of enacting difference within the populations have, for obvious eugenic reasons, not fared well in Western Europe post–World War II (even though, it must be said, that the explicit absence of "race" makes racism by no means an impossibility (Balibar and Wallerstein 1991)). Yet it is important to not simply draw the conclusion that "race" is therefore a thing of the past, or else mere fictitious, only a social construction. M'charek (2013; or see M'charek et al. 2014; M'charek and Skinner 2014) in particular points to the continuing relevance, but absent-presentness, of "race" in contemporary knowledge practices, for instance in genetics and forensics. There, too, specific relationships between "race" and "population" are forged, and there, too, are differences enacted between populations. With the Leiden study, we encounter the phenotype once again coupled with the notion of the national population – this time in the knowledge practices not of forensic scientists or geneticists, but that of social scientific inquirers.

3.5 Returning to the Charge of Racism

This chapter has demonstrated a mode of analysis that concentrates on the reality effects of social-scientific interventions. In so doing it has paid attention not to the politics of its stated effects – the charge of discrimination – but rather the politics that inhere in its enactment of judicial decision-making, criminal law itself, and the population over which it distributes punishment. These enactments of the law as a distribution machine, decision-making as a matter of information inputs and outputs, and the objects of the law as an internally stratified population, I argue, are political through and through: they pertain to the question as to how we order, sort, and make worlds. With Mol (1999: 75) I would point out that this reality, after all, does not precede "the mundane practices in which we interact with it, but is rather shaped within these practices." In that capacity, the term politics is apt, precisely because "it underline[s] this active mode, this process of shaping, and the fact that its character is both open and contested" (Mol 1999: 75).

This emphasis on the politics of the measurement of racism assumes importance in a specifically Dutch context, within which we can discern several modes of dealing and non-dealing with difference more generally. Addressing practices of presumably illegitimate modes of difference-making, my emphasis on the study's performativities is one way to engage with the question as to whether "we are equipped to recognize our racism" (van Reekum 2014: 92). This question contrasts sharply with arguably more dominant social-scientific approaches to difference that posit difference as the source of social problems and the medium (Mitchell 2012) through which these should be measured and governed, for instance in the complex of research practices that take ethnic minorities and "their culture" as objects of measurement and intervention (Essed and Nimako 2006). This proliferation of research about "them" throughout what has been called the "Dutch minority research industry" (Essed and Nimako 2006) has entailed a symmetric move away from "critical explorations of the historical and ideological underpinnings and ramifications of Dutch constructions of 'race' and 'ethnicity'" (Essed and Nimako: 284). It is in this context that the Leiden study's authors' attempts may be welcomed as an opportunity to not speak only about "them," but precisely as a way of engaging with racism on the part of the Dutch self. There are some indications that the Leiden study is cited as evidence of racism in Dutch society, for example in Amnesty International reports on ethnic profiling in 2013, or in articles by those seeking to criticize the Dutch denial of slavery and racism (e.g., Özdil

2014). However, my treatment of this study has suggested we be a little more cautious, specifically in our choice of "equipment." That is, how do our concept and methods render racism intelligible and visible? And, what do they *not* do?

3.5.1 *Due Diligence*

First, some caution is warranted because of the study's reliance on a vocabulary of unconscious bias. On the one hand, the researcher's operationalization of meaningful difference as, first and foremost, a question of nationality and second, of phenotypical difference, seems a plausible mode to construct an object of "unconscious bias." Their reliance on this notion of unconscious bias is, of course, not directly supported by their own data. After all, the discriminatory effects witnessed may, for instance, be the consequence of *conscious* discriminatory attitudes. Indeed, the imputation that certain differences in outcomes are due to unconscious bias presents a palatable, but ultimately quite unsatisfying, modality of shaping the conversation about racism. Moreover, while it is doubtlessly important to make people aware of largely implicit but biased notions they may share, the terms of the discussion leave little room for an appreciation of racism as a *structural effect*, rather than a *mental preference* (a well-known problem in the study of racism, see for example Fanon's warning that racism cannot adequately be grasped as a merely mental quirk or flaw (Fanon 1956)). It is important, then, to note the work an emphasis on unconscious bias is doing in narrowing down the notion of racism itself.

Furthermore, in relation to issues of structural racism, it is crucial to recognize that an emphasis on the "hidden variable" that would explain away discriminatory practices in judges' sentencing decisions might inadvertently bar questions as to the operations of criminal justice more generally. For instance, were we to find, through sophisticated measurement and statistical maneuvering, that ethnic or racial bias in the outcomes of sentencing decisions can be explained with reference to other, heretofore unmeasured variables (for instance, these ethnic minorities' lower educational attainments, lower labor market participation rates, lower "integration" in society, or weaker "social bonds") we might be happy to show that racial or ethnic bias does not exist as such. Note that this is precisely the suggestion made by researchers affiliated with the WODC. When the then Minister of Security and Justice Opstelten asked them for a critical appraisal of the study, their reply suggested that surely the researchers have overlooked an underlying variable that explains these differences and outcomes (Weijters and Leeuw 2012). In any case, following this procedure we would lose the opportunity to ask the question how it is that criminal law seems to target in particular already deprived social groups at all; and by extension, how racism does not have to be present in the heads of individual actors for a system to work out in racist ways.

Further caution is warranted because there is something quite specific in the study's enactment of difference. If critical race scholars treat "race" as an *effect* of racism, this study instead draws matter-of-factly on the state's categorization practices (the distinction between nationals and foreign-borns) and complements it, in case nationality is suspected to be a flawed measure of presumed to be "actual" difference, with an emphasis on physical appearance, that is, the phenotype. As such, difference is partially naturalized, understood to reside on the surface of individual bodies. Assuming the existence of discrete, recognizable, and phenotypically and administratively distinguishable groups in society, the Leiden study hence contrasts sharply with the more critical interrogation of racism, which does not start with "race," but rather with interrogating where and how "race" is produced as an effect of racisms of various (possibly interlocking) sorts. Such interrogations question the self-evidence of both the phenotype and administrative categorization practices, and in doing so allow one to index where "kind and kin" are made. Such a mode of addressing racism would point out that one of the most salient effects of racism is *race itself*, and that a modality of response to racism would need to denaturalize precisely racism's presumed to be stable referent – race.

3.6 Onwards: From Factors to Narrative Typification Practices

Having analyzed the study and drawn out its performative effects, it is now time to return to the issue of *rapport*. In other words: How can we understand the controversial status of the study among the members of the judiciary in light of this analysis? How might we establish rapport between judges and these sociologists?

For a start, I would now point out that the research was in actual fact partial, precisely in the sense elaborated on by Haraway (1988). Even though the study promises political and epistemic detachment, it is partial in the dual sense: partial as in committed to the truth, but also partial as it is engaged in making available of *specific* accounts situated in *specific* perceptual systems. This is not simply a variation on the charge that the researchers' model reduces complexity – of course it does. With Borges (1972) we know that the only map capable of perfectly representing the territory is a map as large as the territory itself, and we can only imagine how unwieldy, how impractical, such a map would prove to be. Even though the study reduces complexity, then, my analysis has concentrated on the way it *adds* complexity: that is, how it enacts worlds that are never quite as self-evident as social scientists may believe them to be. For instance, "law's promise" of equal treatment may not necessarily be adequately translated into a conception of criminal law as a distribution machine taking as its object internally differentiated populations. Moreover, the legal category of the "person of the defendant," part and parcel of judges' sentencing decisions and the locus of the imputed discriminatory sentencing outcomes, is precisely established to move away from an arguably *undifferentiated* and precisely *therefore* unjust treatment of individual cases. Yes, criminal law does promise to "sort people out," but not necessarily by sorting people "sociologically." I have suggested that law's promise of equality should not be misunderstood to imply sociological equivalence between population groups, and that the fact-fiction of the "population group" is doing both productive and perhaps less productive work in the way we conceive of legal practices, of racism, and of "race" itself. While the assumption that reality is in actual fact singular, that is, that both the researchers and judges are actually talking about the same reality, is dominant in the controversies around the Leiden study, my intervention has drawn attention to the fact that we need not make this assumption. It is precisely by deferring this assumption that rapport becomes an option. Not because it suggests that there are different perspectives on "the same" underlying reality, but precisely because social-scientific efforts *make* realities – often in their own terms, using their own equipment.

It is now time to move on and to follow up on the provocative question, posed by the two judges replying to the study, whether the researchers have "any idea how a judge arrives at a sentencing decision?" (Bade and van der Nat 2012: 973). I aim to read this provocation as an invitation, and in the following I will address how judges see their work and go about their adjudicating and sentencing business. If judges do not necessarily "see" individual defendants as exemplars of sociological "population groups," how else do they see these defendants? If they do not understand cases as bundles of factors, how else do they make sense of them?

These questions run through the remainder of this book. The legal case file, conceived as a material-semiotic "optical device" (Haraway 1988) for "seeing cases" is touched upon in Chapters 5 and 6. The following chapter, however, stays somewhat closer to judicial self-conceptions and emphasizes the role played by in-court interactions between judge and defendant, emphasizes the centrality of narrative, and highlights judges' evaluations of the defendants' "remorsefulness." This chapter shows that while members of the judiciary may be quick to contrast the social-scientific, cross-sectional perspective with their own "casuistic" approach – within which each case is considered unique and irreducible – we will see that a concentration on the production and evaluation of remorse in the interaction with the defendant illustrates the existence of vernacular, informal typification practices. That is, even though the social-scientific triad race-class-gender is not explicitly evoked in the course of their decision-making, judges nevertheless make use of informal, narrative typifications that center on the type of defendant and the type of offense in question. Distinguishing between three "typified whole-case narratives" – the typical "drug-addict," the typical "angry young man," and the typical "explosive couple" – I show how defendants' demonstrations of remorse are weighed and prioritized differently, depending on which specific whole-case narrative is mobilized to understand the case in question. In so doing I do not treat the "person of the defendant" as a bundle of factors, but rather zoom in on the way this person is produced as a locus of both moral and legal culpability. In this I am following up on Tata's admonition (2007) that the practice of judging is not to be conceived mechanically but instead as a matter of "judgcraft," which, as we will see in the next chapter, is an admonition in line with judges' own conceptions of their work practices.

4

Situating Remorse

4.1 Following up on the Leiden Study

The preceding chapter has demonstrated the "reality effects" of some social-scientific, statistically oriented approaches to criminal justice practices, suggesting that these kinds of approaches are not to be understood as reductive (only) but as productive. They enact the object of study – judicial decision-making – in a specific way, and simultaneously mobilize and enact multiple "collateral realities," most notably a population that falls apart into distinct, phenotypically and administratively distinct and circumscribable population groups.

Having spent time on the "reality effects" of the Leiden study, I turn now to effects of a different kind, that is the way the study affected judges and my own collaborations with them. In this chapter I suggest that the Leiden study's mode of enacting legal practices contrasts with the emphasis judges place on their own intuitions, their craft, the specificity of individual cases and, especially so, the uniqueness of the "person of the defendant." Aiming to follow up on judges' emphasis on "their own way of dealing with cases," I trace here the kind of judgments judges make about the "person of the defendant" and pay specific attention to defendants' "remorsefulness." Far from a binary given as something either present or absent (Tombs and Jagger 2006), I show how judges' appraisals of defendants' remorsefulness are a doubly situated accomplishment. These appraisals are situated, first, within the legal and moral space of the courtroom, where legal requirements and moral demands may clash and place interactional burdens on the defendant in his or her demonstrations of remorse. Second, the accomplishment of remorse is situated not only in the space of the courtroom but also narratively: that is, within not just the specifics of the case but within vernacular, informal "typified whole-case narratives" (Tata 2007) that judges draw on in their sense-making. For instance, facing either drug-addicted defendants or domestic abuse charges, judges tend to weigh and prioritize defendants' demonstrations of remorse differently. While judges may not work with stereotypes concentrated on statistically relevant population groups, then, their practices nevertheless show some measure of typification, particularly when it concerns their appraisals of the value and importance of defendants' remorsefulness. In other words, I will show how judges make differences (between defendants, between cases), and how these differences differ from the ones made in the Leiden study.

Based upon observations in court as well as case-specific conversations with judges, this chapter emphasizes (much like judges themselves) specific cases chosen for their strategic and demonstrative value. In doing so this chapter offers both a discussion of a specific topic of theoretical concern – the "practical grammar" (Dupret and Ferrie 2015) of remorse, particularly as a both legally and narratively mediated accomplishment – as well as a discussion of my travels in relation to the often-postulated opposition between sociology's cross-sectional approaches to legal practices versus judicial, casuistic self-conceptions. I will conclude this chapter commenting on the situatedness of my own collaborations with these practices as these took place within the largely oral proceedings in court.

4.2 Contrasts and Questions

Let's go back again to that spring of 2012. My first encounters with judges around that time were very much shaped by the publication of the aforementioned Leiden study. In a series of exploratory conversations with retired or practicing judges, the study had a habit of popping up in our conversation. The aforementioned Judge Beech (see the Introduction) was perhaps most vocal about her disagreement with the study's findings:

> This does not do justice to the way we tailor sentences. . . . It's all a matter of taking various steps. You start with the offense in question – is it punishable, is it proven – and then you move onto the circumstances surrounding the offense, and then you move onto to the defendant and his or her circumstances. . . . We might have our weaknesses and our little frustrations [with individual defendants], but we learn to reflect on them to take them into account. But the suggestion that we punish some defendants more harshly than others is just insulting. We have our rules, our procedures, and

> we look at cases individually. The defendant is part of that. Every case is different, every defendant is different, but we follow the same rules.

I have no doubt that some of the discomfort, evidenced here in Judge Beech's words, was in fact partially due to its (implicit) accusation of discrimination, even racism. Yet this discomfort is suggestive, too, of the sometimes fraught relationship between sociological-statistical enactments of judicial work and judges' own conceptions of these practices. This chapter is a way to engage with these discomforts. Sensitized by Judge Beech's rather vehement disagreement, I took her admonition to take seriously judges "own ways of dealing with cases" to heart. That is: if they are not satisfied with the Leiden study's results, how would they say they usually deal with cases?

4.2.1 *Craft, Intuition, and the Unique Case*

I would learn that this question is both the right and the wrong question: right, because judges' modes of response to it cast light on both judges' self-perceptions and their modes of justifying their practice; wrong, because it was asked in a register their answer tended to disavow. That is, while the question is cast in a general and descriptive mode, judges' answers emphasized intuition over "science" or "legalism," the specific over the general, and the "whole case" and the "whole person" over the fragmentation introduced by statistical modelling.

Telling in particular were the moments I would introduce my research to individual judges. Casting my research as an intervention aimed to do justice to "their ways of dealing with cases," I often faced a sympathetic but slightly weary audience. "But so much of it has to do with intuition," one of the judges objected. How would I be able to describe these intuitions, especially when parts of these intuitions may be obscure to judges themselves? For instance, Judge Dempsey suggested that "much of it is unconscious," suggesting that his thinking at times surprises even himself. Conscious or unconscious: with judicial practices, judges asserted, comes a trained, juridical intuition, a cultivated prudence that is not easy to make explicit even to oneself. In evoking the centrality of intuition, these judges tended to agree with Scholten's appraisal of judicial practices as involving, ultimately, an unexplainable "jump . . . that is always courage" [*een sprong . . . die altijd moed is*] (Scholten 2010; see also Hartendorp and Wagenaar 2004). This also means that judicial practices are "not exactly science," to speak with Judge Jamison, and especially so in the relatively minor cases appearing in the Police Judge Court. Neither agreeing with the dictates of rigorous "science" nor with the demands of pure legalism, Judge Jamison thinks of their role as comparable to "village elders": "we arbitrate conflicts, and that's it." The contrast between cultivated prudence and the more rigorous character of "science" was a recurring one in judges' accounts of their practices. Pitting judicial practices against formalism of another kind is Judge Emerald's assertion that "none of this is higher mathematics." Although judges "have an ugly power, the way we can shape people's lives," some of it, Judge Emerald asserted, is "very simple" – that is, as long as judges are trained in the exercise of their prudential sensibilities. "Of course that intuition can be a pitfall as well," Judge Jamison commented, "the risk is that you're working on autopilot, as it were. But it is a craft nevertheless."

Other judges refrained from drawing explicit contrast between this emphasis on the specificity of the individual case and the aggregate level analyzed in the Leiden study, yet their discomfort with the generalization inherent in my questions would become evident in their mode of response. For one, some judges perceived the question "how do you deal with cases" to be an inquiry into different legal-philosophical principles with regard to punishment, including a concern with the proper relationship between the state, the individual, and community. In such cases conversation would swiftly move to more abstract ideals of justice and legal-philosophical questions – should judges aim for retribution or rehabilitation? Whose interests must a criminal judge serve, and how can these be balanced and weighed against each other? – as well as matters of court organization and bureaucracy. When drawn back to their everyday "doings with cases," hesitations and qualifying statements characterized their answers. "It all depends," or a variation thereupon would usually preface their response, and the following answer would usually concentrate on a specific example: a case yesterday, a case last week, a difficult case some months ago ... In any case, "it's difficult to say anything general about it," Judge Curtis sighed. My general questions were either met with equally general concerns with the ideals of justice and the purpose of punishment; or else, once I returned them to their work practices, these generalizing questions were answered only with help of hesitant qualifications and with specific examples.

4.2.2 The Person of the Defendant

These exploratory conversations were helpful, then, precisely because they pointed out the limitations of generalizing questions themselves. However, these conversations also pointed me in the direction of the "person of the defendant" as both a matter of concern and a locus of the specificity and uniqueness of the case. Some judges made the connection between the unicity of the case and the "person of the defendant" explicitly, arguing that their practice is first and foremost one of tailoring the decision to the specific person of the defendant. Judge Beech, of course, suggested as much when she said that "every case is different" and that "every defendant is different" and that their practice is one of "tailoring": "everything must be tailored to fit" [*alles moet op maat*]. Mobilizing conceptions of individualized sentencing (Hutton 2013; Tata et al. 2008), judges suggested that prudential judgment does not only take into account the consequences of the criminal offense for the victim or society at large, but must be "tailored" to the specific defendant. In order to make a correct and proper sentencing decision, judges asserted, it is absolutely vital to arrive at a comprehensive "picture" [*beeld*] of the personal circumstances of the defendant in question. For instance, does a defendant have debt that would cause a fine to be more punitive than called for? Is he or she physically and mentally capable of doing a community service, should that be a sentencing option? Does the defendant risk losing his or her job when sent to prison?

Importantly, however, judges' concerns also incorporate an appreciation of the defendant's character and outlook on life: Do they take responsibility? Are they sorry? Do they have specific and concrete plans to combat that which made them end up in these dire straits in the first place? In a conversation over lunch, several judges comment on the importance of demonstrations of regret and remorse (again with reference, now a familiar gesture, to a specific case):

> The question is, are they *really* sorry? Are they really shocked with what they did? I had a really nasty case some time ago, with a couple of young guys charged with the armed robbery of a store. In court they were trying their best to appear as laconic as possible, making themselves out to be such cool guys. Look, if they tell me they saw the videotapes of their robbery and would say something like, "Gosh, is that really me? I didn't know I was capable of doing such a thing!" But they were indifferent, they didn't see the gravity of what they had done. Needless to say I sentenced them accordingly . . .

Apologies and sincere "shock" is what this judge was looking for; finding it lacking, she saw no reason to opt for a mitigated sentence. The "person of the defendant," then, is both a legal and a moral being: not only someone possibly legally culpable, but also ideally morally responsible.

4.2.3 The Court Session

Now, where are such judgments routinely made? Judges often pointed me to the court session as a salient site to such appraisals. "It all depends on what is said in court," Judge Clarens commented on a specific case: "If he shows up and if he has a clear story and tells me he wants to try and better himself, maybe I'll give him a second chance. There are always extenuating circumstances." Not only do Judge Clarens' comments underscore the importance, for defendants, of showing up in court (they are not legally obligated to do so), they also hint at the storied texture of courtroom practices. In a later lunch conversation, her emphasis on "the story" found resonance among other judges. "It helps to talk," their consensus was: one judge asserted that "when there is a lot of evidence it helps to talk to the police, it comes across a lot more cooperative." Laughing, she added, "Unless the evidence is bad, then you're better off remaining silent!" But not just any talk will do; judges emphasize the value of a "good story," suggesting that both the defendants' willingness to talk and the quality of the proffered story inform their appraisals of the "person of the defendant." These evaluative judgments are, again, subject to that same, prudential intuition. Judge Peters: "I have developed an intuition for that sort of thing."

4.3 Studying Craftwork and Remorse

All in all, then, judges' emphasis on trained capacity for prudential judgment sensitive to the specificities of individual cases contrasts sharply with the Leiden study's enactment of these practices. First, judges emphasize the specific and the unique rather than general regularities. Second, their conception of the "person of the defendant" as a both legal and moral being is at odds with the disaggregation of the "person of the defendant" into presumably "social characteristics" such as gender, age, or "foreignness" effectuated in the Leiden study. Third, to them, a decision is not the function of informational "input," but rather a practice of prudential, sometimes intuitive judgment tailored to the specifics of the case and the specifics of the "person of the defendant." It is for this reason that Tata (2007) warns against the use of statistical analysis reliant on "factors" in understanding legal decision-making practices: "Cognitive-analytical work has tended to equate 'factors' with case 'facts.' So not only does factorial explanation ignore how 'facts' are identified or not, it also ignores their contingent, fluid, synergistic, and constructed nature. Yet . . . the meaning of facts is contingent on the ever-evolving nature of the case" (Tata 2007: 435). Like the judges mentioned here, Tata (2007) prefers to conceive of judicial practices as a kind of "craftwork": a mode of work that relies upon interpretation of "the ever-evolving nature of the case" rather than isolation and the measurement of "case factors" (see also Mascini et al. 2016). Retaining its contrast with the often-evoked counterpoint of "science," "craft" is a productive notion as it is suggestive of training and practice rather than detached "know-what" or "know-why." It evokes situated evaluations of specific cases, and in a fashion similar to the notion of bricolage, prioritizes local modes of problem-solving over the seamless and unproblematic application of rules or plans, introducing a sense of practicality into our conceptions of judging. It is for that reason I wish to mobilize this notion in my effort to follow up on the aporia produced in the Leiden study. If its mode of enacting legal practices fails to address legal practices in terms judges' recognize and identify with, the notion of craftwork promises to apprehend these practices in more acceptable terms. Drawing on this notion, I will follow up on judges' emphasis on intuition, on the "whole case," and on their concern with the "person of the defendant." Specifically, I zoom in on judges' concern with defendants' "remorsefulness" in order to give flesh and bone to their practices of decision-making. In that capacity, defendants' remorsefulness is a local matter of concern capable of casting light on judicial concerns with the unique case.

4.3.1 *Remorse As a Local Matter of Concern*

Now, remorse has a particular history in criminal law. Its importance to judicial decision-makers is contingent upon a rather Western and modern conception of the criminal subject. Where Roman law, for instance, did not treat (criminal) acts as a manifestation of individual intentions, modern law instead "assumes a subject that is answerable for its acts in the world" (Pottage 2014: 153; see Thomas 1977), as it considers deviant acts "expressions of some complex authorial psychology" (Pottage 2014: 153). It is only with this more modern conception of criminal subjects that remorse can enter the picture, as being bound by one's action one now can and has to relate oneself to them. This, of course, is what Foucault points out when he sketches the rise of a modern, juridical concern with the "soul" of the deviant subject (Foucault 1977). This "soul" features both as a locus of threat to society and a site of therapeutic intervention. Indeed, there are strong indications that judicial decision-makers incorporate in their judgments a concern with the defendant's remorsefulness (see e.g., Bandes 2015; Duncan 2002; Eisenberg et al. 1997; Everett and Nienstedt 1999; Martell 2010; Proeve and Tudor 2010; Sundby 1998; Wood and MacMartin 2007).

Although the importance of remorse to judicial work practices is well-established in social-scientific literature on the topic, remorse tends to be isolated from the ongoing practicalities of judicial work practices. For instance, although the Leiden study includes a measure of the defendant's remorsefulness, it is largely unclear upon what specific behaviors or accounts the researchers based their measurement of defendants' remorsefulness. In so doing it fails to address the ways judges themselves attribute, weigh, and evaluate defendants' remorsefulness. Moreover, it treats remorse in a binary fashion as something unproblematically present or absent (Wermink et al. 2012a). A similar emphasis on the supposedly binary character of "signs of remorse" is evident in Tombs and Jagger's (2006) study of sentencers' accounts of their decision-making practices. While "signs of remorse," coupled with "signs of hope," may sway sentencers to mitigate their sentences, it is yet unclear how sentencers in specific cases attribute remorse to individual defendants, and how these attributions are weighed and evaluated. Reifying and dichotomizing remorse this way, these kinds of approaches allows little room to inquire into the way remorse, as a practical and situated matter of concern, is established or challenged: that is, how it is "marked by negotiation, contestation, surrender and opposition, claims and counterclaims" (Weisman 2014: 8). It also fails to address the salience of what judges call "the good story" in relation to remorse: that is, the role of narrative and storytelling in court. Narrative is commonly understood to denote a way of connecting events and people into a temporal and causal arch (Ewick and Silbey 1995) through the device of "emplotment" (Ricoeur 1992). Here, I put center stage the moral uses of such emplotment: that is, the way defendants' remorsefulness is both narratively accomplished and narratively understood by judges.

"We'll have to see what he has to say in court": judges' concern with the interaction with the defendant points to the courtroom as a site pregnant with moral possibility. Their emphasis on the "story" suggests this concern with remorse to be played out narratively and interactively. That in-court communication matters more generally has indeed been the lesson of studies concerned with narrative, storytelling, and interaction in court (see e.g., Atkinson and Drew 1979; Bennett and Feldman 1981; Conley and O'Barr 1997; Jackson 1988, 1996; Komter 2000; Matoesian 1993; Travers and Manzo 1997; for an overview of the field, see Dingwall 2000). Curiously, however, studies of the "doing and telling" of remorse have not as of yet situated remorse within such courtrooms. While there have been important efforts to understand the role of remorse historically and conceptually, and while empirical efforts have concentrated on materials as wide-ranging as narratives in media, in highly publicized court cases, and in written verdicts, there has been little focus as of yet on its narrative production within courtroom dynamics (Bandes 2015: 5). This neglect is all the more striking, as the courtroom can be a rather fraught space for defendants. They may be unfamiliar with legal standards and formats, and – as Dutch criminal law combines, in one setting, both adjudication (fact-finding and judgment) and sentencing – defendants have to navigate both the court's legal and moral demands (Komter 1994).

In an effort, then, to de-reify remorse I emphasize both its "practical grammar" (cf. Dupret and Ferrie 2015) and its situated, interactional character. Questions central in this chapter are: What do judges understand to constitute remorse? How does the interaction with the defendant in court inform judges' attributions of remorse? How do judges weigh and evaluate, moreover, the presence or absence of what they understand to constitute remorse in specific cases? With judges' emphasis on the "good story," I am first and foremost interested in the storied texture of remorse: how, in other words, the interaction with the defendant in court allows attributions of remorsefulness, and how judges draw on narratives themselves to make sense of individual cases, including defendants' demonstrations of remorsefulness.

4.3.2 *Shadowing Judges, Tracing Cases: a Case-Specific Approach*

Aiming for general answers to general questions does not, I had learned by now, assist inquiry into judges' craftwork. An emphasis on specificity – "it all depends," "we'll have to see what happens in court," "maybe he has a good story" – thwarted my questions, focused as they were on arriving at a general sense of judges' "ways of dealing with cases." Having learned, then, that this general question is not the most productive question,

I opted instead for a more case-specific approach to judicial work. Concretely, this meant that instead of relying on more or less structured interviews, I started to ask individual judges if I could "shadow" them in their work practices (see also Halliday et al. 2008) so that I was in a better position to ask them questions about specific cases. Often, I would ask these questions either throughout judges' pre-trial file-work (about which I have more to say in Chapter 5) or before and after specific cases in court, where I was permitted to observe and transcribe the interactions between the various parties to the trial. As the setting within which judge and defendant come face-to-face, where apologies are offered or elicited, and remorse is demonstrated, the courtroom is the primary location of this chapter. While I at first sat in on the court's public benches, in a later phase of the research I was permitted to seat myself, properly attired in robe and bib, at the judges' table next to his or her assisting clerk. There I was able to transcribe the proceedings and conversations on the PCs located on these tables, and there I was in a unique position to ask the judge brief questions in breaks between cases. It is there that I observed the interaction between defendant and judge; and it is there that I would elicit reflection and evaluation from judges on the cases they had just decided on. My efforts to "situate" the question of remorse in judges' work practices, was then itself situated largely in the space of the courtroom – a situatedness upon which I will comment in the concluding notes to this chapter.

4.4 Showing and Telling Remorse: Judge Mason and Jenny Carpenter

By way of an entry into the relationship between judges' concern with the person of the defendant, their evaluations and interpretations of defendants' remorsefulness, and storytelling in court, let's consider the following case involving Judge Mason and Ms. Carpenter:

> On a dreary morning in October 2013, I find myself in a well-lit and unadorned courtroom. Judge Mason is judging 10 cases today, of which Ms. Carpenter is the 6th defendant scheduled to appear in court. Ms. Carpenter, or Jenny, is accused of throwing a broken glass of beer at one of her friends. The victim had sustained rather severe injuries to her face. Judge Mason told me prior to the court session that she expected to see a pliant defendant in court today. On the basis of the case file, she told me that Jenny "is not trying to lie." Moreover, Jenny "hadn't immediately requested a lawyer but was just telling the police her story," – information

which further suggested that Jenny was willing to cooperate. She also approvingly pointed out that Jenny had attempted to get in touch with the victim after the offense, and noted that "girls like this are all in the same group of friends, it is so important for them that they can continue to get along." These meetings also mean, to Judge Mason, "that she never really meant to hurt anyone that badly. This really shows something about her as a person, it tells me something about her willingness to talk."

Enter, then, Jenny Carpenter.

Jenny is short, quite thin, and strikes me as visibly intimidated by the court setting. She has arranged no legal counsel, nor is she accompanied by family members or friends. Judge Mason commences the inquiry in court by asking her a series of questions about the event in question. "Yes, it happened," Jenny immediately confesses, and goes on: "But I just think it's weird that she [referring to the prosecutor's summary of the legal charges] is using the word 'purposefully.' I never meant to do this! I had to spend a night in jail, then sought contact with the victim and we talked a lot, and I've felt bad about it a long time. I even offered to pay her health insurance costs! It was such a difficult period for me back then . . . "

I remember looking at both the public prosecutor and Judge Mason, a little afraid for Jenny's fate: I had seen defendants chastised before for their supposed lack of remorse, and it seemed to me this was about to happen to Jenny as well.

Judge Mason is growing slightly irritated. While she goes on to ask further factual questions – what had you been drinking? Why did you do it? – Jenny seems to have a way of reorienting Judge Mason's factual questions back to the hardships she herself had faced during and after the offense. While unequivocally emphasizing that she is sorry and has done all she can to make up with the victim, Jenny seems to continue to rub Judge Mason the wrong way. After a few of these back-and-forths, Judge Mason intervenes, and tells Jenny sternly, "I see. But I must say, you seem to lack an appreciation of the severity of what you have done here, Miss Carpenter." The prosecutor, seeing her chance, chimes in: "Because this really is about something terrible, isn't it? [Turns to the judge] I don't think Ms. Carpenter is showing a lot of understanding of what she has done, and the consequences of what she has done for the victim, to be honest." Jenny, shocked with the stern tone of both judge and prosecutor, has now started to cry silently: "But, I never expected this . . . "

Judge Mason, unmoved by Jenny's story or tears, finds her guilty and sentences her to 100 hours of community service – "conforming" in her sentence decision to the prosecutor's demanded sentence. Over lunch after the court session, Judge Mason tells me, still somewhat annoyed, "Look, she was talking about herself all the time, about how difficult this

> has been for her." Rather than a meek and cooperative young woman, Judge Mason faced what she perceived as a self-centered and self-pitying defendant. And even though Jenny echoed Judge Mason's perception of her as someone who "didn't mean to hurt anyone that badly," Judge Mason could not, then, in good conscience, mitigate the prosecutor's demands.

This case, I think, is particularly suggestive of the centrality of remorse to judges. It shows the courtroom not only to be a site pregnant with legal narrative, but also as a setting saturated in explicitly moral concerns, questions, challenges, and judgments (cf. Emerson 1969: 204); a setting perhaps even of a "status degradation ceremony" both legal and moral in character (Goffman 1956).

But this case also complicates understandings that would attribute to remorse the status of a given, a "sign" either present or absent (Tombs and Jagger 2006). While judges (and lay-juries, for that matter) may regularly draw distinctions between the remorseful and the remorseless (Tombs and Jagger 2006), and while its role is well-established in the literature (see Bandes 2015; Duncan 2002; Eisenberg et al. 1997; Everett and Nienstedt 1999; Martell 2010; Proeve and Tudor 2010; Sundby 1998; Wood and MacMartin 2007), this case demonstrates that remorse is far from a straightforward "sign." Indeed, this case is suggestive of precisely the uncertainties that accompany such judgments of remorse: on the one hand, some of Ms. Carpenter's actions were understood to be indicative of her remorsefulness, yet others – specifically the way she objected to the public prosecutor and emphasized her own suffering – were suggestive of someone not entirely appreciative of the consequences of her actions. In other words, even though she immediately confessed, Jenny seemed to Judge Mason unaware of, and oblivious to her own responsibility for the offense in question.

In this sense, this case suggests that "doing remorse" does not exactly overlap with either taking legal responsibility (through a confession) or with offering apologies only. Indeed, judges often point out that while "it helps to talk," provide a "story," and to express "shock" or sincere apologies, remorse is not solely established by what the defendant does and does not say. Matters are more complicated, for there is always the danger of insincere expressions of remorse: "after all," Judge Emerald laconically comments, "we are among the most lied to professional groups in the Netherlands, and remorse tends to come only after the fact" [*berouw komt na de zonde*]. Because criminal justice settings are coercive, ritualized, and characterized by unequal power-relationships between participants, "there is always the possibility that expressions of self-condemnation will be more strategic than authentic, more calculated and ulterior than spontaneous" (Weisman 2009: 51). As these expressions of remorse are always already aimed at an interested audience, they are by that definition other-directed and taken to be potentially untruthful. Often, then, judges need further proof that defendants' remorsefulness is a sincere expression of their authentic and "real" selves. In Jenny Carpenter's case, for instance, Judge Mason had been impressed with her efforts to seek contact with the victims: a sign of contrition. In addition, judges tend to look for evidence that the defendant has taken concrete steps to reduce his or her risk of recidivism. For instance, have they found a job, combatted their addiction, and sought help for any psychiatric issues? This initiative is especially important given what judges perceive to be the defining feature of much of their clientele, that is, their shared marginalization. One judge sighed and commented, "Our clients. Well. They have all had a bad childhood. They all have some sort of personality disorder. At a certain point you're familiar with all of it." Judge Kingsley similarly characterized the group of defendants judges encounter on a daily basis:

> They tend to have so many problems. Financial problems. Problems in the relational sphere. Traumatic experiences in the past – abuse and such things. Things are difficult for them, society is complicated. How would they be able to deal with all that? Think of social assistance: you have policy and laws to work through, you have to find and sign the requisite forms … All that stuff is too complicated, especially if you have difficulties reading or writing. So they struggle, have problems of all kinds.

Defendants' "own initiative" and their own motivation are valued precisely because these are taken to be "signs of hope" (cf. Tombs and Jagger 2006): signs that the defendant, given his or her difficult past and circumstances in life, is taking his or her responsibility. Indeed, while judges have the discretionary room to combine a suspended sentence with the obligation that defendants accept certain rehabilitative interventions (individual or groups therapy), it is preferable if defendants seek help themselves. Judges, then, routinely check if the defendant has sought help for drug- or alcohol-related issues, for instance, and gauge to what extent the defendant shows him/herself a "functioning adult" with a job or else with a "meaningful way to pass the day" by going to college or through volunteering. After all, this is taken as defendants' responsibility – and their responsibility only. Judge Emerald comments: "These are people who tend to have ugly pasts. And at a certain point you're done talking. If you don't want help repeatedly, well, then you shouldn't look at me but take a good look at yourself." Judge Emerald's insistence on defendants taking responsibility is widely shared among the judges studied here, and resonates with the oft-noted distinction between defendants who locate responsibility for their crimes externally – that is, locate it outside of their own control – and those who locate responsibility internally (Bridges and Steen, 1998; Mascini and Houtman, 2002). Remorse, then, is about telling a "good story," about expressing apology or shock, and importantly: about "taking responsibility for one's actions," preferably on one's own volition. Doing remorse, then, requires both a "showing" and a "telling" (see also Weisman 2014, van Oorschot et al. 2017). In the absence of either one of these, defendants tend not to be deemed remorseful: hence Jenny Carpenter's fate.

4.5 Situating Remorse I: Courtroom Catch-22s

Jenny Carpenter's case is but one case where the doing and the telling of remorse did not exactly line up with each other. While Jenny may have showed remorse in her actions, she failed to tell it, instead painting herself as the victim and in so doing raising the suspicion that she was insufficiently appreciative of her own responsibilities. Even though remorse is most adequately understood as both a showing and a telling, the telling part still matters a great deal.

Importantly, that telling often takes place in the courtroom, which is as I noted a curiously understudied site in the production, demonstration, and contestation of remorse (Bandes 2015: 5). Indeed, the ample literature on courtroom dynamics (e.g., Atkinson and Drew 1979; Bennett and Feldman 1981; Conley and O'Barr 1997; Jackson 1988, 1996; Komter 2000; Matoesian 1993; Travers and Manzo 1997) sensitizes one to the narrative and interactional texture of courtroom practices and points to the rather intricate tensions that often develop between vernacular language and legal language (see e.g., Conley and O'Barr 1997). Yet how the local, practical grammar of remorse is affected by the space of the courtroom is a question to which scholars have not yet paid sufficient attention. The courtroom, conceived as a both legal and moral space, is where I seek to further situate remorse.

A second case, chosen again for its strategic and demonstrative value, will help to identify the precise issue at stake here. Read in juxtaposition with the case involving Jenny Carpenter it offers ways to tease apart what is expected from defendants in court, and demonstrates how both legal and moral demands of the courtroom may clash in practice. Enter Judge Starr and defendant Harrison.

4.5.1 *Defendant Harrison: Self-Defense or Self-Excuses?*

I am seated next to Judge Starr at her desk. She is about midway through the files making up tomorrow's court session and turns to Harrison Smith's case file. Harrison is accused of assaulting another young man just outside a well-frequented bar in the center of town. Even though she notes small discrepancies between various witness statements, she does not conceive of this case as particularly complex: "I know enough," she says after a few minutes of studying the file, "it's all quite typical. Guy goes out, has a few drinks, gets angry for some reason, and gets violent."

The next day, we find ourselves in court. Harrison is young and well dressed, and seems eager to tell the judge his own story. Like any court session, the time available for Harrison's case is divided into two stages: first the facts of the case will be dealt with, after which Judge Starr turns to questions about his personal circumstances and offers him, as is customary, the "last word" (often an opportunity for defendants to say or reiterate they are sorry). Harrison is obliging. Unlike some defendants I have observed he does not, until the second phase of the court session, talk about himself much. Neither does he deny the charges. He simply tries to answer Judge Starr's questions factually and carefully.

> While Judge Starr guides Harrison through the events with help of temporally and causally-oriented questions like, "what time did you arrive?," "then what did you see?," and "then what did you do?," Harrison provides a neat narrative. That night, Harrison elaborates, he went out for a drink, and while in a bar had accidentally bumped into the victim. The victim had reacted aggressively and had gathered his friends. "Then, they threatened to kill me," Harrison tells Judge Starr, "so I went to nearby police officers and asked them for help, but they said they couldn't help, so I went back to my friend, but those guys approached me. And that's when I felt very threatened, one of them was getting so close-by ... and that's when I head-butted him. I shouldn't have done it."
>
> Throughout his answering of the judges' factual questions, Harrison refers a few times more to the threats issued by the victim and his friends and emphasizes his anxious response to such a threatening environment,

> all the while connecting his statements using temporal and causal sequential markers such as "and then," or "and that's why." Moving onto the "personal circumstances," defendant Harrison opens up and tells the judge that he has sought psychiatric help: "for my aggression, you see. I have been attacked a few times and I realize that I can come across as very aggressive when I feel threatened." He emphasizes that he has sought help from a psychologist to deal with his anxieties. The rest of his time he spends in school: he is working towards a second degree. His lawyer, too, suggests that Harrison's behavior is best thought of as self-defense. Reiterating the threats issued by the victim and his friends, she suggests that Harrison should not be found guilty on the grounds that his actions constitute self-defense. Given the "last word," Harrison states that he is sorry about what happened and that he is aware that he shouldn't have reacted the way he did.

At first sight, Harrison both takes responsibility and has taken steps to mitigate that which made him react violently in the first place (i.e., he sought help for his anxiety). Not only does he express apologies and regrets, he also has a "meaningful way to pass the day" and has sought help on his own accord. However, Judge Starr is not so sympathetic to this defendant.

> Evaluating the case against Harrison before giving her verdict, she tells Harrison that she is not happy with his "excuses" and his appeal to "self-defense," and posits that Harrison "was not justified in his feelings of being threatened." Instead she concentrates on Harrison's lack of responsibility. Even *if* his reaction was due to factors outside of his control – either the threats of the victim and his peers, or his (then) untreated anxieties in certain social settings – he nevertheless had the responsibility to not put himself into such a situation. Indeed, Judge Starr suggests that, given his anxieties, he might have chosen to stay at home. Judge Starr admonishes Harrison: "You are an adult man who is expected to take responsibility for his actions." Not mitigating her sentence, she sentences him wholly according to the judicial sentencing recommendations [*orientatiepunten*], that is, to 120 hours of community service.

We see a by now familiar insistence on taking responsibility. But while Harrison seemed at first to tick all the boxes with his meaningful way to pass the day, his initiative in seeking treatment, and his professions of regret and apology, Judge Starr chastised Harrison for failing to take responsibility. She did not see self-defense, but rather: excuses.

This case, I suggest, is demonstrative of the tensions between the courtroom's legal and moral demands. On the one hand, it is the setting within which events are to be qualified legally, and in legally consequential ways. Self-defense is one such legal qualification, and might have led the judge to dismiss the case. In order to assist such legal qualification, Judge Star herself led Harrison through a long series of factual questions. Emphasizing the messiness of the situation, the role played by the victim and his peers, Harrison aimed to sketch the outline of the chronology of that evening and the circumstances leading up to the offense. On the other hand, however, the courtroom is the setting where Harrison is expected to show contrition, take responsibility, and in doing so express remorse. Indeed, the problem for defendants such as Harrison is one of both trying to cast a story that would be a legal ground for dismissal and – if that argument should fail – demonstrating sufficient levels of remorsefulness. This is a slightly different dilemma than that outlined by Komter (1994), who suggests there is a palpable tension between appearing both cooperative and defensive. In Harrison's case, he faced a Catch-22: For how can he both, as his legal right, claim that the offense was self-defense while simultaneously projecting sufficient levels of responsibility?

Given these intricacies, some argue that remorse should not be incorporated into sentencing decisions at all (Ward 2006) or at least be excluded from consideration in cases involving particularly vulnerable defendant populations, for instance adolescent defendants (de Haan and Hielkema 2005). In such discussions it is often pointed out that defendants who deny the charges or who choose to remain silent cannot, like their confessing counterparts, similarly "take responsibility" and express regrets, for which reason remorse should not play a role in decisions about those who do confess. As we have seen, not just denial or remaining silent but also legal lines of argument – that of self-defense – may interfere with judges' appraisals of the defendants' remorsefulness. Interactional dilemmas of this sort are by no means rare. "Staying factual" does not rarely mean a defendant is forced to talk about other people's role in the escalation of the offense in question; yet it is also a strategy that, to judges, can cast doubt on the extent to which defendants take sufficient levels of responsibility for the offense in question.

4.6 Situating Remorse II: On Narrative Kinds

Now, Harrison's case may seem rare – but to judges it is not. Judge Starr herself had suggested it was "all quite typical: Guy goes out, has a few drinks, gets angry for some reason, and gets violent." It was "just fighting" [*gewoon knokken*]: a formulation in Dutch that does not suggest so much that she treats this fighting as insignificant, but rather that it is something not unusual, something not so unique. Other judges, in their work practices, concur. In a similar case of physical assault, taking place under similar (intoxicated) circumstances, Judge Dempsey notes that the defendant is "playing up" his fear of (what would become) his victim. Adopting a purposefully whiney voice, Dempsey reads an excerpt from the interrogation with the defendant:

> He says [whiningly], "I was afraid he was going to hit me, and something clicked in my head, and then I hit him. I really thought he was going to hit me!" With a sardonic smile, Judge Dempsey looks up and adds, "and that's when I started to cry!" In his normal voice, he glances at me sideways and says, "well, alcohol destroys more than it is kind [*alcohol maakt meer kapot dan je lief is*], doesn't it?"

Cases like Harrison's – "guy goes out, has a few drinks, gets angry" – are, to judges, recurring ones. Often, these are cases of physical assault in public [*openlijke geweldpleging*], and involve similarly young, similarly intoxicated defendants. That Harrison had been drinking, that Harrison was provoked, that Harrison resorted to physical violence: all of these aspects of the case make it a more or less typical incident. These are young men, Judge Clarens tells me, who simply "have difficulties regulating their aggression" (Judge Clarens). One judge comments that it is not uncommon for such defendants to feel treated unjustly. In the circumstances leading up to the offense, there is in actual fact little that distinguishes the aggressor from the victim. Both may exchange increasingly heated words, both may push and shove each other . . . All is unclear, until the situation spirals out of control and becomes the object of investigatory work. Only then, the distinction between victim, defendant, and witness is retroactively drawn: "the one who is there as a defendant is the one who won the fight," Judge Dempsey commented on such "typical" cases. Harrison's appeal to self-defense, then, did not come necessarily as a surprise; indeed, it is not uncommon for similarly charged defendants to concentrate on the role of the victim in the altercations. Neither is it rare for judges to emphasize that it is nevertheless the defendant who is on trial; the victim "is not the one being judged here today," Judge Carol pointedly warned a defendant making a similar suggestion. Judges know, then, on the one hand that the responsibility for these kinds of altercations may in actual fact be distributed over all participants to the fight, yet tend to interpret appeals to self-defense as a refusal to take responsibility for one's own acts.

A typical case: here is something important. On the one hand, Harrison's case is an individual unit of concern – after all, there are his personal circumstances to be taken into account. But to Judge Starr it is simultaneously evocative of a kind of story, a narrative type, summarized by Judge Starr herself in the barest form with "guy goes out, has a few drinks, gets angry from some reason, and gets violent." Note that Judge Starr is hence working not only with a type or kind of offense, but with a skeletal sense of narrative that includes the specific offense in question, an appraisal of the kind of defendant (young, male), kind of setting and timing (a bar at night), a specific kind of victim (another young male) and the kinds of interactions and events leading up to the offense in question. Tata (2007, 1997) suggests we think of these narratives as "typified whole-case narratives." These are not simply summations of offender and offense characteristics, but rather a causal, temporal, and explanatory (but not necessarily justificatory) narrative that ties these together intelligibly. Drawing on prior knowledge (Emerson and Paley 1992), judges come to recognize some cases as variations upon a similar narrative theme. These typified whole-case narratives, Tata (2007) suggests, are important to judges because they provide a "narrative template" and in so doing reduce complexities and impose order. Such narrative forms, Ewick and Silbey (1995) argue, share at least three characteristics, all present in this specific case: narrative relies on the "selective appropriation of past events and characters" (Ewick and Silbey 1995: 200); furthermore, these characters and events become linked in a temporal order: they have a beginning, a middle, and an end. Last, such persons and events are linked not just in temporal terms, but also within "some overarching structure, often in the context of an opposition of struggle" (Ewick and Silbey 1995: 200). Narratives hence offer intelligibility: connecting (imputations of) "character," motive, circumstance and events, the operation of "emplotment" (Ricoeur 1992) ensures meaning. Yet these narratives also reduce moral complexities. The narrative of the angry young man not only renders intelligible Harrison's appeal to self-defense, it also informs Judge Starr's suggestion that there is no excuse. After all, he simply could have walked away when provocations started. Knowing very well that these kinds of incidents are "messy" (Judge Dempsey), it is the judge's task to focus on the defendant's own responsibility.

Now, not all cases are so easily "typified": many cases surprise judges and thwart them in their sensemaking. Nor is the kind of whole-case narrative outlined here the only kind. Let's turn to two other salient kinds of typified narratives and the role defendants' demonstrations of remorse plays in these.

4.6.1 Narrative Kinds: Typical Junkies, Typical "Explosive Couples"

The narrative kinds I am alluding to here are, first, the "typical junkie" engaged in petty theft, and second, cases of domestic violence involving "explosive couples." I concentrate on these two narrative kinds as judges' appraisals of defendants' remorsefulness plays a different role in these cases than they tend to do in the aforementioned cases of physical assault. That is, while demonstrating remorse and taking responsibility is of utmost importance in public assault cases like Harrison's, judges attribute much less importance to defendants' demonstrations of remorse in these cases, albeit for different reasons.

Let's start with the "typical drug addict" engaged in petty theft. Drug-addicted defendants, according to judges, make up a relatively large part of their caseloads (an overrepresentation exacerbated, some of them say, by recent budget cuts on psychiatric healthcare and homeless shelters). Often, judges note, these defendants are homeless and are known to the police (and sometimes to judges as well) and generally have long criminal records with similar property-related offenses. Morally, this typified whole-case narrative reveals some tensions. On the one hand, as the life circumstances of these defendants are particularly dire, judges may find it difficult to attribute absolute moral responsibility to the defendant. Commenting on the host of problems usually plaguing such defendants, Judge Curtis tells me that these are people "without ties to society": "They are addicted, without a job, no education or family around." To Judge Curtis, it is important that "something is done about that addiction." It is not easy to decide what to do in such cases, Judge Curtis goes on: "You can say, he is responsible, and of course you can put him in a cell." But he also notes that "I can only offer help when they are convicted. Without a conviction I can't do anything." Judge Peters is similarly concerned with "doing something." Commenting on a middle-aged, female defendant charged with petty theft, he sighs and tells me, "Wow. She's born in 1962 even. You don't see that often: to be addicted at that age! Well, this is another one of those cases that isn't about the offense as much as it is about the question, what are we to do with you?" However, judges' rehabilitative impulses tend to be thwarted by these defendants' behaviors. If these defendants do not show up in court, for instance, it may be difficult to hear "their side of the story." Or, if they do not accept help, or if they have not accepted help in the past, there might be little judges can do. "You can't force someone," Judge Clarens insists. "If they are not motivated you're just done. It has to be possible and feasible. If you don't take that chance you'll have to sit it out [the sentence]."

Yet even in cases where defendants try their best to show up, apologize, and take concrete steps to "better themselves," such demonstrations of remorse tend to be treated with weary suspicion. Judge Peters for instance recognizes that people may make promises, but that "their addiction is much stronger than their resolution." A case in point is the encounter between defendant Clarence Jones and Judge Emerald. I had not before observed such an overtly contrite defendant, and his investment in his own future seemed, at first, quite laudable.

> Clarence has been addicted to crack cocaine for over six years, he tells judge Emerald in court. During that time, he frequently stole small items from supermarkets and corner shops: crimes for which he was repeatedly charged and convicted. Clarence comes across as quite genuinely remorseful: he looks not only nervous, but ashamed. Clarence is deeply unhappy with the choices he has made in his past, blames himself for everything that happened the last few years, and tells the judge that he has been seeking treatment with help of his parole officer, whose testimony is also present in the file. Yet that previous attempt to combat his conviction had failed: he had returned to his habit. "I really need help. I . . . I really want to do my best. I am sick of the drugs. That's not me. It's my life, but things are starting to go wrong. I really need help." Pleading for a conditional sentence, Clarence tells Judge Emerald he is not afraid of any sentence, as long as he can continue working with his parole officer. A conditional sentence would allow him to do so. Judge Emerald is not swayed, however. "You tell me it is your life we are talking about. Well, I tell you to focus on the opportunities you've had. It is your own responsibility. You are 43! Not 18 anymore. I need you to take control of your own life, and that is not your parole officer's job. The only person capable of making a change is you, not me." Sentencing Clarence to an unconditional custodial sentence, Clarence is on his own – without help of parole services, his addiction might be excessively difficult to combat.

After the court session, Judge Emerald agrees with me that this was a particularly pitiful case. But: "Well, certain of these defendants are certainly pitiable. But what we see every day is a virtually unceasing torrent of pitiable people . . . And those people have been warned before. Better to be clear, then." In this typified whole-case narrative – that of the typical drug addict – defendants' remorsefulness – even if it is established by both a "doing" and a "telling" – is not necessarily consequential to judges' sentencing decisions. At a certain point, the suggestion is, defendants can't ask for yet another second chance. After all, their drug addiction makes them particularity vulnerable to going back to their old habits and tends to eclipse their sense of personal responsibility: "We all know people who try to quit smoking all the time," Judge Fielding comments. It's difficult and they keep falling back into their old habits: "That gives you some sense of how pernicious this is."

Let's compare, then. The "angry young man," exemplified by defendant Harrison, must show remorse, even if that threatens his legal defense. There is no excuse: even if in actual fact responsibility is distributed over all participants in the fight, it is unwise for defendants to point that out to the judge, lest they appear to be taking insufficient responsibility. By contrast, drug addicts may "show" it and "tell" remorse, but it does not always matter even if they do: their addiction is stronger than their resolutions.

In yet another kind of case, remorse plays yet a different role. These are cases of domestic violence. Importantly, this kind of typification is one that incorporates neither only the remorsefulness of the defendant nor only the circumstances leading up to the offense, but the character and responsibility of the (often female) victim as well. Following Judge Roberts, I will refer to this narrative typification as that involving an "explosive couple." Pointing to the role played by the victim in provoking aggressive responses, judges tend to emphasize that these are "difficult relationships" within which people may think it is "normal, to push and shove each other like that" (Judge Starr). "Of course," Judge Starr adds, "you wonder why these women stay with these men." For one judge, this tendency to "stay with him" was tied to "certain strata in society" [*bepaalde milieus*]: "Look, if my guy ever hit me I'd be out of there, crying all the way over to my parents but never going back. It makes you wonder, though, why she stays with him."

"Why she stays with him": this is not an uncommon object of wonder for judges, and in that capacity a question that may cast doubt on the victim's motives. Is the victim as innocent as she makes herself out to be? "Sometimes you see the facts in question and you think, this must be a real brute," Judge Curtis comments, "and then in court you see this tiny little man accompanied by this harpy, this huge woman ... Well, that changes things." The victim's physical size is sometimes referred to, but more common are references to her personality. On the one hand, the victim may be conceived as a strategist, for instance when the couple is caught up in legal disagreement over custody. Such a context casts doubts on the impartiality of the victim's account: a conviction for domestic violence, judges say, tends to strengthen the victim's position in custody agreement negotiations. At other times, judges voice the suspicion that the victims are "difficult personalities themselves," perhaps due to psychiatric disorders (borderline personality disorder is sometimes referred to) or because of their circumstances in life.

Whatever judges may think about these cases in private and express in conversations with a researcher does not always seem to matter to their sentencing. For instance, while both the defendant or his/her lawyer may emphasize the difficult personality of the victim, judges may point out the defendants' own responsibilities. Judge Starr sternly admonishes a young man charged with a case of domestic abuse to focus on his own responsibility when he argues that "even my ex told me she knows she hasn't been the sweetest" [*geen lieverdje is geweest*]. Sternly, she tells him that "You're taking this much too lightly. You say in every relationship there are fights like this. Even so you cannot do the things you did." However, there are some indications that such appraisals of the victim's character and motives do in fact inform judges' responses to specific cases of domestic violence. It is in such cases that defendants' remorsefulness is not necessarily a concern.

An extreme case exemplifying this kind of appraisal is that involving Judge Kingsley and defendant Jeremy Stevens: it demonstrates both what this "explosive couple" typified whole-case narrative looks like, and is suggestive of a particular way of evaluating defendants' demonstrations of remorse (or lack thereof). Jeremy had been accused of beating his wife, and the file included statements by the victim as well as Jeremy's brother and one of his children, who had told the police he had seen his father beat his mother. As we will see, this last statement will become important.

> The day before the court session, Judge Kingsley is quick to point out that the victim of this incident of domestic violence, Jeremy's wife, seems to be suffering from borderline personality disorder. He bases his diagnosis on a statement made by defendant Jeremy's brother, suggesting: "He [Jeremy's brother] is not a neutral party, of course, but I do get the impression the victim is making a mess of things. … God, those women – borderline they call it. Of course such labels are attached to people too quickly. But borderliners are also very manipulative. That's typical for people with borderline." Judge Kingsley also points out that the

> couple is caught up in custody agreement negotiations, which to his mind casts doubts on her statements. After all, does she not have a stake in painting her husband as an aggressor?
>
> In court, Jeremy, a pale and heavyset man in his 40s, tells the story of the circumstances leading up to his arrest. He mentions the complicated divorce proceedings in which he and his wife are caught up, and suggests that she filed a criminal complaint to receive custody of the kids. He also tells the judge he has long suffered from his wife's cheating and her mental ailments: "It hurts. We've been together for 23 years. The first time she cheated on me I tried not to care. I did everything, by then: washing up, cleaning, and cooking. I was always careful to not irritate her." Judge Kingsley, noting a previous conviction for domestic violence on Jeremy's criminal record, asks him about that previous offense. Jeremy tells him that "Back then, I was just cooking, cutting up some vegetables, and she had half a bottle of coca cola in her hand, and she empties it over my head! Normally I walk away, but that time I thought, enough is enough." Judge Kingsley also asks him about the anger-management course Jeremy had taken as part of his previous parole conditions: "Yeah, I took that course. I thought it was me. Therapy and training. Until someone said, it's not you. I'm just a regular guy."

Pointing at his wife's role in previous, as well as this particular offense, Jeremy suggests that he is a "regular guy," that "it's not him." He also seems to suggest he is the *real* victim in this situation, while he brushes the court-ordered aggression-relation course aside as not addressing the real problem, which, again, is his wife. At no point does Jeremy "take full responsibility" for what happened. Strategic or not, this kind of narrative resonates with Judge Kingsley's impression of the case:

> Surprisingly, given the available evidence, Judge Kingsley judges Jeremy not guilty: as one piece of evidence was an eye-witness statement by Jeremy's son, he argues that Jeremy's son was too young to testify: "he's only 12 years old, and you can't expect a 12-year old to testify in such a case without any kind of expert present in the interrogation room." With this piece of evidence disregarded, left is only the victim's statement, which itself provides too little evidentiary weight, Judge Kingsley argues, to convict Jeremy. Crucially, however, Judge Kingsley later tells the researcher that convicting Jeremy was simply not an option for him, but that this did require some creativity on his part: "Leaving out the son's statement is a bit of a ploy, really. I could have used it, but I really didn't want to convict."

Apparently, performing remorse – as consisting of both telling a story through "taking responsibility" and demonstrating it through seeking treatment – is in such cases not as vital as it is in cases that bear more resemblance to the typified whole-case narrative involving "angry young men." In both instances, judges recognize the messiness of the human relationships within which violence takes place, but in domestic abuse cases this does not always translate into the demand that defendants display remorse, that is: take full responsibility and seek help.

4.7 The Case: A Legal and Moral "Grasping Together"

Drawing out these typified whole-case narratives – the angry young man, the drug addict, and the explosive couple – I have demonstrated not only the centrality of remorse to judicial work practices, but also the salience, among the judges collaborated with here, of three different typified whole-case narratives. These typified whole-case narratives may help to reduce *cognitive* complexities in specific cases, but have been demonstrated to serve *moral* purposes as well. That is, they allow judges to evaluate defendants' measure of remorsefulness in relation to the offense and offender in question. The notion of narrative is crucial, here: object of typification is not necessarily the offender, nor the offense itself, but rather the relation between these two. This relation is further typified by including the circumstances surrounding the offense (e.g., time, place), possible motives and reasons for behavior (intoxication, addiction), and to the kind of victim (a stranger or one's spouse or partner).

Remorse, then, is mediated narratively: first, judges face a narrating subject in court, whose "story" has the capacity to inform not only their impression of the defendants' remorsefulness, but also their sentencing decisions. The narratives proffered by the defendant face dual and sometimes conflicting demands: a narrative offering temporal-causal intelligibility, as is the case in those defendants seeking to argue a case of self-defense, for instance, may detract from the successful narration of moral and personal responsibility. Second, defendants' remorsefulness is weighed and evaluated in and through several typical whole-case narratives: recurring and typified "cases" characterized by different modes of emplotment (Ricoeur 1992), including different conceptions of what drives people to do what they do (anger, addiction, a bad relationship), different modes of evaluating the degree to which they are responsible, and different modes of retaining or rejecting the normative expectation that they should take responsibility.

It is in precisely this sense that an emphasis on narrative is indispensable. While studies of legal practices or bureaucratic practices more generally have demonstrated the existence of client typifications or case-typifications (see e.g., Sudnow 1965; Lipsky 1980; Lynch 1998), the crucial role of narrative cannot be glossed over. Providing the conditions of temporal, causal, and moral intelligibility, whole-case narratives tie the specifics of the offender, the offense, the witness, the circumstances of the offense in question, and the biography of the defendant into a more or less orderly and typified whole. I have drawn out, here, the relationship between such temporal and causal orderings and moral modes of ordering; that is, the way a certain narrative plot allows both for legal and moral judgment. Truth about the defendant, including his or her remorseful "soul" (Foucault 1977) is produced narratively: "Narrative constructs the identity of the character" (Ricoeur 1992: 147–148; see also Ewick and Silbey 1995). In so doing this chapter has made some headway in connecting the study of storytelling in legal settings with the role played by remorse: remorse itself is established in narrative and evaluated in and through narrative. These narratives are crucial not only to cognitive, but also moral "comprehension": the activity of "grasping together" heterogeneous elements into an overarching narrative structure.

4.7.1 On Narrative and the Question of "Social Context"

The making of whole-case narratives and their typification is an activity not fundamentally different from other narrative modes of action. People use narrative all the time in making sense of their selves, others, and the worlds in which they move: "we tell ourselves stories," Didion famously wrote, "in order to live" (Didion 2006). Given this affinity between these judicial practices and more fundamentally human tendencies to tell stories, a frequently raised question concentrates on the relationship between these in-court stories and the wider social or discursive context. Critical discourse analyses of legal language, for instance, more generally understand legal narrative to be influenced by and embedded in wider societal discourses. Conley and O'Barr (1997), in their seminal *Just Words*, suggest that the study of courtroom interaction and legal language must be combined with a concern with discourse and power:[1] "Discourse is a locus of power. Different discourses compete for ascendancy in the social world; one is dominant for a time and then may be challenged and perhaps replaced by another. The dominance of a particular discourse inevitably reflects the power structures of society" (Conley and O'Barr 1997: 7). In a similar fashion, I might point out that the suspicion that the female victims of domestic abuse are "not innocent themselves," understandings of addiction as not only an illness but a moral failure, or the idea that hormones or peer pressure are in themselves an explanation for seemingly random acts of male violence, are of course not limited to judges. Exercises in finding resonances between these typifications among judges and more widely shared discourses can certainly be instructive, specifically when they delve into underlying presuppositions that govern both legal and moral conceptions of guilt and remorse. Such exercises, while they are not part of my project here, might also contribute to understanding the mechanisms that produce inequalities in sentencing outcomes (Conley and O'Barr 1997: 13).

However, such approaches do risk portraying these societal or discursive contexts as an unproblematic explanatory "real" in a gesture not dissimilar to those discussed in Chapter 2, in which I highlighted the metaphysics mobilized in efforts to explain the law with reference to the social. In doing so we mobilize the ontological primacy of the social real over the surface effect of legal practices and in doing so, may run into difficulties trying to do justice to the specifically legal character of the kind of narrative mediations involved. In other words: while moral responsibility and legal culpability may not always be so easily separated (see in particular Harrison's and Jeremy's cases!) the narratives in court are not oriented solely towards moral judgment in the name of the social. In the ethnomethodological sense of the term, these narratives are produced in reference to legal purposes and in reference to a legal "overhearing audience" (Heritage 1985), as becomes evident in Judge Kingsley's use of a legal justification to exclude Jeremy's son's witness statement. Both the moral and the legal, then, are narratively accomplished. Moreover, engaging in this kind of theoretical exercise – in which we find behind the legal a realer social or discursive reality – also involves the risk that we become unable to account for our own situatedness with regards with the practices we seek to study. Schegloff (1997), drawing in deliberate irony on the same critical vocabulary as Conley and O'Barr themselves, warns us that analyses of this kind:

> Allow students, investigators, or external observers to deploy the terms which preoccupy them in describing, explaining, critiqueing, etc. the events and texts to which they turn their attention. ... However well-intentioned and well-disposed towards the participants ... there is a kind of theoretical imperialism involved here, a kind of hegemony of the intellectuals, of the literati, of the academics, of the critics whose theoretical apparatus gets to stipulate the terms by reference to which the world is to be understood.
>
> (Schegloff 1997: 167)

In contrast, this chapter has aimed to make the point that, over and against the categories introduced by social scientists, "there has already been a set of terms by which the world was understood – those endogenously involved in its very coming to pass" (Schegloff 1997: 167), that is, the three recurring whole-case narratives elaborated on here. Reducing these "endogenously involved" terms to "power," "discourse," or "the social" tends to place the sociological observer in an epistemologically privileged relation vis-a-vis the actors studied. However, sociologists are not the only "reflexive" actors on the block; nor are the people they study mutes incapable of account-giving, of justifying, of rendering intelligible what they do and why they do so. Instead of placing "behind" these instances of narrative typification a final sociological explanans such as power or the social, the focus has here been on "the methods people use locally to produce the truth and intelligibility that allow them to cooperate and interact in a more or less ordered way" (Dupret 2007: 82). These methods, this chapter has shown, have narrative dimensions: it is precisely in and through explicit and narrative evaluation that cases become intelligible both to judges themselves and to the observer at their desk or at the judges' table in court. My efforts, then, have stayed deliberately with judicial typification practices. Tracing the way judges comment on and make sense of cases, the ways they interact with defendants, and their presentation and justification of their verdicts, this emphasis seeks not to privilege the sociological observer over that of those observed. In so doing I have preferred to focus not on imposing social order on these practices, but rather aimed to trace how legal and moral order is narratively enacted.

4.7.2 Looking Back: Casuistry and Sociology's Cross-Sectional Seeing

Emphasizing the ways judges comment on, evaluate, and justify their decisions in specific cases has led me towards a narrative understanding of cases. This specific way of enacting cases contrasts not only with statistical accounts of these practices, but also with judicial self-conceptions.

Let's concentrate on judicial accounts first. I have illustrated that judges tend to mobilize a casuistic register in their speech about their every-day practices: "every case is different," "it all depends on the particulars." However, my analysis diverges in two ways from the ways judges themselves speak about their practices. First, while judges may understand themselves to be casuistic creatures par excellence, a closer look at their practices adds complexity to what is often understood as this juristic casuistry. Yes, individual cases are specific and unique. But that does not mean that judges do not link cases to recurring, more or less typical narrative kinds. In working with individual cases, judges are precisely engaged in not only *case-making*, but in *kind-making* as well: drawing on typified whole-case narratives, judges routinely employ such narratives to make sense of individual cases, and they do so explicitly throughout their preparations. Second, this analysis shows that these kinds of "intuitions" are not necessarily unconscious, as some judges suggest, nor necessarily preverbal or prelinguistic. Indeed, when talking about specific cases, judges draw explicitly on such typifications. The "social," to paraphrase Hirschaur (2006), is not "silent," waiting for social scientists to "give it voice," but populated by actors capable of commenting on, accounting for, and justifying their actions. The point is not to sideline self-conceptions, but to bring them into relation with the vagaries of practice.

This emphasis on narrative typification practices contrasts, too, with socio-statistical modes of engaging with judicial decision-making. If, for the judges, a case is a narrative entity involving a narrating and narrated character, the fragmentation of cases into factors that is introduced with statistical modelling is bound to alienate. Hence, then, their emphasis on "all the circumstances," on the "whole case," on the "person" and his or her "story." This point pertains equally to judges' appraisals of the "person of the defendant." In the kinds of narratives just elaborated on, the "person of the defendant" appears not as a collection of static factors, but rather as a narrative character with a biography, a character relationally connected (or not) to the victim, and a character whose needs, wants, and regrets are to be taken into account (even if these wants, needs, and regrets are then to be sidelined when, considering the defendants' prior biography, they appear unreliable or untrustworthy). This also means that the disaggregation of the "person of the defendant" into social factors such as gender, age, class, and ethnicity or race does not resonate particularly well with judges' way of approaching cases. Defendants appear primarily as typified characters in typified whole-case narratives, not as bundles of factors or exemplars of certain population groups or strata in society.

Hence, this account has brought us closer to the conditions for a *rapport* between judges and socio-statistical researchers. It has suggested that statistical researchers and judges are in fact speaking about two different realities. Both are populated by cases, but the case is a different thing in both. For judges, the case is first and foremost a narrative thing: involving times, places, events, and characters inextricably linked both to the offense in question and to their biographies, their previous actions, and the narratives they in turn provide the judge with. In sociology's cross-sectional world, cases are bundles of factors that refer back to population groups. Questions asked about these cases are different, too. In these legal practices, the question with regard to the case is: *what's its story?* In the second, the question with regard to the case is the quintessentially sociological question, *what lies behind it?* (see Luhmann 1994). Both kinds of cases – narrative or statistical – also demand different kinds of observers. Judges' familiarity with different whole-case narratives comes as a result of professional intimacy, prior knowledge, and practice: trained, but not necessarily pre-discursive intuitions and narrative capacities that help to distinguish between the relevant and the irrelevant, the remorseful and the remorseless, the typical and the atypical. In these practices, objectivity demands not the cancellation of the individual observer in an appeal to mechanical objectivity (Daston and Gallison 1992), but precisely the mobilization of his or her prior knowledge, expertise, and prudence.

4.8 Onwards: Beyond Narrative

If the preceding chapter has demonstrated the "reality effects" of some social-scientific, statistically mediated approaches to criminal justice practices, this chapter has placed emphasis instead on the morally charged and narrative character of judges' evaluations of the case, the defendant, and his or her remorsefulness. In so doing it has put center stage the storied texture of legal work practices. It has treated judges as reflexive and accountable actors, engaged in the typification of individual cases in order to assist their legal and moral judgments. As such this chapter has connected an emphasis, in the literature, on storytelling in legal settings (e.g., Jackson 1988, 1996) with that of the production, contestation, and evaluation of remorse (cf. Weisman 2009, 2014).

In so doing this chapter itself enacts judicial practices in a certain way: it enacts these practices as narratively mediated. And in so doing, it produces its own aporia once again: an aporia rooted in the fact that its emphasis on narrative is itself partially a performative effect of the largely orally mediated collaborations upon which this chapter is based. Indeed, the observations related to you here are based on moments within which judges told me about their appraisals of cases, or on recorded instances of courtroom interaction: all largely "oral" moments. This chapter's emphasis on narrative, then, is itself situated within the performativities of oral modes of engaging with the object of study: in asking questions, I place the "informant" (itself a performative effect!) in a confessional and reflective relation to his or her own actions and thoughts. Such an approach tends to yield comments, justifications, accounts, and: narratives. Of course such an account is inevitably limited: not, as is often the argument, because what people say they think is not necessarily what they actually think. Such a gesture depends for its rhetorical efficacy on the "head of the actor" (Garfinkel 1967) and is for that reason not as sociologically relevant. No, this approach to judicial practices is limited precisely because it is grounded in specific collaborations mediated by oral modes of engagement with these practices (my questions and the conversations I had with judges) and focuses on oral moments in sociolegal life (the court session). What happens, however, when I start to observe what judges *do* backstage? Taking into account that realities do not await discovery but are enacted within such collaborations, is it possible to raise another question? What are we missing out on if we remain content with this appeal to practical and narrative "real"? How can we move on to different situations, different tools, and different collaborations? Are there different ways to enact judicial realities?

The following chapter aims to take up these questions. It emphasizes not narrative mediation in judicial case-making, but instead draws attention to the rather quieter and protracted episodes of routine "file-work" taking place "backstage" (Scheffer 2004, 2007). It raises the question how judges "visualize the case": how they order documents, summarize evidence, and produce additional artifacts to help them in their sense making. Based on observations of judicial work practices and their rearticulation as a consequence of a large-scale digitization project in the court, it highlights the case file in its materiality. Concentrating on the case file and judicial documentation practices it emphasizes writing, not speech, and in doing so it departs from more "phonocentric" (Derrida 1967) approaches that highlight interactions between copresent participants in interaction settings. It draws to a lesser extent on conversations with judges and instead mobilizes observation of their work practices, specifically their pre-trial face-to-file interactions.

5

Visualizing Cases

5.1 From Story-Telling to File-Work

Born out of largely conversation-mediated and interaction-based collaborations with judges, the preceding chapter demonstrated the centrality of defendants' remorsefulness to judges' appraisals of individual cases and demonstrated how such remorsefulness is narratively established and narratively evaluated. In so doing it resonates not only with those studies taking seriously the way language and narrative come to matter in legal settings, but also with judges' emphasis on "a good story." Guilt, responsibility, and remorse are narratively mediated accomplishments, not unproblematic "signs" or "case factors." Legal practices, specifically as they pertain to the remorsefulness of the defendant, have a storied texture.

Yet an exclusive focus on spoken language, both as something in and of legal practices, that is, courtroom interaction, and as a method we use in collaboration with these legal practices, that is, by talking with judges, introduces its own limitations. That narrative and storytelling make up an important part of legal practices cannot be denied. Yet there is a real risk, here, of forgetting that legal practices are not just that. They also, Dupret (2007: 85) argues, "constitute an activity accomplished on a daily basis, of an overwhelmingly routine character, the place of production and reproduction of professional practices." Scheffer (2010) similarly warns against the tendency to concentrate exclusively on the verbal production of order (cf. Atkinson and Drew 1979) or on interactions in court (cf. Conley and O'Barr 1990). Doing so runs the risk of "phonocentrism" (Derrida 1967): of treating as more primary the spoken word over writing. Of course, legal practices are themselves notably phonocentric: many jurisdictions for instance privilege oral testimony over written testimony. Yet there is no reason for us to reproduce this phonocentricity in our accounts, especially not if in doing so we miss out on large swaths of file-work (Scheffer 2005, 2007). In this chapter, I concentrate on these practices of file-work. Instrumental in judges' pre-trial "visualization of the case," these practices of file-work demonstrate both the centrality of the case file in judicial practices in particular, and the materiality of knowledge practices more generally.

This chapter, then, speaks to a curious hiatus in legal as well as socio-legal understandings of legal practices. Focused on the technicalities of legal reasoning (Riles 2005) or on verbal interaction (Conley and O'Barr 1990; Atkinson and Drew 1979), dominant approaches to legal practices tend not to pay much attention to the case file. Reasons for this neglect of backstage file-work are not difficult to fathom. There is a real attraction in the tragedy of the courtroom: promising unity of place, time, and act, the courtroom evokes and dramatizes the encounter between the subject and the law. It also speaks to the sociological imagination, calling upon researchers to understand, in classical fashion, the intricate relationship between personal troubles and public issues (Mills 1959: 226). On a more practical level, courtrooms tend to be publicly accessible and as such raise fewer barriers to curious researchers. Documents, in contrast, do not perhaps make for the most exciting of research objects (Latour 1986: 28) quips they may be among the "most despised of all ethnographic objects"), and in their association with backstage legal practices make their use and operation difficult to access. Nor are different national jurisdictions equally reliant on written materials: Anglo-Saxon courtrooms tend to emphasize speech over writing, whereas Dutch criminal law draws more extensively on the official dossier as a carrier and transporter of evidentiary materials.

5.1.1 *"Seeing the Case Clearly"*

However, these official dossiers are a principal object of and for work for the judges studied here. Indeed, much of judges' time is spent in their offices, where they try to "see the case," or attempt to "see the full picture," all the while remaining sensitive to their "blind spots." While these visual metaphors, like many of such metaphors (Haraway 1988, Dewey 1929), seem to suggest this is quite an unproblematic, cognitive operation, their work practices are revealing of active, sometimes fraught, *practices of visualization.* I arrived at these practices not from a vantage point in the courtroom, but rather through the observation of judicial practices of file-work backstage. This place, seated next to the judge, tracing and recording the judges' file-work, afforded me a unique sense of these practices of visualization. An exemplification:

> This morning I join Judge Roberts in her office to observe her preparation for tomorrow's court session. She is almost ready to start, she tells me, as she drops a large stack of files on a corner of her desk and takes seat behind her desk. "There are a couple of big ones," she tells me as she points to a set of particularly thick files, "I hope we have enough time to discuss these in court tomorrow; it looks like they're going to be complicated." In front of her, she has a smaller stack of single sheets of paper. These are copies of the summons sent out to individual defendants detailing the charges. These copied summons all have hand-written notes on them. I know that these have already been "prepared" by the clerk who is assisting Judge Roberts with tomorrow's court session. On her left is a small collection of colored pens, post-its, and yellow markers. I am seated to her right, and glance over her shoulder while she studies the case files. "Can you see it alright?" she laughs, and starts her preparation of tomorrow's court session.
>
> Methodically, Judge Roberts first takes a yellow marker and marks certain phrases and words on the summons accompanying the first case file. "See, you have the tendency to delve right into the file. But it is important to first look at the charges. With that in the back of your mind you then enter the file." Reaching to her left to pick up one of her colored pens she tells me, "I like to use colored pens when I work with the clerk's written preparation on the summons. That way it's clear what exactly I wrote down myself, my own notes stand out." Opening the case file, she takes out a letter from the defendant's lawyer; with a red pen, she then writes down, on the summons, the name of the lawyer. This type of back-and-forth between the case file and her own notes is repeated throughout her preparation: leafing through the file and reading several documents, she uses her pen to cross off the clerks' notes and occasionally exchanges her red pen for a yellow marker to highlight specific phrases and words in the case file. She says, "See, I am checking each and every part of the charges now," and shows me how, having found the relevant information in the legal case file, she checks off the location of the crime, the name of the defendant, and the specific acts that were involved with small, v-shaped scribbles on the text of the written charges. "What I am looking for is whether the clerk has written everything down and whether all of it is in the file." Getting ready to close the file she hesitates: "I forgot to read the parole service report!" Rummaging through the file she halts when she sees a small, pink post-it peeking out from the now slightly messy-looking file. "Ah, there it is!" Slipping the document out of the file, she reads the concluding section in the parole service report, and mumbles, "So, this guy probably left the Netherlands again while he was still on

> parole . . . " Having taken some notes again on the copy of the summons, she is done with this file. The elastic binder snaps the case file closed.

Taking some twenty minutes, this case was not very difficult to "see clearly," she told me: the case file was complete, the evidentiary materials mostly in order, and the clerk's preparation was up to par.

5.1.2 *Doings with Paper or Digital Documents*

What appeared, in Chapter 3, as an input-output system distributing justice, and in Chapter 4 as a highly morally charged, narrative practice, now starts to look slightly more mundane. Seated at the judges' desks to observe their work I learned that judicial work is also a practice of lugging heavy files to one's desk; of ordering documents in the file; of leafing through them, in search of that one piece of testimony or that one expert witness report; and of using pen, pencil, and paper to distill, from the file, an operative sense of "the case." These judicial practices are practices of *extraction* (Latour 2010): of extracting from the case file "the case" it supposedly enfolds. For many court workers, then, "ordinary case work seems to a large extent a face-to-file interaction" (Scheffer 2005: 75) rather than face-to-face interaction. "The case" is buried in the file – and the judge's task is to see it clearly.

Such extraction is not always easy. Case files themselves may resist the effort: their sheer size, incompleteness, or their "messiness" may thwart judges' pre-trial preparations. These little recalcitrances were exacerbated, for judges, when the Court introduced digital case files. Part and parcel of a broader program aimed at streamlining the organization of the Court and its communication with its "chain partners" [*ketenpartners*], for example the public prosecutorial offices, parole services, digital files held the promise of reducing administrative personnel costs and, particularly so in civil law cases, of rendering access to legal procedures easier and swifter. Judges however were not quite enamored with these digital files. Indeed, many lamented the transition. "I kept thinking, you know, if only I could see that stack of files in front of me!" a judge sighed wistfully when recounting her first difficulties with the digital case files. Her colleague added, "if only to get that first impression, even! Like, what case files are thick, which are thin, that kind of thing." Clerks, too, complained: "It's presented to us as a time-saver. I can tell you, it's not!" They, too, faced new demands as they were asked to work digitally, and they, too, only gradually settled into this unfamiliar medium of work.

These observations sketch the outlines of the central problem addressed here: the relationship between the materiality of the case file on the one hand, and on the other, judicial visualization practices. They point towards not only the centrality of the case file as a material entity in, and active constituent of, judicial sensemaking and visualizing practices, but also to the ways this materiality starts to *matter* in the migration of one medium (paper files) to the next (digital files) (Lanzara 2009). The question is hence how, through various types of file-work, an elusive "image of the case" emerges in the interaction between file and file-worker, and crucially, how such taken-for-granted sensemaking practices are variously disrupted, rearticulated, or painstakingly maintained when judicial professionals face a shift in the tools of their trade.

5.2 Judicial Thinking, Seeing, and Visualization

Unpacking the implications of these observations leads not only to a rearticulated understanding of just how we may inquire into "judicial thinking" (cf. Possner 2008) or Hart's "internal point of view" (1994 [1961]); accompanying this effort is also an account of the challenges that attend to our efforts to take the abundance of written artifacts in our fields of research seriously.

In this sense, this intervention takes place against a background of conceptualizations of judicial work that are, explicitly or implicitly, cognitivist. As an example of such cognitivism, take Possner (2008). Drawing on experimental and survey data, he raises the question as to "how judges think," suggesting that psychological mechanisms or economic incentive structures shape and structure judicial thinking. In so doing, legal decisions are first and foremost understood as a product of cognitive processes upon which other cognitive biases, for example psychological mechanisms or economic, profit-maximizing orientations, exert their influence. A similar emphasis on judicial cognition is present in Wermink et al. (2012a), who suggest that different sentencing outcomes are due to processes taking place in the "unconscious." As I have argued in Chapter 3, such an approach to judicial decision-making treats not only the legal system at large as an input-output system; it also places within that black-box yet another, explanatory black-box: the head of the judge. The implicit assumptions that action is the product of cognitive processes, and that such cognitive processes exist only in the "head of the actor," contrasts sharply with approaches to cognition that treat it as embodied and situated. Combining insights from a wide variety of sources, for example activity theory and developmental psychology, practice theory, and American pragmatism, these approaches treat cognition not as a consequence of detached and unmediated knowing activity, but intimately bound up with the material environment (see e.g., Hutchins 1995; vom Lehn et al. 2001; Orlikowski 2006; Schatzki et al. 2001). Intellectual tasks conceived in this way often "appear to be highly embodied activities, in which on-going interactions with the immediate surroundings play a key role" (Berg 1996: 504). People think not only with their heads, but with their "hands," too (Latour 1986). An appreciation of file-work hence defers the necessity to "black-box" judicial thinking in the "head of the judge," and treats it primarily as a situated and materially mediated activity. In contrast with a cognitivism that leaves us with a "'dematerialized' understanding of conduct and action" (vom Lehn et al. 2001: 208), this understanding of judicial knowing practices also opens these activities up for empirical inquiry, rather than locking it up in the "head of the actor."

5.2.1 *Permutations of Perspectivism: Point of View, Vision, Visualization*

Some of this situatedness of knowing is attended to in approaches to legal work that draw, like the judges studied here, on a perspectivist register. Judicial thinking is not just any kind of thinking: there is something uniquely "legal" about it. It is, according to Hart (1994 [1961]) the attitude of the practical-rule follower: seeing the rule is an immediate and unreflexive grasping of the rule (see Shapiro 2006). Not only does this emphasis on the internal viewpoint resonate with judges' own conception of what they are doing when they are doing file-work (after all, they are trying to "see the case clearly"), it also resonates with those seeking to study "vision" in relation to specific professional practices. Goodwin (1994), for instance, suggests that different professional practices rely on cultivated and materially mediated modes of distinguishing figure from ground, information from noise. Yet while Goodwin (1994) treats these professional practices as intimately bound up with specific socio-material sites and settings (e.g., collecting soil for testing, recognizing, and pointing out, for others, "aggression" in a defendants' behavior caught on videotape) Hart's perspectivism remains rather cognitivist: for him, the grasping of the rule is a disembodied, immaterial process.

Hart's internal point of view, however, does allude to something specific to legal practices: that is, the legal rule itself. These legal rules are central to legal practices: in ethnomethodological terms, legal practices are "oriented to" these rules. It is through this very act of orienting oneself to the rule that these rules become implicated in action. While legal rules, then, may preexist their implication in concrete practices, the very fact that they preexist concrete instances of implication does not make their "hold" on concrete practices unproblematic. For sociolegal scholars, the question remains: how, as a matter of practical activity, are rules oriented to at all? In the social study of legal practices, this problem is also known as the "missing-what" (Dupret et al. 2015). Lynch summarizes this "missing what" as born out of a tendency to "describe various 'social' influences on and implication of the growth and development of legal institutions while taking for granted that lawyers write briefs, present cases, interrogate witnesses, and engage in legal reasoning" (Lynch 1993: 114). Accompanying this tendency is treating legal categories and rules as self-evident "prescriptions and proscriptions for action" (Dupret et al. 2015: 4). Yet the practical and concrete question is one that would highlight precisely how legal rules are "oriented to" at all as a matter of situated and practical activity. File-work, as the location of coming to the case, of grappling with it, of turning it around in one's thoughts while browsing the file, is a plausible candidate to start to begin inquiry into this kind of apprehension.

5.2.2 *Legal Case Files*

Latour (2010) and Scheffer (2005, 2006) are notable here, as they have explicitly traced the "doings with documents" (Harper 1998: 3) in legal settings. For both, legal practices take place in relation to both spoken word and written text. For both, the case file is a crucial agent in these practices. For instance, Latour (2010) locates the quintessential legal activity of finding the means (the legal argument) in the file-workers' attempts to build a "fragile bridge of texts" between the case file and the letter of the law (2010: 83) in a series of sequentially distributed note-taking and summarizing operations. Especially helpful is his attention to the distributed character of such practices over various kinds of file-workers, and his sensitivity to the sheer amount of work that goes into extracting, "like diamonds . . . from the ore" (Latour 2010: 102), the case in its purest form from the case file. Scheffer (2005, 2006, 2007, 2010), too, concentrates on the implication of the documents in the case file in the formation of a criminal defense in his study of defense lawyers' file-work, focusing on the interplay between written and spoken text in the construction of lawyers' defense pleas. Emphasizing the intricacies of file-work, both authors move away from treating case files as unproblematic representational devices: the file does not speak for itself. At the same time, both authors highlight above all else the *textual contents* of the case file, and in so doing risk reproducing some of the cognitivism or dematerialized perspectivism I seek to make problematic here. It treats knowing as a product of unfolding and practical "microformation" (Scheffer 2005), yet loses out of sight the fact that the case file is not only a container of information but a material object as well.

Combining both a concern with the practical ways legal actors orient their action to legal rules and an emphasis on the materiality of such practices, I suggest we think of these practices as practices of visualization. With Goodwin (1994), I would suggest that these practices may be rather specific to certain professions or communities of practices. With Lynch (1993), Scheffer (2004, 2007) and Latour (2010), I would suggest the "missing what" of much sociolegal scholarship lies precisely in its disregard for the practical and material activities of orienting action towards legal rules and categories. Unmooring it from its dominant coupling with discussions about big data (Halpern 2014) or new media technologies (Mirzoeff 2015), the notion of visualization is suggestive of purposeful and operational modalities of "seeing" that require active schematization and ordering. Drawing on this emphasis on schematics and ordering, I want to concentrate on the small acts of apprehending, of coming to the case, as these takes place in relation to the case file. The notion of visualization helps me to do so, as it precisely "straddles the actual practices of depicting and modelling the world, the images that are used, and the forms of attention by which users are trained to use interfaces" (Halpern 2014: 23).

In order to demonstrate what such an attention to file-work may yield, I now take you to the offices and file-rooms making up the court's "backstage." I give up my position as spectator in the courtroom and interrogator of judges for an observational mode of inquiry that traces case files from their entry into the court to the judges' desk.

5.3 Visualizing the Case: A Paper-Specific Account

What does it take, then, to visualize the case? It takes, first of all, a case file. Gathering together evidentiary materials, expert witness reports, and documents testifying to the specifics of the case, the case file promises to enfold the case. In their paper form case files arrive in the court's administrative offices; there, their arrival is registered in one of two digital registration systems (the older Compas or the relatively new GPS). Administrative workers must then check these files according to a checklist that is attached to their inner sleeve. Among other things, they check whether the case file meets certain procedural demands and take note of its components. For instance, does it include a separate binder for information on, and correspondence with, a possible victim? Does it include a parole service report? Most files, however, are far from complete upon arrival: not only may further reports be added to them once they are sent to the court's administration, but ongoing correspondence between the prosecutor or the defense attorney and the Court must similarly be added to the case file. Latour (2010), drawing on colloquialisms shared by the administrative workers in the Conseil d'Etat, speaks of these processes as one of "ripening." In the court studied here, files stored in the file-room are considered quite "open" and even "alive."

5.2.3 "Reading" a File: Material Clues

To the uninitiated, files look very much alike. As standardized objects, files are precisely instruments of deindividuation, physically and materially embodying procedural "equality before the law" (cf. M'charek, Hagendijk and Prainsack 2013). Yet seemingly slight differences between them assume importance to both clerks and judges. For instance, paper files in police judge cases may be quite thin or quite thick. Their sleeves may be worn (when the case has been adjourned, perhaps more than once, in its past) or rather new and sleek. Clerks' and judges' first encounter with their cases, then, is visual and perceptual: they simply face a stack of files, which they might have to move from one location (the file room) to their own offices. This stack itself, as well as the thickness and age of individual files, allows clerks and judges to gauge the case load, that is, it allows them to assess not just exactly how many cases are scheduled to appear in court in a single court session (done by counting), but also the relative complexity of individual cases. Clerks and judges regularly make distinctions based on the thickness of individual files, as they have come to learn the bigger files are usually more complex cases, with more evidentiary materials: a case of physical assault, perhaps, in which victim's, witnesses', and defendants' statements are notoriously incomplete and contradictory, and in which correspondence with the victims may have generated more paper. Thinner files are perceived differently; these are probably simple cases of petty theft, in which defendants are caught red-handed and (usually) confess.

Once the paper file is opened, the physical qualities of its component parts afford the same intuitive gauging processes to take place, prior, even, to reading one word of its textual content. For instance, a thick folder of evidentiary materials suggests not only that the case is more (legally) complex (as more evidence has been gathered), but also that the judge will be dealing with a defendant who pleads innocent: a clerk explains that in such cases, "police officials have to work harder to find the two pieces of evidence we need to convict someone and, well, they use a lot more paper." The criminal record, as a physical object, is particularly suggestive here, too: it allows clerks and judges acquire an "image" of the defendant as for example a particularly troublesome repeat offender or a one-shotter, which "image" in turn helps them evaluate punishment options if the defendant is found guilty. Leafing through the file, Judge Dempsey, with a surprised look on his face, showed me a particularly thick criminal record: "Look at this! You can seriously injure someone if you hit him on the head with a criminal record this thick. Well, if he's found guilty we won't have to explore the option of a community service; he passed that station twenty-five cases ago!" Here, the physical qualities of the paper case file become instrumental in conceiving of the case as characteristic of a certain narrative kind. Concerning "offense types rather than specific individuals" (Dupret 2011: 142), judges' narrative typifications may already be mobilized at this early stage of their file-work (see Chapter 4). Gauging the physical qualities of the case file and its component parts provides file-workers with a set of material clues instrumental in structuring and timing their pre-trial preparations. Their informational value is not limited to their textual or graphic content: case files are both texts and physical objects.

Of course, it takes experience to be able to make such distinctions. For a novice, the case file is utterly bewildering. Looking all very much the same on the outside, their insides are a jumble. Documents are not necessarily ordered chronologically. Folders within folders raise the question what logic guides their inclusion into each other. And what are all these scribbles about? Why all the stamps? What do all these abbreviations mean? "Reading" is a word ill-suited to describe my first studies of the case files; "struggling with" being an arguably much more astute nomer. Case files very much resisted a "politics of immediation" (Mazzarella 2006) that promises immediate and unmediated access to "what really happened." Judges and clerks, then, have developed ways to "tame" the file in order to extract the case.

5.2.4 Taming a File

Before the file arrives at the judges' desk it has first passed through the hands of an assisting court clerk. These clerks are tasked with making the file a more easily navigable and structured object. Kirsch (1995) calls such practices "informational jigging": these are practices in which "an agent will arrange items (consciously or sometimes unconsciously) to draw attention, to cue cognitive events or processes in himself or herself or another agent" (Kirsch 1995: 38). Coding, for instance, is the practice by which court clerks physically mark some parts of the paper file with color-coded stickers. Showing me his selection of red, orange, blue, green and pink post-its, clerk Lee explains:

> So what they want from us is to mark the documents in the case file, so that they can switch to whatever documents they are interested in right away when they are preparing cases. We use orange for the criminal record, red is for his statement in the police interrogation, blue is of course for the police findings [referring to the color of police uniforms], the victim's statement is marked green and then there is the pink sticker for the parole service report, if one is present.

Showing me a drawer full of these colored stickers, he chuckles and adds, "By the way, it is really annoying when we run out of these post-its, so I and some other clerks are hoarding them."

Here, clerks' coding practices assist judges' future navigation of the case file. Court clerks may also draw out relevant passages from the police observations or interrogations by highlighting, with a pencil, certain important words and sentences in the case file, hence directing attention to those "sensitive text zones" (Fraenckel et al. 2010) in which the judge is anticipated to find answers to questions of legal relevance: "it's just to sort of underline the things a judge might be interested in, like the defendants' statement or a witness' observations, stuff like that," a clerk tells me. In their highlighting, they also "transform the future reading of the copy" (Scheffer 2006: 308), drawing attention to salient phrases or accounts.

Judges, too, engage in such informational jigging activities – although they, unlike clerks, may prefer to use yellow markers in their highlighting practices. Assisting both clerks' and judges' "reading" of the file is yet another affordance of paper files, that is the fact that component parts can be spread out on a desk. Especially in cases involving multiple witness accounts, the "ecological flexibility" (Luff et al. 1992) of paper files allows file-workers to easily switch between different accounts.

5.2.5 *Making a Summary: Disentangling and Assembling Work*

Throughout their gauging, jigging, and juxtaposing work, clerks and judges are first and foremost concerned with making a summary or "extraction" [*uittreksel*] of the case. Their extractions are always oriented to the official charges, which charges they use to "apply a filter" (Judge Beech) and to distinguish signal from noise. These charges are legal-formulaic in nature, and are drawn up in order to cover various modalities of the crime in question (e.g., whether the person committed the crime alone or in association with others, whether the person hit or merely slapped a person), for example:

> That he, on or about [date] in [place] together with and in association with others, or alone, maliciously maltreating a person or persons, hit/kicked a person [name victim] multiple times (with force) on/against the head and/or back and/or leg/legs and/or on another part/on other parts of the body, as a result of which [the victim] has suffered pain and/or injury.

These charges are, to speak with Latour (2010), a tentative bridge between the case file and the letter of the law. They fold within the formulation of the legal rule – "maliciously maltreating" – the specifics of the offense in question – the date and place of the offense, the name of the victim, and the precise alleged actions, that is "hit/kicked . . . on/against the head and/or back/ and/or legs." The file, once ordered and jigged, is read and summarized in relation to these summons. These charges, one judge emphasizes, "anchor" her navigation practices.

Some judges additionally visually draw out the case as a more or less provable entity using the text of the charges on the copy of the summons. Translating the information in the file into an "image of the case" may for instance be done through the marking of specific terms, or crossing through terms in the charges that the judge expects cannot be proven, superimposing the facts of the case onto the formal charges:

> That he, on or about the [date] in [place] ~~together with and in association with others~~, or alone, maliciously maltreating a person or persons, hit/~~kicked~~ a person [name victim] multiple times (with force) on/against the head and/~~or back and/or leg/legs and/or on another part/on other parts of the body~~, as a result of which [the victim] has suffered pain and/or injury.

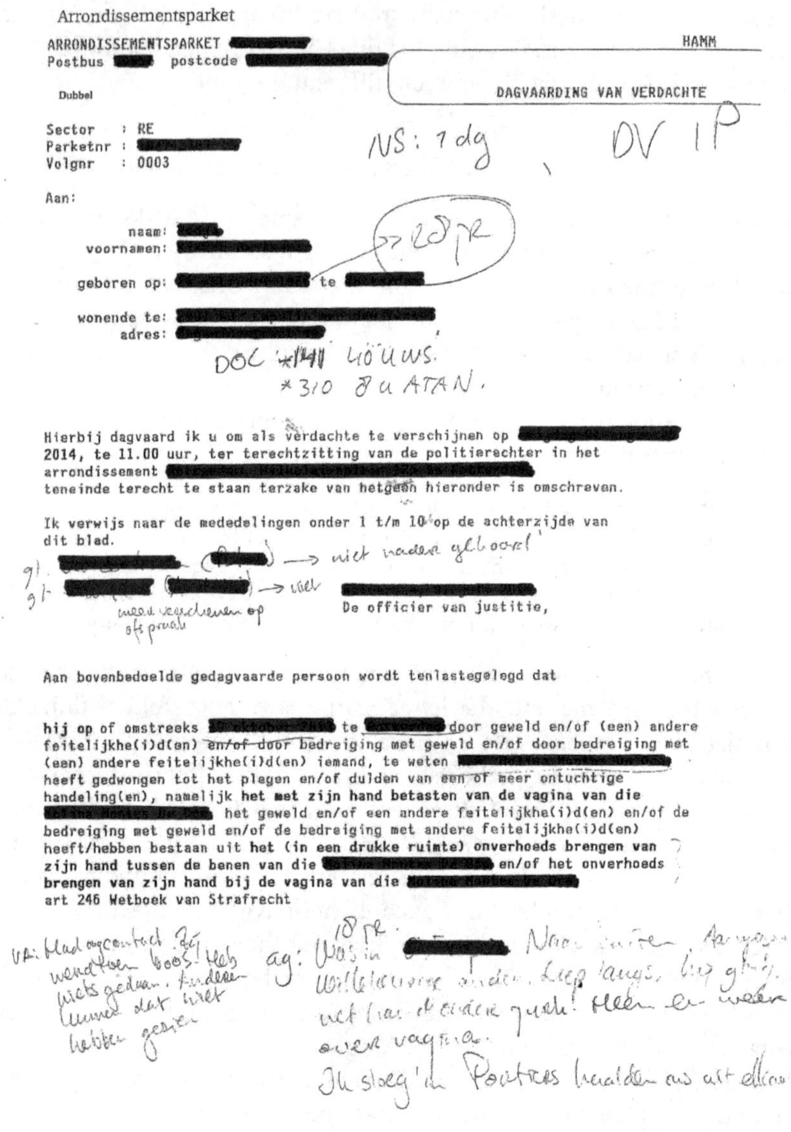

Arrondissementsparket

ARRONDISSEMENTSPARKET HAMM
Postbus postcode

Dubbel

DAGVAARDING VAN VERDACHTE

Sector : RE
Parketnr :
Volgnr : 0003

Aan:

naam:
voornamen:

geboren op: te

wonende te:
adres:

Hierbij dagvaard ik u om als verdachte te verschijnen op 2014, te 11.00 uur, ter terechtzitting van de politierechter in het arrondissement teneinde terecht te staan terzake van hetgeen hieronder is omschreven.

Ik verwijs naar de mededelingen onder 1 t/m 10 op de achterzijde van dit blad.

De officier van justitie,

Aan bovenbedoelde gedagvaarde persoon wordt tenlastegelegd dat

hij op of omstreeks te door geweld en/of (een) andere feitelijkhe(i)d(en) ~~en/of door~~ bedreiging met geweld en/of door bedreiging met (een) andere feitelijkhe(i)d(en) iemand, te weten heeft gedwongen tot het plegen en/of dulden van ~~een of meer~~ ontuchtige handeling(en), namelijk het met zijn hand betasten van de vagina van die het geweld en/of een andere feitelijkhe(i)d(en) en/of de bedreiging met geweld en/of de bedreiging met andere feitelijkhe(i)d(en) heeft/hebben bestaan uit het (in een drukke ruimte) onverhoeds brengen van zijn hand tussen de benen van die en/of het onverhoeds brengen van zijn hand bij de vagina van die
art 246 Wetboek van Strafrecht

Afschrift aan raadsman SL 2012 II W 1/2 21 - 01

Figure 5.1 The product of the Judges' case-extraction on the (copied) summons (anonymized)

Yet the surface of the summons is not only instrumental in extracting the case-as-event. Further bits and pieces are added to it, in particular information with the case as a procedural entity and information with regards to the "person of the defendant" and his or her personal circumstances. Often, these bits and pieces are spatially clustered on the surface of the summons. Take, for instance, the anonymized copy of one of the judges' notes in Figure 5.2.

Here, we see in the upper right-hand corner information with regard to procedural elements of the case. This specific defendant has spent one day in custody, the judge notes ("IVS: 1 dag"), and the summons have been handed over in person ("DV: IP"). It also includes a brief summary of the defendant's criminal record ("DOC"), which has in this case two counts specified with use of the Dutch Criminal Code's numbering: one a count of public assault ("141") and another of theft ("310"). Detailing, too, the specific sentence decided on (e.g., "40 u ws" means forty hours of community service), this preparation form allows the judge not only to place the current event in a more or less criminal history, but also to take into account the (relatively new) statute stipulating that defendants do not receive a community service for a similar offense within five years after their first conviction.

Moving on, what appears is information with regards not to "the case" as a procedural entity, but as an event. The judge has noted that two witnesses to the offense ["gt" – *getuige*] to the offense, a case of sexual assault, have only been heard in situ and have presumably not been invited to the police station for further interviewing. Below the charges, we also find a brief summary of the defendant's words, drawn from the process-verbal of his interrogation: "had eye-contact. She got angry. Did not do anything. Others could not have seen it."

Included, too, is a rudimentary version of the victim's account. Its use of both the first- and third-person evokes the activity of *stitching together* both the first-person account of the victim and the third-person summarization of the judge while simultaneously allowing the judge to distinguish between the victim's statement and his own summary: "was in [bar name]. Went outside. Addressed by random person. Passed her, he put hand under dress, rubbed her vagina. I hit him and security guard intervened." In extracting the basic informational coordinates of the offense in question, judges may sometimes take care to summarize the offense as a narrative. For instance, Judge Roberts adds to the summons the following note: "big fight, two stages. Def.[endant]. issues threat, tapping knife on window, throws table through door -> police. Def. sleeps. Again fight + verbal threats, grandmother and daughter now present. Kicks in front door." Yet not all judges do so, as it may render it more difficult to keep apart exactly what was said by whom. Drawing distinctions between the account of the defendant and victim, as in Figure 5.1 assists judges especially in cases where different accounts diverge significantly.

The case as event, and the case as a procedural entity: both are now neatly separated. While this judge has not included notes on the defendant's personal circumstances, many judges do so in the lower corner of the copied summons. If the defendant is found guilty, these notes assist judges in accounting for the defendants' personal circumstances in crafting a suitable sentence. Judge Dempsey, including information about the defendant's addictions to heroin, cocaine, and alcohol, notes down the following on his preparation form: "her/coc, alc, no fixed income, daughter, debts up to 30.000 euros." The case's "microformation" (Scheffer 2006), then, is a practice revolving around a move from a first glance towards a more specific form of visualization, that is a visualization that distinguishes between the case as a procedural entity, the case as an event, and the case as involving an individual defendant. Yet together, these three spatial clusters also do something more: they mutually elaborate each other (Berg and Goorman 1999). They are not discrete bits and pieces of information, but are interpreted together. For instance, whether the summons has been handed over in person or not is important in a legal-procedural sense; at the same time, this legal-procedural element of the case structures judges' expectations with regard to what kind of defendant they will be dealing with. If the summons has not been handed over in person, judges know that the defendant is probably homeless, an association, we know by now, that evokes not only drug addiction, but petty theft as well (see Chapter 4). Similarly, the precise nature and modality of the crime charged may (or may not) seamlessly "line up" with the type of defendant into a more typical narrative. For instance, assembling the information from the defendant's criminal record, a parole service report, and the specificities of the event in question, judge Roberts, having taken some notes giggled and told me: "See why I am laughing? He's still on parole for a previous offense, and part of his parole conditions was participation in an anger management course . . . So him kicking in that door [one of the offenses in question] doesn't come as a surprise!" Jigging, coding, highlighting, juxtaposing, and summarizing work, then, produce what we may call a "story-before-the-trial" (cf. Jackson 1988, 1996). After such preparation, one judge proclaims, "you can send me into the courtroom with this one piece of paper!"

5.4 Digitization: Struggling to Visualize

Against this background of socially textured and materially mediated practices of visualization, the digitization of case files was met with hesitancy and frustration. Judges lamented the presence of computers in court, suggesting that these notoriously slow computers perched on the judicial desk would significantly hamper their interaction with defendants. But backstage, too, the digitization of case files led to some confusion. On the one hand, paper case files continued to trickle in; linked to an older registration system (Compas), these paper case files tended to be part of the prosecution's backlog of cases. As such, the court was not, at any point of my fieldwork, wholly without paper case files. Yet more and more cases were not delivered to court in the form of paper files, but rather "made available" through the new file viewer, Divos 2. Throughout my fieldwork, these digital files were all scanned copies of paper files; only in a later stage of digitization will all documents in the file be produced digitally.

I received access to these digital files as part of a broader digital access to the court's computers. While judges and clerks could use Divos 2 to check up on their own caseloads, I had access to all PR caseloads through Divos 2. While this slow but sure "infrastructural inversion" (Bowker and Star 1999) would present court workers with practical hurdles in visualizing cases, it turned out an unexpected, methodological boon for me. As clerks and judges were able to highlight passages in the file and draw up digital, rather than paper, preparation forms, I now was able to trace (even in real time) clerks' and judges' preparations. Divos 2 rendered available and visible especially clerks' preparation practices and their both formal and informal standardization over time. While the preceding observations are based, then, on close observation of work practices through the "shadowing" of individual judges, the following part of this chapter draws additionally on these digitized preparation forms.

Let's first discuss the digital file viewer. First of all, working with digital files is no more or less material than working with paper files: it still requires of judges that they be seated in a particular place and engage with specific materials (desk tops, desk chairs, computers). However, the file viewer quite radically disrupted judicial methods of gauging cases in relation to the look and feel of individual case files. Instead, the perceptual field of an as-of-yet unknown caseload is materialized as a digital interface in the digital file viewer, Divos 2. This is a basic, visual interface that allows judges to open and close specific files, which in turn are listed as belonging to a specific court session. Crucially, this file viewer indicates only the number of pages as an indicator of the file's severity or complexity. Without any clue as to how thick the file would be, judges had difficulties structuring their workflow. In fact, this indication was only added to the software after judges expressed discomfort with an earlier version of Divos 2. Yet even the number of pages in the file detracted from the more immediate gauging afforded by the physical look and shape of the file. Both clerks and judges reported having difficulties translating the number of pages of a digital file into a sense of how thick or thin the paper equivalent would have been. Similarly, the component parts of the case file (a criminal record, the evidentiary folder of the police) lack a material "body" or physical substance. In a similar vein, judges and clerks were not always happy with the software as it disallowed their navigation-by-thumb. Capable only of displaying two separate documents at the same time, the file viewer did not allow its users to juxtapose more sources of evidence, a technique especially useful in cases involving more than two pieces of evidence.

The file viewer did, however, allow them to "tame" the file in ways not dissimilar to what they were used to. For instance, it allowed its users to digitally highlight selected sentences and words in the various components that make up the case file. When selected and highlighted, these phrases and words appear as marked in yellow – a format that replicates visually judges' use of markers when navigating the file. Also, the file viewer anticipated existing summarizing practices: it provides the option to open and save a digital preparation form, in which information can either be typed out or copy-pasted from the digital file. Last, the digital file viewer offers its users a way to code the information using hyperlinks, which appear as underlined and blue text in the digital preparation form (e.g., "statement defendant," "parole service report"). Clicking on a hyperlink, the user will open the hyperlinked file in the right half of the screen, in which the hyperlinked phrases will appear highlighted.

Yet these digital affordances, while they seem ways to meet existing practices and "user-demands," in effect had significant consequences for the social distribution of these work practices between clerks and judges. Take, for instance, clerks' preparation forms. In the case of paper files, clerks' tended to write these by hand, either on a separate sheet of paper or, like judges, on a copy of the summons. Judges could then either start their own preparation practices with a second, clean summons or, often using a different color pen, add their own notes to the prepared summons.

The paper-based preparation of clerks, performed through manual note-taking onto the copy of the judicial summons, had as an advantage that it tended to be brief and to the point. After all, writing can be rather arduous and slow, and the physical space on the paper copy of the judicial summons is simply limited. The graphic layout of the preparation form, and the informal routine of presenting information in two or three separate spatial clusterings, further assisted the visual extraction of the case. However, faced with the affordances of the digital preparation form, clerks tended to present significantly more information and text. Not only is typing less arduous than writing and the space on the digital preparation form unlimited, the file viewer also rendered it possible to copy-paste whole swaths of texts into the digital preparation form. Copying and pasting text from the file into the digital preparation form is easier than writing a summary oneself, while the digital preparation form can incorporate as much information as the clerk deems necessary – the space it offers is, in principle, unlimited. While some clerks used headings and subheadings to present the information, the preparation form would often take the visual form as a list (of bullet pointed bits of information or quotes) or a text. Some clerks, too, would neglect to incorporate the charges, hence requiring judges to navigate not only the documents "in" the case, but also to keep yet another document in sight, that of the official summons.

The possibility to present large swaths of texts, sometimes literally copied from the texts in the digital file, met clerks' user-needs very well: their task, after all, consists of *being complete*. However, used in this particular fashion it failed to meet those of judges, some of whom in turn missed the brevity, clarity, and spatial clustering of information on the one-sheet, paper preparation forms had offered them. Without the brief and visually concentrated presentation of the facts of the case, the digital file viewer in effect shifted more of the summarizing work to judges, who now not only had to navigate the wealth of information in the file, but the large swaths of text in the digital preparation form as well. It was only as a result of feedback from individual judges and the introduction of summarization guidelines for clerks that clerks started to strive once again for brevity. Commenting on a clerks' preparation, Judge Jamison said:

> What I like about these here is that they include the charges in the same [digital] field: that way, I immediately have some image of what we're talking about. Very good is also her brevity, in particular her summation of the defendants' criminal record. Some clerks in contrast simply copy all kinds of texts, while I will still have to check in the file whether that is all the relevant material. Copying like that, by the way, is a sure way to make the preparation form almost as unclear and extensive as the file itself, and that doesn't work for me at all.

Taking the shape of a list or a text, the digital preparation form was not, furthermore, spatially clustered in two or three visual fields. In response to what they perceived as extensive preparation forms, then, judges tended to continue to work with their own copies of the summons. Perceived as more trustworthy than the digital preparation form, the paper copy of the summons continues to be the preferred way for judges to prepare their cases. Their fear that the computer may fail them in court motivated many judges to continue to rely on their own note-taking on the summons. Perceived as more "comfortable" and "stable" to work with, the paper summons continued to act as the surface of the visual concentration and mutual elaboration of information. It also supported judges' reliance on manual note-taking and their interweaving of reading (the digital file) and writing (by hand) without having to switch screens on their computers (cf. Sellen and Harper 2003), which, seeing as the computers in court are notoriously slow to operate, significantly speeded up their preparation practices.

It is salient that the use of paper preparation forms came over time to be reserved mainly for the judges. Clerks' digital preparation forms were not completely sidelined: some judges would print these out and read the digital file in relation to both the paper summons and the clerks' preparations. Checking their own work against that of clerks was also deemed necessary when the digital case file had been highlighted and hyperlinked digitally. On the one hand, these digital hyperlinks facilitate a "horizontal" and flexible navigation through the file, jumping immediately from digital preparation form to the information the clerk has highlighted without the necessity to scroll through the entire case file. Similarly, digitally highlighted text allowed judges to arrive at crucial bits of information almost immediately. Yet some judges remain hesitant to only use the clerks' digital directions: after all, a clerk may overlook a piece of information or fail to select (and hyperlink) an important passage in the file. In paper files, this is not necessarily a problem: the feel of the file affords some sense of how much text preceded salient information in a witness report or a transcription of the interrogation of the defendant. After all, it matters, to judges, whether a defendant confesses at once or is guided towards confession; it also matters whether a victim or witness has important things to say about the circumstances leading up to the event, or is rather brief about these. Post-its and penciled highlights, coupled with a tactile sense of the number of pages preceding a confession or description of the event assisted judges in their visualization. Yet precisely this tactile dimension was lost: left only were the hyperlinked, but dematerialized and decontextualized passages. It is for that reason judges expressed some hesitancy in following only the clerks' digital "directions": it would disallow precisely such judgments about the texts surrounding the case, its literal "con-text." Using only the clerks' hyperlinked passages might mean they not only fail to read salient texts presented in other parts of the file; it would also mean they might not fully understand the context of the offense itself. Pointing, for instance, to a defendants' offhanded remark that he always carries a knife in the process-verbal of the defendants' interrogation, Judge Masons suggested that it is precisely these bits and pieces that inform her "image" of the case: "This is important. It isn't related to this specific case, perhaps, but it strengthens the idea that there are significant problems there, that he moves in strange circles" [*milieu*]. As these bits and pieces, the "context," are instrumental in building that "image" of the case, judges rarely rely on these hyperlinks only.

Of course, over time and with practice judges and clerks seemed to slowly but surely "settle into" (Lanzara 2009) the new medium. For instance, while clerks may have copy-pasted long swaths of texts, the digital preparation forms are slowly but surely decreasing in length, and judges may ask of clerks to make use of the newly introduced standardized digital preparation form. The relationship between specific individual clerks and judges may also play a role in how judges work with the (digital) file: when judges have worked with a specific clerk before, and were satisfied with his/her performance, the selection of information made by the clerk is trusted, while in other cases the clerks may not have a particularly good reputation, or such trust may as of yet not had a chance to develop (with new clerks). Both these inter-professional claims to professional legitimacy, control, and ownership of the judicial decision, as well as individual relationships between judges and clerks are without doubt to play a role in the further development of digital work practices.

5.5 Visualization and "Doings with Documents"

The preceding pages have demonstrated how cases, over the course of practical face-to-file work, are visualized; how, in other words, case-workers render both the truth of the matter and its legal qualification visible both textually and graphically. In doing so this chapter "materializes" our understanding of both legal practices of truth telling and practices of legal qualification: that is, it treats these practices as materially mediated. Apprehending the case is coming to an operational sense of "what really happened" in relation to the letter of the law. The paper summons operates, in these practices, as a both conceptual and physical "bridge" between the text of the file and the text of the law (Latour 2010). "Micro-formation" (Scheffer 2005) of cases is enacted over the course of distributed and materially mediated activities of glancing at files, of gauging them, of ordering and taming them. If Hart's internal point of view (1994 [1961]) is that of the practical rule-follower making his or her intuitive leap into the rule-governed dark, judicial work practices first and foremost suggest that "visualizing the case" is a practical activity that unfolds over time, that is helped along or thwarted by the specific affordances and recalcitrances of case files, and that is distributed over judges and clerks. It is not a purely textual practice: instead, it draws on the para-textual and non-textual affordances of (paper) case files. In emphasizing these distributed, materially mediated practices of visualization it makes problematic both cognitivist appeals to "how judges think" as well as an insistence on a dematerialized, unmediated "point of view."

5.5.1 *Praxiography: A Practical Understanding of Writing and Infrastructure*

Such an emphasis on practices of visualization, rather than on points of view or ways of thinking, would necessarily demand of us a practical understanding of the production and use of artifacts in the sites we study. Bureaucratic settings especially are rife with files, documents, and administrative forms. The problems they pose are diametrically opposed to that of the metaphorical anthropological fieldworker who confronts a "society without writing" (Levi Strauss 1961: 292). These are settings that, in contrast, depend on and hang together by virtue of writing: bureaucracy, the "rule of the desk" (Weber 1978 [1922]) alludes precisely to the desk, where files are compiled, ordered, and processed. Yet a decidedly phonocentric reflex (cf. Derrida 1967) remains tempting. In other words, there is a tendency, within social inquiry, to not spend too much time on these artifacts, and instead to focus on the richness of face-to-face interactions. It is this same tendency, I think, that makes the court's frontstage such a well-studied setting relative to its backstage. As a result of this phonocentric reflex, the fact that bureaucratic actors *themselves* are very much concerned with administrative forms and artifacts can hence be glossed or itself be made into an exotic curiosity: look at how they fetishize these objects! Look at how they place excessive trust in writing! Such ironic readings, in my view, do little to appreciate just how much of bureaucratic or legal practices hang together not or not only because its human members share a professional worldview or culture, but by their shared (if diverging) engagements with the bureaucratic "mutable mobile" (cf. Latour 1986) of the case file. Speaking of Prussian bureaucracy, Latour marvels that:

> The "rationalization" granted to bureaucracy since Hegel and Weber has been attributed by mistake to the "mind" of (Prussian) bureaucrats. *It is all in the files themselves.* . . . The "cracy" of bureaucracy is mysterious and hard to study, but the "bureau" is something that can be empirically studied, and which explains, because of its structure, why some power is given to an average mind just by looking at files. . . . Common sense ironically makes fun of these "gratte papiers" and "paper shufflers", and often wonders what all this "red tape" is for . . . . In our cultures "paper shuffling" is the source of an essential power, that constantly escapes attention since its materiality is ignored.
>
> (Latour 1986: 26)

Similarly, Dorothy Smith comments that "the formality, the designed, planned, and *organized* character of formal organizations depends heavily on documentary practices, which co-ordinate, order, provide continuity, monitor, and *organize* relations between different segments and phases of organizational courses of action" (1984: 66). The centrality of these travelling documents in these settings also means that "the social" is not mutely awaiting a researcher to give it voice (Hirschauer 2006). In contrast: bureaucratic practices are shaped and structured by their own many documentary secretions. While documents may exercise a "pull" on the researcher (Riles 2008: 8), taking them seriously as actors is not always easy. Garfinkel (1967) notes for instance that organizational documents are quite difficult objects in and of study. They are drawn up with specific audiences in mind and produced in reference to specific organizational contexts, and the researcher hoping to learn from them may be very much disappointed to learn he or she was not among the intended audience. Berg (1996) similarly draws attention to medical records, which have different organizational uses and as such cannot simply be used to "learn more about the patient." Representation of "the case" may be only one, and even subservient, of the purposes of a document. Those interested in textual or graphic or textual "inscriptions" (cf. Latour and Woolgar 1979) in various settings may surely take this to heart: representation is not necessarily the organizational point (Riles 2008).

Nor is "representation" a given. Even if documents may "want" to represent this chapter shows that these case files still have to be "brought to life" (Berg 1996: 501) through organized and distributed practices. A case file never speaks for itself. Successfully navigating its information relies on material work, like highlighting, coding, and summarizing practice; the case as such interactively emerges and is not in any simplistic way "contained" in the case file. Case files may mediate epistemic access to a specific event in history, but it requires a professionally-situated set of techniques to organize this access to be able to "see like a judge" (cf. Law 2009; Scott 1998). In these kinds of "epistemic practices" (Lynch 1993) documents are better analyzed as concrete "technical objects" that are deployed in making out a more abstract "epistemic object," which epistemic object is the case to be decided on (Ewenstein and Whyte 2009). What is more, the file is operational in ways that have nothing to do with its textual content proper, but instead with its material properties (wear and tear, its thickness, weight). Approaching documents in this manner allows us hence to put the senses back into our conceptualizations of sensemaking activities, and appreciate the relevance of these sensemaking activities for practitioners faced with high caseloads and the requirement to efficiently "get things done" (Garfinkel 1967). If there is one thing to learn from this chapter it is that such representation takes not a simple glance or reading, but a specialized kind of "professional vision" (Goodwin 1994) or rather, *professional practices of visualization*, to make case files do representational work at all. It is only by becoming familiar with these objects, and through developing ways to "boil them down," that it becomes possible to "read" them representationally and visualize the case.

The emphasis I have placed on digitization as a potentially disruptive event should interest researchers at the intersection of knowledge practices and digital artifacts more generally. In a context where digitization is increasingly understood as both a money-saver and a catch-all solution to public services' presupposed lack of transparency and efficiency, this chapter is in many ways a cautionary tale. An understanding of documents that treats these as transporters of information may do little to apprehend how knowledge practices are both profession- and medium-specific and implicated not only in individual, but also collective work practices. For instance, case files are, as I have shown, subtly implicated in the reproduction of the professional boundary between judges and assisting clerks (see for a similar case in medical settings, Berg and Bowker 1997). For instance, judges may use yellow markers to highlight text while clerks use erasable pencils, and continue to use the paper summons while clerks are expected to adapt to the digital files. These observations also point to the way technologies do not simply mediate individual sensemaking practices, but are deployed in "rich, densely structured landscape[s] of identities and working relations" (Suchman 2002: 141). Also, at stake in intra-professional struggles over control and legitimacy is in this case not merely the question as to who can "legitimately see" (Goodwin 1994), but also, who, and with help of what specific instruments, can "legitimately visualize." At the same time, it is important to avoid a technological determinism that treats human activity as fully dependent on its material parameters. While following digitization some work practices become irretrievably lost, other practices are rearticulated or maintained. Indeed, digital practices may also come to exist alongside paper-based practices that to participants simply feel more comfortable, reliable, and flexible (Sellen and Harper 2003). And even where such digital media may attempt to replicate paper-based practices (e.g., the coding and highlighting affordances of the file viewer), work practices may not "naturally and unproblematically adapt to the new technology," nor will workers automatically "take advantage of the 'obvious' benefits afforded by new computer based systems" (Heath et al. 2000: 301), as existing practices are maintained or rearticulated. In other words, materials matter – but where, how, and to whom are questions badly attended to in either overtly human-centered or technology-centered accounts. The trouble is, as always, in the middle: in the relations between files and file-workers.

5.6 Onwards: Matter and Time

The preceding pages have demonstrated what an attention to materiality may do to our understanding of legal practices. That is, an attention to the medium-specificity of judicial work practices has assisted us in taking seriously the material mediation of both judicial "thinking" and "seeing." I have paid specific attention to the various affordances and recalcitrances of case files. As physical objects, they allow for an intuitive gauging and sequential operations of "taming" of the case; as digital objects, they lose some of these recalcitrances yet they gain some, too: digital files remain difficult to gauge and summarize.

Case files, then, matter. That is: their materiality is consequential in and material to judicial visualization practices. Yet case files have yet another mode of mattering: not in the spatial sense of the term, but in the temporal sense. That is, their purpose is rendering the there-and-then of the event in question available in the here-and-now of judging activities; their role in allowing action-at-a-distance is one of creating a passage from the court setting towards the event in question. If they duly perform this task, time is folded: the there-and-then rendered accessible in the here-and-now. But they do not always succeed. Drawing attention not to the time and place of the event in question, but rather to their own history of production, case files may fail to mediate this temporal folding. The following chapter concentrates on the ways case files mediate this folding of time – and what happens when they fail to do so. As such, it is both a discussion of the temporalities in and of objects more generally as an account of the enactment of procedure in this legal setting. In order to make this point, I stick to no place in particular but am led only by legal procedure. I switch from file to courtroom and back again, tracing the ways time, histories and futures are implicated in the making of a decision in the here-and-now.

6

Folding Times, Making Truths

6.1 From Here-and-Now to There-and-Then

The preceding chapter suggested we think of judicial work as materially and socially textured practices. Distributed and sequentially organized practices of visualization extract, from the file, an operative sense of the case. Active in, and constituent of, judges' visualizations of the case, case files matter both materially, as physical or digital objects, and semiotically, as containers of texts. This kind of action, of course, is oriented towards the courtroom future. A good visualization is a helpful, productive visualization that serves both communicational and fact-finding goals in court, allowing a decision in the here-and-now of the court session to be made about the there-and-then of the offense. It is in this sense that the case file is not only a mediator in the physical, spatial sense, nor only a semiotic object. It is also active in allowing retroactive truth finding and future-oriented courses of action. In other words: it is an object that renders available different times and places in the here-and-now of the decision.

Sometimes, however, such temporal bridging is barred. Take the court cases involving defendant Jack Ross. He is accused with the breaking and entering of his ex-girlfriend's house and additionally charged with the damaging and theft of some of her belongings. According to the prosecutor's version of the events in question, Jack climbed into his ex-girlfriend's house through a rooftop window in the summer of 2013 while she was vacationing abroad. Jack is quite young – twenty-four years of age – but does not make a nervous impression when he is questioned by the judge. After all, his lawyer has prepared an elaborate closing argument. His lawyer begins his plea:

> Your honor. I will start by saying that there is only one witness to the breaking and entering, and [the statement] is far from sufficient. This witness does not describe any of my client's defining physical characteristics. So how can we be sure that it was indeed my client who was seen entering this apartment? The police never organized a line-up either, so we can't quite identify the person who was seen breaking and entering. Then there is this other statement, the statement made by the affected party. Well, this statement is completely contradictory: the victim mentions different time periods in which she would have been abroad, for instance. And some of her statements are simply incorrect: for instance, she told the police she did not know that my client, her ex-boyfriend, had been under electronic house arrest. But she *did* know, because she has previously assisted with the electronic surveillance of my client [after a previous conviction], that is, when they were still together! Baffling are also the damage claims she filed against my client: in her first statement she never talks about what goods had been stolen, while, in the damage report she later files, she speaks of stolen goods with a value of 1000 euros. As for the damaged goods: in the case file I don't see pictures anywhere of those electronic appliances that my client allegedly damaged.

Referring, again and again, to the evidentiary materials in the legal case file, Jack's lawyer aims to cast doubt on the public prosecutor's version of the events in question. The legal case file is implicated in his storytelling, focused on answering the question: What really happened? Can we rely on the identification made by the affected party's neighbor, if this neighbor – who is supposed to remember and know the defendant, who lived together for a while with his now ex-girlfriend – tells the police that he *recognized* the defendant, but has not explicitly *described* the defendant's physical characteristics? Can we trust the statement made by the victim, considering the fact that she denies any knowledge of her ex-boyfriend's previous conviction while she must have known very well he had been convicted earlier? Does it furthermore not seem she is frustrating the court's truth finding, as she sees the trial as the opportunity to claim money? And was she not caught lying about the period she spent abroad? Seen in this light, can her statements be considered trustworthy enough to merit conviction of the defendant? What can these statements tell us about what really happened?

Jack's lawyer goes on:

> Besides, when we look at the process-verbal of the interrogation with my client, I see, typed down, in the middle of one of my client's questions, the phrase, "theft, unqual.", which arguably stands for "theft, unqualified." But my client would never express himself this way, nor would other defendants, presumably. So who is speaking here? The police officer or the

> defendant? Furthermore, the victim has told the police, and I quote, that "all the neighbors have seen it." So why was their testimony not taken? I think the police has indeed talked to these neighbors, but that they [their statements] are not present in the case file. My last point is that the police suggest, in the file, that they would further investigate the site for traces of my client's presence, but the results of this investigation are curiously lacking from the case file. It seems to me that exculpatory evidence has been excluded from the file, so that the evidence is wafer-thin.

Jack's lawyer here enters a different mode of asking questions about the "truth-value" of the file. Here, he does not only offer an interpretation of the different stories present *in* the file; he also tells us a story *about* the file. This lawyer first challenges the neutrality of the written transcription of the interrogation with the defendant. He suggests that the police officials have been so set on shaping and rewriting his client's words that it has now become unclear who precisely is speaking – something clearly at odds with the demand that defendants' statements must be "verbalized" [*geverbaliseerd*], that is, written down, in accordance with the defendant's "own words." If police officials complement his client's words with phrases like, "theft, unqual.," then how can we be sure that the rest of the client's statements in this process-verbal are truly his, and not added by zealous police officials? Secondly, this lawyer suggests that the case file offers only a partial rendering of the full police investigation: the police, he suggests, have indeed spoken with more witnesses but these statements never made it to the legal case file. Police officials also mention additional investigation into traces of his client's presence in the house, yet he cannot find the results of such testing anywhere in the file. Does this imply that the prosecution failed to exercise due diligence? At stake, at this point in his plea, is not a set of statements or stories in the file, but their absence.

All in all, a smooth transportation from the here-and-now of the court session towards the time and space of the offense is barred: not only because the individual witnesses are necessarily unreliable (although according to Jack's lawyer, they are that, too), but also since the case file is the product of specific modes of translating oral statements into written evidence and of practices of partial inclusion and exclusion. In other words: the case file itself has a history, and it is that history Jack's lawyer mobilizes in his attempt to thwart conviction.

In this chapter I am interested precisely in the case file's status as both a neutral transporter and carrier of evidence and a non-innocent, perhaps treacherous, object that inevitably transforms reality, an object with a complex history. As such this chapter does not highlight its material and physical recalcitrances, but its temporal ones. It asks the question, first, how the case file manages to build a bridge between offense and court session, and secondly, how traces of its own disavowed histories allow actors, most notably defense lawyers, to question the validity of the facts it presents. It is interested in the relationship between legal procedure and fact-finding, yet refrains from treating legal procedure as an unproblematic "legal context" to practices of fact-finding. Instead, it highlights how both "factuality" and "procedure" are enacted in and through the case file. The notion of the folded object (M'charek 2014) is particularly useful, here: offering a vocabulary within which to begin to understand the multiple and dense temporalities of objects, it is especially suited to inquiry into the relationship between law, truth, and time.

6.2 Law, Truth, Time

In its concern with the histories and uses of the legal case file, this chapter is meant as a respecification of dominant approaches to the relationship between legal procedure and legal truth making. There is a clear connection between procedure and legal modes of truth making, especially so in Dutch criminal law. While civil legal procedure may work with a more "virtual" sense of the truth (the truth of the matter is simply and a priori established by virtue of agreement between parties) criminal law has a more subtle and hybrid relationship with the truth. Cleiren (2001: 16) for instance notes that "the criminal process is aimed at finding truth in order to punish those guilty. Verification of the facts of which the accused is charged is therefore prime goal of the criminal process." But because there is a real danger of convicting innocent suspects, such "verification" must be safeguarded procedurally: "The function of criminal law is to be formulated hybridly: on the one hand, it is the finding of truth in order to punish transgressions of material law, and on the other hand, the protection of citizens against far-reaching governmental breaches of their constitutional rights, understood to include the prevention of the punishment of those innocent" (Cleiren 2001: 18). On the one hand, then, the truth of the matter is carefully guarded by procedure – not just any fact may come to bear on the matter at hand, for instance when evidence is attained by illegitimate means. On the other hand, it is not entirely up to the affected parties to deliver the facts and agree, among each other, on the delineation of the case: it is the judge, in Dutch criminal law, who decides on both the facts (their admissibility and relevance) and the law.

The "material truth" matters, and precisely because it matters so much its establishment is guarded by procedure.

It is tempting, within this rather general mode of addressing the relationship between legal procedure and the production of legal facts, to treat procedure as an unproblematic "context" to the production of legal facts. Procedure then functions as a "frame": something that both structures and contains practices aimed at the truth of the matter.

Such an approach effectuates several things at once. First, it glosses over the question how facts with regard to the specific offense in question are *made*. In other words, it treats the facts as already established and of equal relevance and weight to the decision at hand. Of course, facts may be contradictory – as was the case in Jack's case, within which different witness statements did not cohere very well – but they are already there nevertheless. In doing so such an approach fails to address the question of how and where such facts are made, and how these are made to matter to the decision at hand. This question, crucially, is precisely the question Jack's lawyer raises with regard to the case file as a producer of facts: How is the case file made? What is lost? What is distorted? Not only does this vignette alert us to the intricacies involved in "doing procedure" and "making truth"; it also points to the case file as a central artifact in the production and contestation of the facts. Second, and vice versa, treating procedure as a context risks treating that same context as similarly already there as a stable frame and container for practices of legal truth telling. But did not Jack's lawyer precisely implicate a concern with procedure in his plea? That is: Is not procedure drawn on, evoked, made consequential within and to the decision it is supposed to merely "enframe"? Procedure, then, does not enframe "the truth" in any straightforward matter: it is a "moving horizon" (Scheffer 2010: 45). Both truth and procedure, then, have to be done somehow, somewhere.

6.2.1 *Doing Procedure and Time Together*

Taking the simultaneity of "doing procedure" and "doing truth" seriously positions this effort also in relation to questions about legal temporalities more generally. As such it draws inspiration from approaches to legal temporalities that treat temporality not as a backdrop or temporal container of practices (in which legal events happen "in" time) but rather as something that is effectuated within practices, giving rise to multiple and specific ways of making pasts, presents, and futures. Latour (2010) points for instance to law's strange timelessness. The law, he states, never fundamentally changes – at least that is the conception of the law the counsellors are working with. Lawmaking, among the counsellors of state, is always understood as a practice of *finding* law, not *creating* it. Law evolves, sure, but it does so always with reference to precedent, that, the counsellors suggest, always already incorporates its future application and interpretation. But taking place in reference to precedent does not quite make law a historical being itself: as something that can be found, it was always *already there*, a timeless totality that places itself outside of chronological time. Law knows no beginning or end; only a perpetual now. Yet this sense of timelessness, of a-historicity, contrasts with the slow pacing of the counsellors' work practice, Latour notes (2010): there, predictability is ensured through doubting, through hesitations, that is, by *not hurrying*. The timelessness of capital-L Law contrasts with the temporal pacing of its practices, yet both are specific ways of "doing time" that coexist within the practices of the counsellors. Luhmann's efforts resonate to some extent with those of Latour. If Latour emphasizes the production of predictability, Luhmann (2004) emphasizes normative expectations. Legal norms, according to Luhmann, presuppose an unknown future. In relation to this unknown future, they make the promise that whatever may happen, the legal norm will hold. As such legal norms allow for the stabilization of expectations in an operation of "time-binding" (Luhmann 2004). Grabham, in taking seriously the temporal products of legal regulation, instead turns her attention towards specific modes of analogizing of time spent working and time spent off work in work-life legislation (Grabham 2011, 2014). Legal practices, then, both take and make time.

6.2.2 The Case File: Mediating Time and Truths

With procedure and facts, we hence enter the problem of *legal temporalization*: the way pasts, presents, and futures are made and remade in legal practices. In doing so it treats neither procedure nor time itself as a container of or for action; instead, it suggests that chronological time and procedure are themselves the outcome of specific modes of "sorting time" (Latour and Serres 1995). Here, my efforts diverge somewhat from Latour's treatment of temporalization: while he concentrates on law's "timelessness" and contrasts it with the diachronic pacing of file-work, I am interested instead in the way the case file itself folds time, and how such folds create the very possibility of unfolding and refolding in other sites, in other times.

In so doing, I follow up on M'charek's (2014) crucial contribution to the study of temporality: that is her suggestion that objects are not to be understood solely in spatial terms, but in temporal ones. With the help of three narratives on the history of the first genetic map of human beings – the Anderson sequence – M'charek illustrates how objects fold time within themselves. Folded into them are their histories, which in turn are entanglements of places and times: "the essence of the folded object ... lies in the intricate ways in which it gathers heterogeneous spaces and temporalities together" (M'charek 2014: 33). This Anderson sequence has a taken-for-granted status in some practices, for instance in laboratory practices where it allows comparison with other genetic sequences. Used in this taken-for-granted way, this sequence hides the places and times that have become entangled within it, and have been folded into it: "Once made, they appear to be independent of human action, 'thrown at us' and assuming an allegedly stable state" (M'charek 2014: 30). M'charek (2014) further argues that the times and places folded into objects remain, however, present – perhaps absently present. A folded object "indexes and enacts its history" (M'charek 2014: 29) even though that history may not be immediately visible. M'charek's analytical work consists precisely of attempting to unfold this object and trace the times and places within it, showing how racially charged classifications and population genetics are folded into it. Faced with such objects, important questions are: Where and how is this object made? In what precise ways have various times and places become entangled? But also: Where and how does this object make its own history invisible, and where and how does it inadvertently betray itself by showing traces of its past?

With the folded object, then, we are closer to understanding the relationship between the sorting and folding of time and the making of legal truths. It suggests that objects are not simply used "in time," but that they both enact and render invisible different times themselves. Drawing on this notion, I am interested, first, in how the legal case file folds within it multiple histories in its effort to render history (the offense in question) available; and second, how the case file may itself become the object of un- and refolding practices in the making and remaking of that same historical event. The following is an elaboration.

6.3 How to Transport an Event: Traceable Materials

"We weren't there when it happened," one public prosecutor insists. "And that is why we press the world onto paper." The Dutch phrasing "*op papier persen*" is not only suggestive of the preferred medium of storage – paper – but simultaneously evocative of reducing something, of transforming something into something else. Indeed, this is the case file's first method of rendering an event available in the future. Entrusted to paper are heterogeneous entities such as spoken words, observations, traces of blood, plastic bags of weed, video materials, and decisions made by police officials and prosecutors. Indeed, while digitization may have plagued judicial "end-users," not much has changed in these sites of production (yet): all these various kinds of things are translated into paper documents (which are only later scanned and digitized). Case files are hence "comprehensive recording devices that register ... events, voices, gestures, appearances" (Vismann 2008: 10). They do so through the medium of writing, through schematic and graphic materials, and through photography. Together, these materials must allow its users access to "what really happened." Yet reading these materials is by no means easy. They require not only a trained capacity to work with files (see Chapter 5), but also require a forensic sensibility: the ability to trace clues, to connect statements, to consider the plausibility and reliability of these various human and nonhuman witnesses. Figure 6.1 and Figure 6.2 are not just evidence, in an age of CSI and the "silent witness" of DNA profiling, of the persistence of proverbial good old-fashioned police work, but suggest, too, that arriving at "what really happened" is practice of tracing clues and of re-tracing investigatory steps.

However, not all sheets of paper can become documents. They must, in other words, acquire the status of being "evidence in support of a fact" (Briet 1951: 7; see Buckland 1997). Procedure plays a crucial role in elevating certain papers to the status of evidence. Importantly, procedure is inscribed on the surface of the paper, now a document, so that future users may trace the document's procedural history. In order to allow access to the event in question, the case file must trace itself. That is, it must account for its own history of production as proof "procedure" was followed. This tracing has two modalities. On the one hand, *correspondence* between the evidentiary materials itself (e.g., a spoken word, a trace of blood on a curtain, plastic bags of marijuana) and its paper "double" needs to be carefully traced. The legal case file ensures such correspondences by tracing precisely where, how, and by whom the piece of

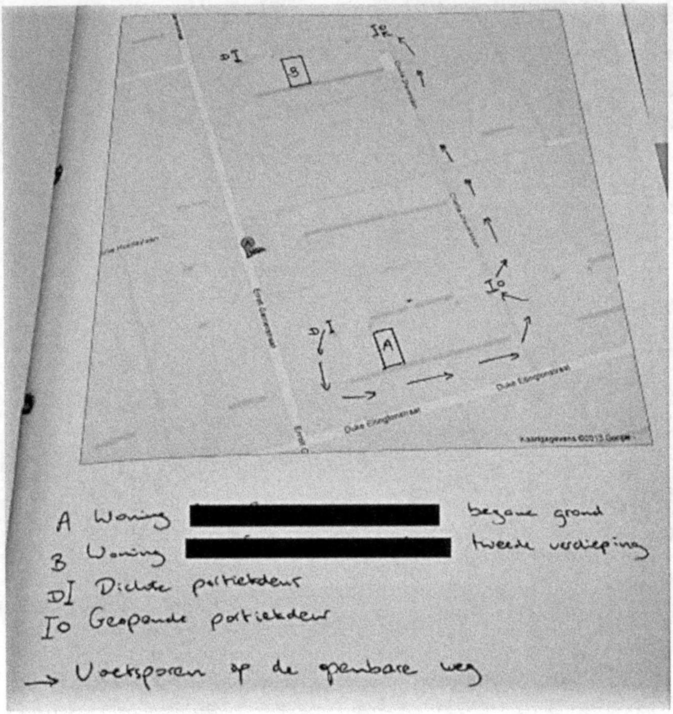

Figure 6.1 Photographic evidence of the traces of the suspect's shoes

evidence was found, elicited, or investigated. Tracing these "chains of reference" is key to ensuring the "chain of custody" (Lynch and McNally 2005): the case file must ensure these small correspondences between, for instance, that trace of blood on a curtain, a numbered sample of this trace, and a report of the Dutch Forensic Institute that matches this trace with a known offender (see also Toom 2010).

A second kind of tracing is that of *authentication*. Sheets of paper become evidence through signatures of the various (human) actors contributing to the file: witnesses, defendants, victims, police officials. Stamps, furthermore, meticulously trace the dates documents were sent, received, or filed. Copies of original documentation are similarly stamped with "copy conform original" (in rare cases, these stamps themselves need to be authorized with a signature). The case file's production needs to be accounted for, procedure "observed": that is, procedure must be enacted by testifying, in writing, how, when, and where an investigatory "act" has happened. Only then are statements

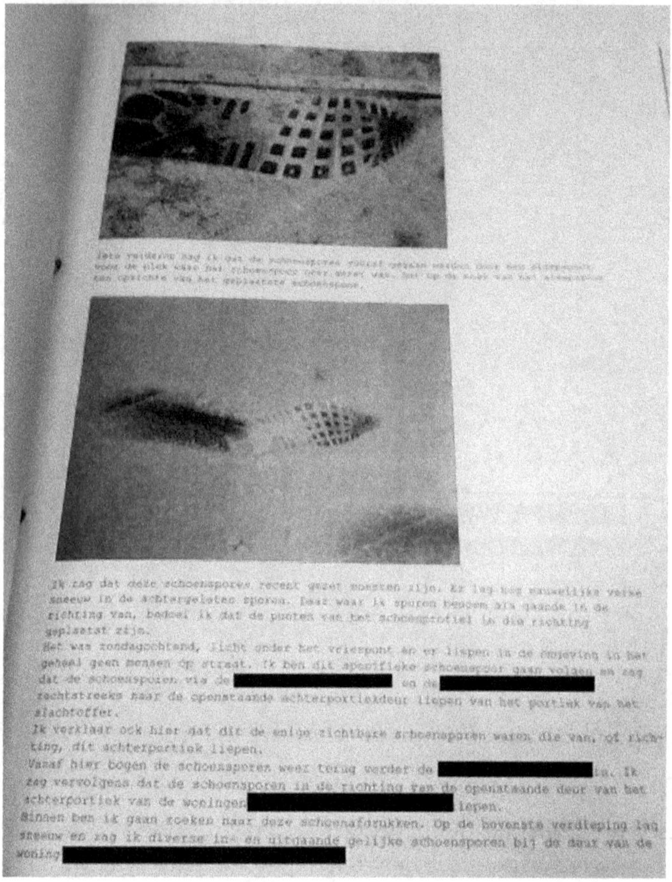

Figure 6.2 A map tracing the direction of the suspect's footprints

able to become legally relevant. The case file as such participates in "a specific social economy" (Kozin 2007: 195), an economy concerned with the attribution of statements to "authors," or rather, "authorizers" (Pottage 2012: 177). Considered in this light, the etymological connection between "act" and "enactment" is surely no coincidence (cf. Vismann 2008).

The case file as a whole also traces its own development: within it are not only primary documents testifying to the case at hand, but also documents that offer official notification of decisions made throughout the investigation. On its paper surface, the case file's travel through the legal-bureaucratic networked is traced by, again, stamps, signatures, and

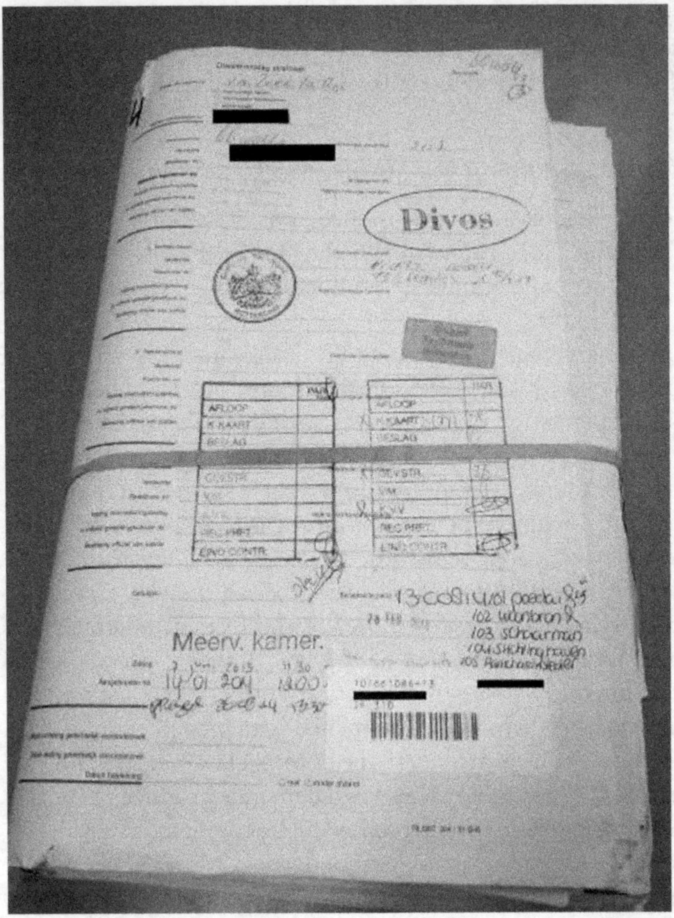

Figure 6.3 Stamps, signatures, and stickers testify to the case file's trajectory

stickers (see Figure 6.3), so that "signs of its history are continuously and deliberately inscribed upon the artifact itself" (Hull 2003: 296). As such, the case file is a "chronicle of its own production, a sedimentation of its own history" (Hull 2003: 296).

Through these techniques, which allow decisions to always be traced back in time and place, the case file also becomes compatible with its anticipated future use in court. Only if it has carefully traced small correspondences and attributed accountabilities it can be employed in the investigation in court. This way, it folds both history and future within itself. Tracing is a crucial way to "index and enact" its own history

(M'charek 2014). Rendering available, through documents, acts in the past the case files allows both retroactive tracing of past events and ensures the file's forward push along legal-procedural paths.

6.3.1 *Writing Up in Anticipation of the Future*

However, the case file has another existence, too: "it is [both] and object and a story" (Kozin 2007: 195). And in the stories it tells, it similarly anticipates its future, and similarly produces its own visibilities and invisibilities.

Take the process-verbals in the case file. These process-verbals are documents composed by police officials that report on the police's findings, witness statements, or interrogations with defendants. These process-verbals are written in a field of tension: on the one hand, victims, witnesses, and defendants are required to tell their stories "in their own words." Only if the document permits no doubt as to who precisely said, saw, or witnessed what, can it be used in court. On the other hand, these documents have to be able to make clear precisely how the event in question can be related to one (or more) of the formal description of illegal activities found in the letter of the law. In other words: these process-verbals must anticipate the operation of legal qualification, that is, the question whether "what really happened" can indeed be subsumed under a description of illegal activity in the criminal law code (see for this point Komter 2002, 2003, 2006). These two demands produce particular visibilities and invisibilities. Take the following fragment from a process-verbal reporting on a criminal complaint, lodged by Nancy Carr, female victim of domestic abuse:

> I wish to lodge a criminal complaint of assault against my ex-boyfriend, named Stan Dwyer. I will tell you exactly what happened this afternoon. This afternoon, Thursday the 3rd of May, around 3:15 p.m., I was at the TileStore shop on Regent street number 70 in [place]. . . . I went outside and saw that Stan was indeed in front of the door. . . . Stan said he wanted to talk to me. I told him I did not want that. Stan asked me if it was really over between us. I told him that I thought it had been over for a while. . . . heard that Stan repeated to me that it was really over then. Subsequently I saw and felt that Stan hit me with a flat hand on the right side of my face. I felt an enormous pain in my face.

Reporting on her story this way, the process-verbal anticipates the criminal charge of physical assault with criminal intent, this being defined in the Dutch criminal code as the "intentional infliction of pain or injury or other physical harm or suffering onto the body of a person." First, the victim reports that it was *Stan* who hit her (and not someone else); she reports that she *felt* his hitting, which she felt on the *right side of her face* (the hit was hence directed against her body); and she reports *having felt pain*. This report also localizes the event in space (a specific address in) and time (the 3rd of May, 2012). This, too, is legally relevant, as the formal charges have to similarly describe the event along these spatio-temporal coordinates. Indeed, the charges read as follows: "that he in **[place]** on or about the **3rd of May 2012**, intentionally abusing a person (namely **N. Carr**), has **(forcefully) hit/slapped in/on/against the face multiple times or at least once**, as a result of which this person has suffered injury and/or pain." Note how the bold text, original to the documented charges, refers to the particulars of the event in question: they refer to the time, place, name of the victim, and the specifics of the event, which here cover slightly different accounts. The regular text refers to the formal definition of assault as found in the Dutch criminal code. As such these charges weave together both event and criminal code. In this case, like in other cases involving material damages or physical injuries, additional photographic material of the injured body part is included in the file (materials I have, for obvious reasons, not reproduced here), adding to the victim's statement that she felt pain also the visible fact of injury.

Let's take a closer look, however, at the victim's statement. This process-verbal has effectuated a couple of things. A dialogue taking place at the police station has been translated into a written, first-person narrative. The dialogue itself however has been rendered invisible: we only know that it took place, but the particular ways police officials elicit this story have been rendered inaccessible. These prompts and suggestions, of course, are precisely how the story becomes formatted to anticipate the criminal assault charges (see for this point Komter 2002, 2003, 2006). Komter (2006) hence argues that "considering the way in which this text has emerged, it will be clear that the interrogator's activities are 'noticeably absent'." Or perhaps: absently present. After all, in this translation of talk into text a certain history has been written (a particular story about "what really happened" on the 3rd of May 2012) but another history (the history of a conversation between police officer and victim) is at first sight erased. But is it lost?

Working towards the time and place of the court hearing and the text of the law while tracing actions and times in its past: this is how the case file mediates access to "what really happened." Making the event in question "judgment-compatible" (see Latour 2010) here consists of rendering histories visible as well as invisible. It is precisely these temporal in/visibilities that allow the case to proceed, that is: move forward in time and space. Yet all its histories are not lost: history, we will see in court, "can strike back capriciously" (M'charek 2014: 31).

6.4 The File on Trial: Times-in-Use

The case file folds within itself multiple histories: a historical occurrence which is simultaneously a potentially criminal event; the bureaucratic time of legal acts; and the times and places in which written and graphic materials are made. If all goes well, these temporalities are kept separate and partially invisible, so that the time of procedure functions smoothly as a frame, the time of the file's production is conveniently glossed over, and the historical event of the alleged offense becomes an object of concern.

The question, then, is how to keep these temporalities separate; how, in other words, to trace some histories while forgetting others. Within the court, such practices are distributed over various court workers. When a case file arrives in the court, administrative workers for instance check whether the file meets a set of procedural requirements, which is work that in many ways is both "logistic and legal" (Latour 2010: 79). It consists of tracing signatures, stamps, and dates: When did the file or document arrive in the court? Where is the authorized process-verbal of the interrogation with the magistrate judge? Is the original "process-file" (the subfile that reports on the criminal investigation) present, and, if not, at least a properly authenticated "copy conform original"? Clerks and judges similarly take note to trace the file's histories, knowing full well that in its legal-bureaucratic temporalities lay possibilities for the undoing of a case. In particular, the presence of a document testifying to the receipt of the summons is crucial. The court must know that the defendant knows he or she is charged. Hence, in the previous chapter, the judge's care to include on the paper summons the note that the summons had been handed over "in person" (on the form, this is abbreviated to "IP"). Only if the case file, and the documents within it, has correctly traced its procedural path can the file be used in court.

It is however on the court session I wish to concentrate here, as it is there that the case file becomes implicated in a complex "intertextual field" (Lynch and Bogen 1996; Scheffer 2006). The judge in criminal justice practices "inquires mostly paper testimony and technical reports"

(Otte 2015: 102), which, in court, are added to, challenged, or given new meaning: "There is hardly any gathering of new evidence, but rather the gauging of the value of the already gathered evidence. . . . if witnesses are heard at all, those tend to be witnesses who have, throughout the earlier investigation, have been heard before" (van Veen 1985: 3–4 cited in Otte 2015: 103–104). In this intertextual field, written and photographic evidence are weaved together with the spoken accounts of the defendant, and the questions and pleas of the prosecutor and defense attorney. Written testimony here structures the interaction between prosecutor, defendant, lawyer, and judge in a practice that Lynch and Bogen (1996), nodding to Garfinkel's "documentary method of investigation" (1967), have coined "documentary methods of interrogation." It is in this setting that the case file sometimes remains folded, allowing for smooth travelling between the here-and-now of the court session to the there-and-then of the offense, while at other moments, it is unfolded, that is, employed as a material object with a complex history. At such points its "truth-function" (Vismann 2008) is endangered in the here-and-now of the court session.

6.4.1 *Histories of Production*

Take yet another case, that of Martin Galloway, a private security guard of a nightclub. Martin was charged with the physical assault of a young woman, which offense he allegedly perpetrated in his capacity as a security guard. This woman, Helen Amis, had been quite drunk and rowdy, and had resisted Galloway's attempts to isolate her from the small crowd outside the nightclub. Having restrained her Galloway tried calling the police, at which point the woman tried to escape from his hold. In the brief, physical struggle that ensued, Galloway allegedly hit her in the face, which the public prosecutor sought to qualify as physical assault. The case file includes some contradictory accounts of various eyewitnesses: two accounts of bystanders, and two accounts of colleagues of the accused. Galloway himself strenuously denies that he hit the victim: in the struggle that ensued, he argues, she tried to hit *him*, while he only tried to ward off her assaults.

Let's listen closely to the way in which these statements are used in court. Take, first, the prosecutor, who concentrates on the two witness statements from Galloway's colleagues. These two statements may appear exculpatory, the prosecutor suggests, but she has an explanation for their content: "Yes, your colleagues tell us that they didn't see anything untoward in your conduct. Well, I've seen things like this before, where people in your business stick up for each other. Bearing that in mind I can't say that these are, strictly speaking, exculpatory accounts." Here, the prosecutor expresses her reservations with regard to the truth-value of these two documents. She casts doubts on the impartiality and hence reliability of the two witnesses. They may, in other words, be lying. Of course, Galloway's lawyer draws on precisely the same two documents to argue the opposite: these two statements clearly contradict the victim's account. While they know that the process-verbals are not "exact representations" of what was said to the police, the prosecutor and the lawyer nevertheless treat these documents as "at least . . . reflection[s] of what has been said in the interrogation room" (Komter 2006: 222) or indeed at the scene itself. And precisely because these process-verbals are relatively truthful reflections of what was really *said*, they enable the production of potentially competing, but ideally plausible and coherent accounts of what really *happened*.

Yet this kind of use of the file does not exhaust its possibilities. The histories of the case file itself can become implicated in lawyers', defendants', and even prosecutors' truth telling activities. In such cases, these parties do not concentrate on the stories *in* the file, but rather tell stories *about* the file, bringing to life its partially invisible histories. Galloway's lawyer leverages precisely this strategy when he commences his concluding plea, which concentrates on the eyewitness account of the victim's friend:

> My client insists that he has only warded off her attempts to assault him. One of Miss Amis' friends says here [pointing to the process-verbal] that she saw the movement of my client's arm, but it must be said she did not see that mister Galloway indeed hit Miss Amis. Things like this have to do with the way police officials write things like this down, you see. They will ask, "did you see the accused hitting her?", and then the eyewitness might say "no," or something else. But the police will write down, "did not see *whether* the accused hit the victim." Which makes the statement neither an exculpatory, nor an incriminating statement: this way, it just seems that the eyewitness simply didn't see anything. *But it could have been an exculpatory statement*: maybe the eyewitness saw *that* something or other did not happen, and then we would have ended up with an exculpatory statement.

Here, the interrogation of the accused about the events in question shifts to an interrogation of the document itself (cf. Lynch and Bogen 1996). Placing us in the interrogation room, where police officials are busy translating talk into text (Komter 2019), the lawyer suggests that the statement can be read in two competing ways: either the eyewitness saw *that* Galloway did not hit the victim, or the eyewitness did not see *whether* he hit the victim. In this case, the exploitation of this ambiguity in the process-verbal works: the judge, "unwillingly" declares the defendant not guilty. The process-verbal reporting on the conversation with the eyewitness is no longer successful in corresponding to what was really *said*, so that it can neither tell us something about what really happened in that nightclub some months ago.

6.4.2 How Police Officials Write Things Down: Institutional Writing in a Bind

Galloway's case casts "the way police officials write these things down" into sharp relief. As we have seen, these writing practices take place in a zone of tension: on the one hand, police officials must aim to retain people's "own words" and "own observations"; on the other, these process-verbals need to render the event in question judgment-compatible. This is their conundrum: emphasizing the naturalist portrayal of interaction as it actually took place risks not only including swaths of irrelevant material; the risk is also that parts of the charges cannot be substantiated. Focusing, on the other hand, on massaging the text to be able to meet legal rules and definitions may lead the document to betray its own history of production. Judge Fielding commented ironically: "Some things they can't seem to write down anymore. They never say [write], 'I felt I was being hit,' but rather say something like, 'I saw and felt I was apparently receiving a blow to my body.' It's a kind of fear – after all, they know how we work." The problem is magnified, for judges at least, when police officials write down their own observations in the official, "*ambtshalve*" process-verbal [*proces-verbaal van bevinding ambsthalve opgemaakt*]. These kinds of process-verbals tend to be used more widely as indications of what the police officials in question observed when arriving at the scene of the alleged offense, but may also be used to write down observations of what they heard (or overheard) the defendant say after the offense. Such process-verbals may include incriminatory utterances by the defendant without his or her counsel being present or without the defendant even knowing that certain words are committed to paper (for instance, the defendant tells someone else in a temporary holding cell that he did it; this comment is overheard by a police official checking in). Aside from the obvious legal problems accompanying such "overheard talk" committed to writing, judges tend to comment largely on the *practical* difficulties that accompany reading, evaluating, and using such process-verbals. For instance, as police officials tend to work in pairs, such process-verbals tend to be signed by two persons. Of course, the question is whether both or merely one of the two officials saw an incriminating act, which is a question that may come up in Court. At the same time, police officials are to be believed at their written word, even if that written word does not specify the observations individually: the relationship, Judge Jamison suggests, is one of necessary and "institutionalized trust."

6.4.3 Graphic Materials: Photography and Film As Mediators

Similar concerns play out in relation to the evidentiary value of photographic materials. While photography, so much less fallible than human memory, has historically promised transparency and visibility to decision-makers in legal settings (Mnookin 1998), like written materials it, too, can either be mobilized as a neutral carrier of evidence or an active transformer in itself. It is not uncommon, especially in cases of physical assault, for court actors to focus their attention on what is and is not rendered visible in the photograph taken of the victim's injuries. The fact that copied versions of the file are in black and white adds to the problem: if the victim's injuries (e.g., a swollen lip, a bruised nose) are not immediately visible on the photographs in the file, does that mean that there was in effect no injury, or that the photograph merely distorts the actually existing injury? It is not uncommon for lawyers to request they see the photographs in color; requests judges summarily deal with by showing them the relevant photographs in court. The transforming character of photography can also play a role in different kinds of cases, for instance the case of Abbas. Abbas, having a long history of various migrations from the African subcontinent to the Netherlands and back, had been charged with carrying of false identification papers. In a routine check, his passport had come up as nonexisting in the national registry. Abbas' lawyer went to great lengths to describe the way Abbas had requested a renewal of his passport in his home country and had received the document that would prove later to be falsified. As "things are done differently there," meaning in his home country, the lawyer argued that Abbas could not have known that the passport he received was tampered with; as such he was not to blame either. Based upon Abbas' testimony and a scanned copy of the falsified passport, the judge acquitted Abbas. Later, the prosecutor suggested it was a shame the actual passport was not present in the courtroom: the judge could have seen that its first page detailing the passport holder's identifying information, seemed tampered with, "as if someone just glued something on top of it." Even if Abbas had not himself falsified the document, the prosecutor felt that these obvious marks of falsification should have alerted him to the possibility that his passport was falsified.

Both writing and visual materials, then, introduce into the court session not only a concern with what actually happened, but with the times and spaces of their production. These times and places, absently present in the file, may be successfully mobilized: "history is never lost" (M'charek 2014) indeed.

6.4.4 *Unaccounted Histories: The Decisions Not To*

A third way within which the file's hidden histories of production are rendered relevant in the here-and-now of the court session is in its erasure of the decisions to *not* act. For instance, while the case file always traces its *growth* (by attributing authorship to, and hence accounting for every step in the criminal investigation) it does not similarly account for the decision to *stop* the criminal investigation or to refrain from undertaking certain investigatory actions. In other words, while the case file accounts for the evidentiary materials present in the file, it does not similarly explain the absence of other possible pieces of evidence. These unaccounted decisions, inaccessible to the parties in the courtroom, may come to haunt the proceedings in court. For instance, the lawyer in the introduction of this piece suggested that the police had actively barred competing and exculpatory eyewitness accounts from the case file. Defendants, too, may level similar objections to the judge, like for instance this young man accused of stealing a mobile phone in a bar. This young man was accused of theft of a mobile phone, but the phone had not been found on his body, but rather on a couch close to where he was sitting:

> So why have they never checked the phone for fingerprints? They tell me I would have been the last to have it in my hands before they found it in my vicinity, according to their story, but they never bothered to check. And by the way, it's a bar, there must be security camera footage they could have checked? Again they didn't bother. All this seriously hurts my defense!

Even though the file itself, having moved from prosecutorial offices to the court, is pretty much an indication of the case file's presumed completeness, the "decision not to" is unaccounted for in the file. As files become inserted into the intertextual field of the courtroom, their supposed completeness may however be cast into doubt. A partial file inexplicably missing crucial pieces of potentially exculpatory evidence, for lawyers, is proof that the prosecution has failed to exercise due diligence. Sometimes, lawyers couple this line of reasoning with a request for additional witnesses to be heard, or security camera footage to be collected. These appeals are, at times, successful in that they lead judges to require additional evidence to be gathered. However, lawyers may also be quick to point out that hearing additional eyewitnesses is not going to help the defendant in his or her defense much: after all, (chronological) time has passed since the offense, human memory is fallible, and witness testimony is likely to become less trustworthy over time.

When judges grant requests like this, concerns with the correct "folding methods" take center stage again: not just any document can be folded into the case file. Decisions like these are recorded by assisting clerks and later expanded into a formal document testifying to the reasoning behind these decisions. Having been signed by the presiding judge, these documents will be added to the file while the file itself will await additional documentation, like authorized process-verbals drawn up by police officials or expert witnesses. The case files are then kept "open" and "alive," that is, until the newly appointed court date. All in all, defense practices do not only consist of coming up with a better story. They also consist of playing with the case file's temporalities, of leveraging invisible and inaccessible histories to thwart a guilty verdict in the here-and-now, or at least, to adjourn the case; to allow the case file to proceed further into a deferred and uncertain future.

6.5 Making Facts, Unmaking Cases, and Temporal Interferences

This chapter has been an attempt to start accounting for the intricate relationship between law, time, and truth. In the previous pages I have attempted to show how struggles over what really happened in courtrooms do not simply draw on the stories present in the file, but that such interpretative struggles are extended to the file itself. Understanding how and why this happens is assisted by a conception of the legal case file as an object that has folded times, places, and actors within itself that nevertheless may come to haunt the procedures in court. A focus on these histories, either explicitly accounted for, or made absently present, allows one to carefully trace the way the case file mediates epistemic access to the event law seeks to judge. That is, it takes seriously the way the case file builds correspondences with "what really happened," while it simultaneously underscores how this particular way of building correspondences and tracing histories offers the parties to the case unexpected possibilities to make or unmake a case. This way, the legal construction and deconstruction of cases is shown to be not only a matter of "disturbing the social and cognitive networks that surround and strengthen ... [truth-] claims" (Fuchs and Ward 1994: 482); the making or unmaking of cases extends itself precisely to the objects in these practices: "the strength of the case usually depends on the careful choreography of several witnesses, expert testimony, [but also] physical evidence, documents, and so on" (Fuchs and Ward 1994: 487).

It is in this sense that this chapter diverges from Latour's treatment of case files and the legal mode of existence (2010, 2013). As elaborated on in Chapter 1, Latour (2010, 2013) quite rigidly distinguishes between the legal and the scientific mode of existence ([LAW] and [REF] respectively). Delegating all factual questions to the mode of existence [REF], his purified sociology of law becomes unable to attend to precisely the ways truths are legally made, and the ways procedure and the case file's history of production become themselves objects of epistemic attention in court.[1] Of course, differences between legal and scientific modes of making facts cannot be glossed over. For instance, scientific truth making often relies on what Latour and Woolgar (1979) have coined the "deletion of modalities": the deletion of contextual qualifications, among which are authors' names, which deletion transforms these statements into general facts. The case file draws on a similar kind of operation when it renders invisible the context of the interrogation, that is, in the transformation of a complex face-to-face interaction into a written document. However, legal truths can only be made when other kinds of qualifications and "con-texts" (semiotic artifacts like autographs and stamps accompanying these texts) *remain present*, at least until the hearing. Certain precise dates, times, persons, and bureaucratic "authors" (or rather: "authorizers") can emphatically not be deleted, as the case file is not only active in the transportation of evidence, but also in the enactment of procedural justice (M'charek et al. 2013).

Furthermore, this chapter has made problematic a rigid distinction between procedural context or frame on the one hand, and legal modes of arriving at the material truth on the other. "Observing procedure," it has shown, is a practice of enacting procedure; "acquiring the facts" is similarly a practice of folding statements and utterances into legal space-time.

Highlighting, furthermore, precisely the connections between "doing time" and "doing truth," this chapter has refused to treat one as a context for the other. The case file, transporting and transforming evidence, is a crucial object doing both legal and truth telling work.

6.5.1 Temporal Interferences

In emphasizing the making of multiple temporalities this chapter has paid specific attention to phenomena we can now start to recognize as moments of *temporal interference*: that is, the moments in which the time of procedure, the time of the file's production, and chronological time cannot be neatly kept apart but rather interfere with each other to produce barriers to truth making. In each of the cases drawn on in this chapter, the time of procedure, the time of the production of the file, and the time of the offense are evoked and "brought to life" simultaneously, producing a situation both propitious (for the defendant and lawyer) and challenging (to the prosecutor). These moments of temporal interference demonstrate that, while great care is taken to set the procedural stage for truth making, such efforts do not necessarily succeed. Procedure, as well as the times and places of the case file's production, can be evoked to bar access to the truth. To speak with Barad (2003), processes of mattering (i.e., of something becoming material to and consequential for, of making differences that make a difference) have, then, both spatial and temporal dimensions. Or rather, spatiality and temporality are themselves the product of "ongoing open process of mattering through which 'mattering' itself acquires meaning and form in the realization of different agential possibilities" (Barad 2003: 817). Both "temporality and spatiality emerge in this processual historicity" (Barad 2003: 817–818).

The case file's multiple temporalities play a crucial role in these practices of translating between the there-and-then of the offense and the here-and-now of the court session. By folding, ordering, and sorting different temporalities, the case file is both what allows procedure and facts to be kept apart as much as it presents the possibility of such temporal interferences, and with these, the undoing or unmaking of a case. Indeed, M'charek (2014) locates politics not necessarily in what is "contained in" objects but rather in the ways they are folded: how they make certain histories immediately present, and how histories linger on in obscurity. Building upon this recognition, this piece has suggested that this temporality is also key to understanding not just power, but also its subversion. As it is possible to make these histories present again, it is possible to turn the tables on this object, to act in the face of an accusation, to keep, in other words, a human body in movement. Recognizing that objects are political things, recognizing, too, that part of their politics resides in their temporal fold, is hence key to understanding how they can be unfolded and refolded.

6.5.2 *Process/Event Distinctions*

In highlighting practices of temporal sorting, this account has similarly bracketed distinctions regularly drawn between the *process of inquiry* that precedes the trial, and the *event* of the court session. Such distinctions are not necessarily made explicitly. Conversation analytical approaches to legal practices, for instance, tend to emphasize courtroom interaction, glossing over inquiry into the practices that chronologically "precede" and structure these interactions, especially file-work (a tendency commented upon in Chapter 5). In working with a very narrow conception of "context" as utterances produced in court, such approaches gloss not only over the fact that these in-court interactions are "bound" in crucial ways to previous utterances and statements (see Scheffer 2010), but also the way these accounts are bound to written accounts. In other words, the pasts of the case "reaches out into the present" (Scheffer 2010: 53). Similarly, accounts that focus exclusively on the in-court production of narrative or discourse also disregard this sense of historicity (e.g., Conley and O'Barr 1990). While they may work with a broader sense of societal or discursive context, histories of frequent and local relevance to in-court actors are glossed over. This analytical presentism (M'charek and van Oorschot 2019) risks underestimating the extent to which the dramaturgical unity of space, time, and act so central to court proceedings is itself made possible and plausible only by virtue of active and partial ways of accounting for and erasing of histories. It also shows that the "process" that precedes, in chronological time, the "event" of the court is itself always already oriented towards that event, so that process and event interpenetrate each other. Indeed, it is only through the spatial and temporal enactment of a "cut" (Barad 2003, 2007) that process and event are separated: only then it makes sense not to speak of an unfolding process but an event with a before and after; only then can both procedure and investigatory process appear as "context" to the event in question (Scheffer 2010: 186–188). Of course, the verdict itself offers precisely such a cut: after all is said and done, the defendant is found guilty – or not.

6.6 Visionary and Forensic Approaches to Documents: or, What to Learn from Lawyers

There is another lesson, here, and it is one that pertains to documents and to our modes of treating them. That is, while I warned, in the preceding chapter, against both our "phonocentric reflex" and a "politics of immediation" (Mazzarella 2006), I aim now to add a further note to these praxiographic concern with the study of documents in legal practice. I want to warn against a third habit of thought in relation to the documents we encounter in fieldwork settings: the tendency to treat these not as unproblematic representations of the world, but rather as documents that can be read hermeneutically, in search of authorial intent, or else interpreted as signifying dominant world-views, (sub)cultures, discourses, or mentalities (Hull 2012; Prior 2008). Of course, both approaches are useful to some extent. From presentencing reports we may, for instance, aim to distil not just information with regard to the defendant but also try to read them as the product of the author's intentions. Did this or that parole officer really think this defendant is willing to change, or is he or she subtly letting the judge know rehabilitation is not to be expected? Indeed, this "hermeneutic" reading of presentencing reports is in fact a local mode of approaching presentencing reports, both in the site studied here as elsewhere (see Tata et al. 2008). For instance, it is not uncommon for the judges studied here to treat standard, routine, and very short presentencing reports as an expression of the individual parole service worker's lack of confidence in a specific defendant. Secondly, elucidating as well is the mode of reading that treats documents as signs of wider societal or cultural logics, discourses, or worldviews. Take presentencing reports again: we might wonder how presentencing reports reflect wider societal shifts in conceiving of and dealing with crime, deviance, and risk (see e.g., Maurutto and Hannah-Moffat 2006; Hannah-Moffat and Maurutto 2010). These two ways of approaching documents, however, contrast sharply with the kind of understanding of documentation developed in this chapter. Indeed, both these approaches treat the document as a sign of something else, for example the author's intentions or sociocultural or discursive realities. In a way, its treatment of documents is almost visionary: the gesture places behind the document an intentional subject or a world of which the document is mere testimony.

In contrast, I would like to develop here an understanding of documents in a different key; an understanding for which we do not need a visionary, but rather, a *forensic* sensibility. It is concerned not with the meaning of documents or their authors; instead it seeks to understand their operation, their effects, their moments of mobilization, production and use. And if (but it is a big "if") such operations include meaning or truth, both can be analyzed not as something given or exterior to the document, but as operations of the document itself. A forensic sensibility with regard to documents is interested less in treating them as signs of, but rather as *clues to* (cf. Valverde 2008: 13). It treats them, at first sight, superficially, "dermatologically" (Deleuze 1990: 120). Tracing their moments of production, mobilization, and use, this mode of inquiry is concerned with finding a trajectory through different practices. It is a kind of approach quite close to what lawyers, with their skilled forensic eye, do when they aim to mobilize documents' histories of production. Leading us from different "heres" to "theres," from presents to pasts and to potential futures, this forensic approach treats the document as a trajectory. Keep following it – as lawyers may do – and we may end, not in the generalities of "procedure" or "truth," but rather in local, concrete modes of doing both.

6.7 Onwards: Productive Fictions for the Description of the Law

Highlighting the doing of truth and the making of multiple times, this chapter has suggested, crucially, that these legal practices are characterized by sophisticated practices of making and sorting time. As such this chapter contrasts sharply with a conception of law that places it outside history and time; a conception within which the law, Derrida writes, must always be "intolerant to its own history" (1992: 112). Instead, this chapter has concentrated on different operations of sorting and making multiple times.

Looking back and pushing forwards, the following chapter will aim to relate my travelling so far to the question that has been plaguing us ever since the beginning of this book: that is, in essence, a question about the relationship between capitalized abstractions of science and law on the one hand, and the practical and concrete robustness of both scientific and legal practices. What is it these ambulations, these different ways of collaborating with and within concrete legal practices, have taught me?

What can we learn, both about the law itself and about our methods, approaches, and descriptions? What abstractions will help us "hop, skip, and jump" some more? In the following chapter, I argue that we need productive fictions that set us in inquisitive motion, that ground our trajectories, that alert us to specificity and concreteness, and that defer generalizing abstraction itself. The notion of the hyper-object (Morton 2013) does exactly that. Onwards, then, once more.

7

Productive Fictions for the Study of the Law

From Hyper-Explanation to Hyper-Object

7.1 An End to Journeying

Jurists write arrêts (Latour 2010): statements that want to bring discussion to a close, to bring us to halt. Scientists, in contrast, write "please-go-ons" (Latour 2010): efforts that call upon others to try for yet another approach, make yet another leap. In this sense, a scientific *case* is always a *cause* hoping to mobilize, in that it "obliges those who belong to this [scientific] field, forces them to think, to act, to invent, to object" (Stengers 2015: 91). Whether this characterization of the status of legal and social-scientific writing can be elevated to a defining characteristic of both practices as a whole I dare not say anymore. For that, I have grown much too weary of sociological purification and totalization. But as a reflection on the different purposes of much legal and scientific writings, it is quite apt. Beholden, as I am, to description, the final thing to do for me here is to allow inquiry to go on.

The following chapter, then, looks back as much as it aims to push inquiry onwards and outwards. It aims to pause with the fact of multiplicity, or: the way in which different collaborations, different methods, and different ways of experimenting with legal practices yield quite radically different realities. The law, this book has shown, is irreducibly multiple. And while it may be comforting to reduce these multiplicities to a singular reality, I propose that we *stay with multiplicities*. Emphasizing the multiple ways the law has been enacted throughout this book as well as the categorical troubles evident within both scientific and legal practices, I will suggest we choose to understand legal practices through the prism of a fiction that effectively bars us from having the final word, a fiction that stops us stopping. The notion of the hyper-object (Morton

2013) allows us to do precisely that: it stops us from stopping. As a fiction to think with, the notion of the hyper-object suggests we are never quite "inside" or "outside" of the law; instead, it asks that we find concrete passages, paths, and burrows. It does not prioritize contemplation but calls us to find, like Joseph K., yet another entrance, and behind that entrance, yet another door, yet another office. Indeed, if we are truly interested in description, I think we must refuse the theoretical and methodological confinement of purified abstractions. Instead, we must insist on our capacity to engage in real conceptual movement (cf. Deleuze and Guattari 1986: 45). Deferring totalization and finalization, the notion of the hyper-object keeps us in inquisitive motion.

7.2 Looking Back

Let's first, however, briefly revisit the three central questions that have guided this inquiry. The first pertained to sociological accounts of the law and the work they do, inquiring into the performative dimensions of sociological knowledges about the law. The second question concentrated not on sociological "case-making," but rather focused on the legal case-making practices I encountered in the Court and aimed to pay particular attention to the role of the legal case file in mediating epistemic access to the events and persons in question. The third question required me to introduce accountability into my own account and focused on tracing the performativity of my own methodological collaborations with these legal practices.

All three questions were born out of the observation that theorization regarding the relationship between sociological description and legal practices itself is largely unhelpful when confronted with the vagaries of both scientific description and legal practices. On the one hand, there is always *more* to legal practices than the application of norms or rules: legal practices need knowledge of and reference to events and persons for them to proceed to become anything else than self-referential. Nor are legal practices in any real sense dictated by legal rules; the question is rather how rules and cases are brought into relation with each other as a matter of practical activity. On the other hand, while an emphasis on accurate representation of the world "out there" may sound like a worthy scientific goal, it nevertheless fails to address the performative dimensions of scientific practices themselves, that is, the way social-scientific methods inquiry introduce their own orderings in the realities known and made. When taken to its logical extreme, the norm–fact distinction underlying these two mandates gives rise to paradigmatic conundrums (see Chapter 2). Even though social scientific commentators of the law and legal positivists differ in the way they "ground" the law, they nevertheless share a disregard for concrete representational and legal practices. Even Latour's sociology of law, grounded in robust, fine-grained ethnographic fieldwork falls prey to the purification inherent in any effort to isolate law's proper, true being. Nor is perspectivism of the kind advocated by Bourdieu or Hart a solution: Bourdieu's sociology of law presumes an impossible "view from nowhere" upon legal practices, while Hart's internal viewpoint is in effect no epistemic viewpoint at all. Again, the choice seems to be one between either an understanding of the law's true being, or a description – but not both. And because the law is identified with norms or rules and science with the accurate representation of reality, it becomes increasingly difficult to account for the impurities and troubles represented, first, by performative dimensions of knowledge practices – the fact that accounts of the world do things in and with worlds – and second, by epistemic practices within legal settings – the fact that judges need a sense of what they are talking about when they are judging. While it may be the case that the law has at its purpose the provision of legally sound judgments, and while science may have at its telos the provision of serviceable, operative truths (I find nothing objectionable in either standpoint), neither of the two practices is adequately grasped in these binary terms. For within these practices dwell impurities and troubles: performativities attending to scientific efforts at representation, epistemic practices necessary for legal practices of judgment. Of these troubles, the Leiden study is but one exemplar, but – as I hope to have shown throughout this book – in this case a worthy exemplar to think with.

In contrast to purified conceptions of the law or a problematic, unmediated perspectivism with regard to the law, I aimed to develop a more pragmatic and concrete appreciation of both scientific and legal practices. This reorientation away from abstraction towards the concrete – what I have come to call a pragmatic respecification – aimed to conceive of both "law" and "science" as firstly and irreducibly local and concrete practices. This pragmatic respecification means turning the question "what is law?" into a more open-ended, anti-definitional inquiry that takes seriously how, where, and when that abstraction "law" is practically and concretely done. Similarly, this pragmatic respecification also entailed a shifting away from "pure theory" or "pure description" towards an understanding of description and theorizing as themselves methodologically situated, practical, and concrete accomplishments. Characterizing this pragmatic respecification is further an attendance to the agency of objects in these legal and scientific practices: in the first case, I introduced case files as crucial to an understanding of concrete legal practices; in the second case, I pointed to concrete practices of measurement, of "gathering" data, of moving about the Court's frontstage and backstage, of sorting, ordering, and hence making realities.

This pragmatic respecification offered me the tools to start my journeying. Starting with the categorically troubling Leiden study, Chapter 3, "Dealing with Difference" is an attempt at both diplomacy and accountability. It seeks to create if not harmony, then some understanding between practicing jurists and social-scientific observers. It demonstrates to jurists precisely what kind of reality statistically inclined social scientists tend to enact and speak about when they engage in statistical modelling of sentencing practices. It shows that criminal justice, in and through such statistical modelling, is enacted as a distribution machine taking as its object of knowledge a population internally stratified along several axes of difference. In this case, the meaningful differences made pertain to both "legal" and "extralegal," that is social, "factors," most notably in this instance defendants' phenotype and administrative category as a Dutch citizen. In so doing, Chapter 3 cautions us against making two assumptions about criminal justice practices and the role played by the individual judge. First, it suggests that the legal promise to "treat equal cases alike" is not a promise made based on sociological equivalences between population groups. Such an epistemology of legal practices not only introduces equivalences and differences where legal actors make *different differences* (e.g., in terms of individual defendants' remorsefulness, as I show in Chapter 4) but also risks expecting criminal law to combat institutional and structural racisms. Second, placing that burden not only on criminal law, but on the individual judge and his or her (un)conscious thinking may be an unhelpful, even harmful, gesture, precisely because it treats racism itself as something that structures only "outcomes," and not people's "starting positions" in highly unequal structures of inequality more generally.

Chapter 4, "Situating Remorse," is the result of a different kind of entry into the practices of the judges I studied. Empirically, it is an effort to stay with judicial conceptions of practice as an intuitive, partially moral and evaluative kind of work, including a concern with the legal category of the "person of the defendant." At the same time it has zoomed in on a friction between these judicial, casuistic self-descriptions and the three recurring typified whole-case narratives, suggesting that these typified whole-case narratives are instances of cases not existing as a singular whole but rather as an exemplar or instance of a narrative kind. Relying on conversations with judges and the observation and transcription of in-court interactions, this chapter has tried to connect two separate bodies of research: on the one hand, research into the role of narrative and remorse in legal settings, and on the other, research on the role and production of remorse in such settings. Both audiences may find things of value in my account of these practices: those concerned with "signs of remorse" (Tombs and Jagger 2006) may come to appreciate the interactional and narrative complexities of "doing remorse" in courtroom contexts; those concentrating on the in-court production of stories and facts may appreciate the centrality not only of legal modes of storytelling, but their relationship with moral modes of interrogation and evaluation (see e.g., Jackson 1988, 1990).

Taken together, these two chapters demonstrate and contrast the performativities of statistical modelling of sentencing practices (Chapter 3) and those accompanying a more verbally mediated emphasis on account-giving and narrative (Chapter 4). However, these two modes of collaborating with these legal realities do not exhaust our possibilities; indeed, once I ventured "backstage" and delved into files and started to trace file-work, a phonocentric emphasis on the spoken word made way for an appreciation of largely silent and protracted instances of file-work. Chapter 5, "Visualizing Cases," is rooted in yet another mode of collaboration with the practices at hand. Grounded in observations of backstage file-work, this chapter has called attention to the material texture and social distribution of judicial work practices and the implication of the case file in coordinating and distributing clerical and judicial visualizations. In that sense this chapter is also a meditation on the role played by objects, and the strange and shifty part they play in our relationship with the world. Objects, Heidegger (1962) suggests, have a tendency to withdraw from us when they are implied in ongoing action; that is, when they are ready-to-hand [*Zuhanden*]. However, when people are asked to switch tools – as was the case in the Court's digitization project – they spring to consciousness again, asking for reflection where previously their use had been taken for granted. Moments of such naturally occurring "infrastructural inversions" (Bowker 1994; see also Star 1999) commonly represent ruptures in everyday work practices. They are moments when the tools of one's trade become not an object implied in action, but objects of contemplation: not only did judges reflect on the affordances of the paper versus the digital file viewer, implied in that reflection was also a recognition of their dependency on clerk's brief and to-the-point summaries. This chapter has also demonstrated the conceptual limitations of both cognitivist and perspectivist understandings of judicial work practices, as both judicial "thinking" and "seeing the case clearly" are by no means wholly individual nor purely mental practices. Visualization of the case, I have shown, is a distributed and materially mediated practice involving the affordances and limitations of both paper and digital files. The "internal point of view," in so far as one wishes to speak about it, is better grasped not as *one* point, nor does it involve an *unmediated* view but rather distributed, networked, and mediated practices of visualization.

Chapter 6, "Folding Time, Doing Truths" took up the case file not as a material, but as a temporal, "folded object" (M'charek 2014). It has paid attention not to law's supposed timeless being, but rather to the vernacular and multiple ways times are enacted as a matter of legal practice. The event of the offense, the time of procedure, the time and space of future-oriented production of evidence, the retroactive reading of documents to retrieve, from them, a sense of these times and places lost, all this taking place, again, within the pacing introduced by statutes of limitations and the fallibilities of human memory: these are the temporal ingredients of making a decision in the here-and-now about the there-and-then. The timelessness of abstracted "law" (in which law is only "found," never "made") contrasts with these multiple ways of sorting, ordering, and folding time, or rather may in fact be predicated upon them. After all, there can be no event, no cut, no rupture between past and future, without these many ways of "following procedure." In a way, this chapter has also offered a way of understanding the relation between the legal archive (precedent, rules, and case-specific communications) and the decision. The archive, Derrida (1995) suggests, can be thought of as a site of the command and of the commencement, or in more familiar terms: of a rule and a beginning. Folding an event, as the beginnings of a "case," into the circuitry of legal practices is an *archival* practice, much like the decision is itself a mode of making a relation between the case and legal rule. This chapter has zoomed in especially on the doing – enacting – of procedure and its crucial role in the doing of the law.

Looking back, it is evident that my journeying has yielded distinct chapters. Staying on the move, moving from different epistemic positions vis-à-vis legal practices, has meant that these different chapters all make contributions to different bodies of research, and are grounded in different modes of collaboration with sociological and legal realities. They place different interventions in different bodies of literature: for example in examinations of the performativities of social-scientific measurement (Chapter 3), in elaborations of the role of narrative and remorse in legal settings (Chapter 4), in accounts of the materiality of legal work specifically, and work practices more generally (Chapter 5), and theorizing regarding truth telling, time, and procedure in legal settings (Chapter 6). These different chapters are in turn rooted in specific and varying kinds of collaborations with realities, for example reading peer-reviewed articles, in correspondence, in gathering newspaper clippings, in talking with judges, in transcribing courtroom proceedings, in observations of backstage file-work, and in struggles with the case files themselves. Methodologically, each chapter similarly makes a contribution to our understanding of both sociological and judicial ways of case-making. Chapter 3, "Dealing with Difference," enquires into the making of an "external point of view" upon the law, and pays specific attention to both affordances and limitations of such a statistically mediated perspective. Chapter 4, "Situating Remorse," is suggestive of what a concentration on verbal interactions in court and a method of pre- and post-trial informal conversation helps to render visible, and, importantly, what it fails to address. Chapter 5, "Visualizing Cases," is as much a reflection on backstage practices of case-making as it is a demonstration of how "access" to these backstage practices significantly rearticulates just how we collaborate with legal practice. It also draws attention to that mundane object of legal work: the case file. Chapter 6, "Folding Times, Doing Truths," offers a methodological discussion of the fraught collaborations with case files and is suggestive of challenges facing researchers in bureaucracies more generally. Drawing on judges', prosecutors', and lawyers' selective mobilization of the case file's histories of production, it develops a forensic sensibility with regard to organizational documents: an approach that focuses not on what documents mean or signify, but rather on their trajectories through bureaucratic networks and their moments of production and mobilization.

Letting go of the demand that description be pure, letting go of a perspectivism blind to mediation, this book has sought to stay with the troubling presence of both social-scientific enactments of reality and of epistemic work in legal practices. Such an effort has required methodological agility and has emphasized the finding of paths over the stability of established and rather static "points of view." Indeed, in contrast with approaches that emphasize stable and static epistemic situations – *one* method, *one* theory, *one* well-defined object of study – I have sought to expunge from my account neither the fact of journeying itself nor the multiplicities my concrete collaborations with legal practices have yielded.

7.3 Staying with Multiplicity: Towards a Sociology of Hyper-Objects

Although the preceding chapters are all rooted in the same pragmatic respecification, these disparate chapters yield multiple realities, demonstrating how "the law," depending on one's methodological and conceptual engagement with it, is variously enacted as a distribution machine, a both legal and moral being, a file-bound and rule-oriented practice, and a practice of making times and doing truth. To get to this multiplicity, I have moved from one epistemic situation to the next and to the next again; mine has been an ambulatory approach that never forgets that it moves across a terrain rather than glides across a frictionless plane. Conceptually, I have moved away from a purified understanding of law and science towards an appreciation of the impure, the troublesome, and most of all, the practical and concrete dimensions of social-scientific and legal practice. I have moved away from a conception of description as unproblematic mirroring of the world towards a more performative and mediated understanding of knowledge making. I have also collaborated with the things designated as "legal" in many different ways, and in so doing have produced "the law" in many different ways. There are real multiplicities here, and facing that multiplicity it is tempting to ask just how they can be brought together once more.

Bringing together multiplicities, Mol (2002) shows, is often effectuated with reference to a singular reality. In medical practices, different ways to measure or diagnose a disease can, for instance, be calibrated and compared against each other in reference to a real, biological reality (Mol 2002). What measure of atherosclerosis, after all is said and done, reflects the disease best? Which is to be prioritized? This question hovers over other scientific practices as well: Which measurement comes closest to what we assume is an underlying, singular real? In the study of the law, we have seen such an effort before. We have encountered it in appeals to "law's truth," presumed to be hostile to description itself and only apprehensible in reference to a basic norm or through an internal perspective. Of course, in order to make this theoretical gesture plausible, one has to postulate the existence of an underlying, singular reality to begin with, and secondly, disregard the performative dimensions of actual scientific practice. It is only then that one can order different accounts, for instance hierarchically, as more or less approximate to the "real thing." This desire for hierarchization and ordering, then, is a question that tends to erect, once again, a "real" thing that precedes and transcends actual occasions of collaboration and experimentation. Giving in to this tempting gesture, we might wonder how the four realities enacted in this book can be ordered. Which one is more accurate? Which one approaches the law best? As such, singularization is also a gesture that desires both closure and totalization: when all is said and done, this or that is what the law *actually* is. In that sense, it is a question that wants, again, a hyper-explanation (Dupret et al.): something definite, essential, and final about the object of study. However, giving in to this totalizing impulse, we erase the fact of multiplicity and veer off into abstraction again – losing out of sight, of course, that our own practices of grappling with "the law" are themselves productive in the making of such multiple worlds to begin with.

In these last pages, I will not provide you with such a definite answer and produce a stop to these debates. After all, I am not in the business of writing arrêts. In fact, I will do the opposite. Instead of proposing an abstraction that captures something pure about the law, I will hand you one that suspects totalization, defers finalization, and as such allows multiplicities to persist. It is, in other words, a notion that asks you to *please go on*. This is the notion of the hyper-object.

7.3.1 Sociologies of the Hyper-Object: From Climate Change ...

Inspiration is found in unlikely places. I found mine in Morton's *Hyper-Objects: Philosophy and Ecology After the End of the World* (2013), in which he sets out to understand the unique problems the object of climate change poses to human observers. A brief discussion is necessary here, for it is in this example – global warming – that we can detect ways to do justice to the law multiple without, crucially, suggesting that we can ever have the last word about it.

Global warming, Morton (2013) argues, is a thing so vast and complex that it challenges the way we tend to think about objects more generally: that is, the conception that objects are "out there," that we can feasibly situate ourselves in an external position vis-à-vis their objective reality, and that they have a stable existence across and within space and time. Hyper-objects such as climate change, however, defy such habits of thought. There is a mystery to them we fail to grasp, however hard we might try: "The more data we have about hyper-objects the less we know about them – the more we realize we can never truly know them" (Morton 2013: 180). Global warming is so vast a thing that it encompasses us, making impossible a relation of (epistemic, political, ethical) exteriority: we are never quite outside of them. Hyper-objects like global warming, Morton argues, are also "molten" and "nonlocal." They exist not "in" time and space but "emit" these: they shape, direct, and disrupt flows of time and shapes of space. These material and temporal forms of mattering, to adopt a phrase from Barad (2003), are multi-scalar, "phased," and nonlocal: it is as if hyper-objects occupy a wholly different plane of reality than us mere mortals. These higher dimensional phases are, Morton (2013) suggests, not directly available to human perception. Indeed, its multiple forms of temporalization (e.g., of natural cycles, of the durée of change over millennia) contrast with modes of doing time more familiar to us (e.g., a human life, a calendar year, a season). Also, climate change is nonlocal in that it is not adequately grasped as a purely local phenomenon: a rise in average temperatures or a rise in sea levels do not begin to account for the full complexities of global warming. Climate change also messes with the categories of causality and scale we are used to: "tiny" events may have "large" consequences. And human beings may not always be able to make differences and to act successfully in the face of this hyper-object: yes, we play a role, but climate change is also an inter-objective process, shaped by relations between ice, sun, oceans, vegetation, etc. With the impossibility of taking up a relation of exteriority comes also the impossibility of ever seeing these objects in their totality; instead, all we ever arrive at are *glimpses of the traces it leaves*, for example a rise in sea levels or average temperatures. This is the mystery of the climate change, and with that, of hyper-objects: they defy the possibility of looking at them "directly" and seeing them "in full." For that, we are far too limited and enveloped. Above all else, then, hyper-objects resist hyper-explanation. There is no one "theory" of climate change: climate change is itself far too distributed, multi-scalar, and phased to allow such singularization.

7.3.2 . . . to the Law Multiple

The kind of conception of legal practices I have been working towards will surely start to resonate with this conception of the hyper-object. Let's start with the issue of multiplicity. Like climate change, "the law" is not *one* thing upon which one may have *different perspectives*. Rather, it is multiple: depending on our collaborations with it, it does not so much shift in appearance as change entirely. From a distribution machine, to a morally dense narrative practice, to a practice of paper-shuffling, to folding multiple temporalities: these are but four of the "beings" of the law, and by no means the only ones. None of these can lay claim to capturing the law in its totality, but none of these are entirely divorced from its machinations either. What we have encountered along the way are glimpses of the traces the law multiple leaves on bodies ordered, on words spoken and written, on time folded and refolded. These are always situated glimpses, mediated glimpses, and therefore glimpses that deny us a view onto its totality. Hyper-objects are also nonlocal: there is always something more than only the here-and-now of local enactments. Something escapes the here-and-now. This, too, is a dimension of the law in my account, in which every chapter created aporias, every chapter as such set the stage for another line of escape: there are always yet other offices, other doors to enter. That the law is both "here" and "elsewhere" is, for Deleuze and Guattari (1986), a sign not of the law's fictional, perhaps even transcendent character, but rather of its serial and contiguous character. If the law only provides glimpses, if in other words it *hides*, Deleuze and Guattari write, that is only an effect of it always partially taking place "in the office next door, or behind the door, on to infinity" (Deleuze and Guattari 1986: 45).

Like the hyper-object climate change, the law multiple also shapes and reconfigures – "emits" – time in many different ways. We have encountered not only the time of procedure, the time of events, the time of production and use of its artifacts, but there is also the image of a timeless law that knows no beginning or end. The law multiple is a "phasing" thing: time "percolates" (Latour and Serres 1995) in legal practices. Procedure allows for periodization, times and spaces are rendered absently present, there-and-thens become available in the here-and-nows of the court session so that, once all is said and done, a lasting, impersonal judgment, as if out of nowhere and no-time, can strike the accused. How are these ways of making and taking time related? I would venture the suspicion, here, that both the law as a *folder of times* and the law's placement *outside* of history are related: perhaps the image of ahistorical Law functions precisely as a way to "align its [the law's] gears and make them function together" (Deleuze and Guattari 1986: 43). Indeed, if there is one way this book has made a contribution to situating law's claim to transcendence – to tracing how an appeal to transcendence "aligns gears and makes things function together"

(Deleuze and Guattari 1986: 43) – it has been in its attention to the tension between the making and doing of multiple temporalities in legal practices, and law's paradoxical placement outside of chronological time. This is my suggestion: it is that timeless, transcendent "law" is precisely an *effect* of the very different ways of folding, sorting, and ordering times.

The law multiple, finally, is both inter-subjective and inter-objective: it relies not solely on inter-subjective agreements between human actors (as a conception of the law as a culture or institutions would have it) but on written reports, post-it notes, files, folders, staples, digital programs, law books, case files, desks, chairs, computers ... These nonhumans are the infrastructure of legal memory and of legal action. The case file in particular is testament to the traces the hyper-object law leaves, its preferred trace being, of course, the *signature*. Referring both to its human authorizer and the mandate of impersonal (nonhuman), transcendent "law," the signature is the objective-subjective nexus around which the legal machinery turns.

Adopting the productive fiction of the hyper-object, we face a law multiple that is a many-scaled thing, parts of it too big to fully see, other parts immediately available, a thing that has no center nor definite boundaries, a distributed and tentacular thing (ten Bos 2015). It is also too big, or rather too multi-scalar, to ever "see in full": there is no "outside" of the law, and therefore it has no "inside" either. Instead, we can only hope to move through it and capture some of the traces it leaves. Crucially, the notion of the hyper-object is not meant to operate as a definition, but rather as a warning: in saying that the law "is" a hyper-object, I am simply saying that there is not one privileged, pure abstraction to which its concrete existence may be reduced or against which it may be measured. The notion of the hyper-object is one that consistently confronts researchers with the complexity and multiplicity of the law itself and therefore, with the limitations of any one methodological approach. As such, the notion of the hyper-object makes hyper-explanation impossible, and does not hold out the promise of unmediated vision of totalities. It only asks us to consider opening yet another door, finding yet another passage, another escape.

7.4 Joseph K.'s Murder: A Note on Life and Death

Nearing the end of this book I have but one (for now) last thread to follow up on. These concerns are related to the end of *The Trial*, that is, the scene in which Joseph K. is killed "like a dog" at the hands of two shady representatives of the law. While I have highlighted the differences between the "man from the countryside," stuck in contemplation, and Joseph K.'s frantic travails, this ending of *The Trial* seems to collapse the distinction between the man from the countryside and Joseph K. After all, they both die.[1]

These two deaths seem to call into doubt my suggestion that it matters how, where, and when we collaborate with things qualified as legal. I have insisted that we cannot "arrive at truth" without departing and travelling roads. And in making ourselves ambulatory, we arrive at different truths and enact different realities depending on the tools we use and the situations in which we find ourselves. This ambulatory attitude contrasts with the man from the countryside's contemplative approach. While static contemplation yields sterile abstractions, tautology, or reduction, Joseph K. teaches us that ambulatory action, by contrast, yields multiplicity, specificity, and concreteness.

Yet irrespective of whether they prefer to contemplate or investigate, both the man from the countryside and Joseph K. meet their deaths. Is this, then, perhaps the law's final truth? That it does not matter what we do, for death awaits us in the end? In this interpretation, there is something vampiric about the law. Both deaths seem to function as symptoms of law's timelessness, its immortality perhaps: "for in the exercise of violence over life and death more than in any other legal act," Benjamin writes, "law reaffirms itself" (1978 [1921]: 286). Is this, perhaps, law's final and foundational capital-T Truth? Is its deathly grip on life itself, to speak with Benjamin (1978 [1921]: 286), at its "rotten" core?

In essence, this is an interpretation that highlights the relationship between the law, life, and violence. Benjamin (1978 [1921]) especially zooms in on this aspect of the law. The law's violence, Benjamin writes, is mythical: it does not express a will, neither a command, nor a project or plan, but first of all existence of the law itself (1978 [1921]: 294). Agamben's elaboration on sovereignty and the law displays a similar insistence on the relationship between violence and the law. The sovereign, in a precise mirror image of "bare life," stands both within and outside of the law: within it, as ostensibly constrained by its imperatives, and outside it, as that body which is capable of suspending the law itself in a state of exception (Agamben 1995). Investing bureaucracy with a similar violent capacity, Graeber (2015) suggests that those studying bureaucracy should not close their eyes for the fact that, at the end of the day, bureaucracies rely on the legitimate mobilization of "men with guns." Command theories in legal scholarship similarly seek behind the force of law a "gunman": Austin (1995 [1832]) notoriously suggests that law consists fundamentally in the command of the sovereign, backed up by sanctions. Indeed, my approach to legal practices has been largely silent about this crucial operation of the law: an operation Deleuze and Guattari (1986) define as simply the capacity to keep you from going about your own business. Rendering bodies in motion static: this is what the law does, and this is what it grasped at with recourse to an emphasis on violence and sovereignty. Is this, then, the final truth I have failed to capture? A truth of violence, death and confinement? A truth of violence against life as such?

I would argue, first, that to equal the law with violence is a problematic gesture precisely because it is a way to purify our accounts once more, a way to distinguish between the mess and machinery of concrete practices and their guiding logos. In doing so we gloss over not only the concrete "remainder of things" (Whitehead 1953) so crucial to this book but may also end up mistaking the *effects* of the law for their *foundational truth*. Could the relation between the law and death not be drawn, however, in the other direction? Perhaps the law's power over life and death is only a transcendent-seeming effect of a whole machinery of moving parts. In the words of Deleuze and Guattari: "the divisions of oppressor and oppressed, repressors and repressed, flow out of each state of the machine, and not vice versa" (Deleuze and Guattari 1986: 56–57). And as death or confinement "flow out of" this machine, they do not in and of themselves explain much about its machinations. Indeed, I think my sustained attention to the technicalities of "the force of law" – for example practices of police investigation, of producing, using, and circulating that which incriminates, of judgment and decision – speak precisely to the question as to how sovereignty and violence are *done*, drawing attention to the law's multiple, concrete, perhaps even banal, beings. And as we know, it is only with an emphasis on banality that we become able to truly understand the affective texture of this compromised, bureaucratized world we live in (cf. Arendt 1963). Here, my emphasis on the concrete, moving parts that go into producing the effect of abstract "force" or "power" is perhaps better suited to come to an appreciation of our responsibilities within these worlds.

Indeed, a second thing to consider in light of Benjamin's emphasis (1978 [1921]) on the inevitability of violence in lawmaking and law-positing is, crucially, what we want our accounts of this strange, seemingly interminable machinery of moving parts to be able to do. Even *if* death and violence are law's most fundamental truths, may we not want to refuse to build abstractions in their names? The problem, I think, is related to the cynicism that is our dominant affective response to hyper-objects. Given their sheer size and scale (or multiple scales), hyper-objects commonly inspire fatigue, complacence, or cynicism: after all, we are far too small to make a difference. Indeed, scaled-up analyses of the law as an instrument of bourgeois, patriarchal, or neocolonial powers frequently inspire a similar kind of fatigue: for how might we hope to make a change for the better? For William James (1911: 226), this tired complacency also makes it tempting to take a "moral holiday." In this case, this moral holiday would look like a few days off in which we learn not to worry about the law, waiting perhaps for Benjaminian divine violence to bring the law, violence, suffering, to an end (Benjamin 1978 [1921]). In the meantime, we might as well lean back and contemplate the view.

This attitude strikes me as wholly unsatisfactory. Only the most hardened cynic maintains that nothing matters for death awaits us all. Precisely *because* death gets us all in the end almost everything matters almost all of the time. Even if death and stasis are the keys to unlock law's mystery, we nevertheless have concrete living to do, concrete paths to seek out, concrete hurdles to take. And this is where I think our primary ethico-political imperative comes in as researchers, that is as those charged with making knowledge. This imperative, in my view, is the demand that the moves we make, the abstractions we fabricate, and the accounts we give, serve *the living* (Schinkel 2014).

While the law's deathly, rotten core may (or may not) be one fact, then so are our lives. And this, again, is why the hyper-object is a productive fiction: it accepts grand-theoretical failure and precisely in doing so makes us cling on to real things, concrete things, *for dear life*. It does not expunge all mysticism from life – for there is a mystery to the law, but not a mystery that is "hidden by its transcendence," but one that exists simply because there is always something in "the office next door, or behind the door, on to infinity" (Deleuze and Guattari 1986: 45). This political and affective sensibility only asks where transcendence is done, how mysticism is sustained, how abstractions are made and mobilized, and then goes on to wonder how such abstractions sustain what forms of life.

Indeed, a sociology of hyper-objects, in my view, is a sociology for life: it finds its impetus, its jurisdiction, its telos not in the realm of purification, contemplation and finalization, but in the only task we really share: that of living-with. Living with what, whom, when, and how? Now, that's a start. Please go on.

NOTES

2 Abstractionism, Revisited

1. As I show, this is in fact a rather superficial reading of Hart's account of the internal and external point of view. However, it is worth noticing that this kind of misreading of Hart's point – the unproblematic mapping of the internal view onto members and the external view onto observers, sociologists included – surfaces again and again in legal and sociological scholarship. See e.g., Tuori's characterization: "the legal scholar is supposed to adopt an internal, participant's point of view, whereas the sociologist is said to approach law from an external observer's perspective" (Tuori 2006: 28), or Cotterrel's admonition: "in order to understand law, the legal sociologist has to understand it as a participant, or as a participant does, or rather as many different kinds of participants do – lawyers and citizens, for example, living in the world of Law," so that the sociological study of the Law "samples, inhabits, imagines, explores, compares, questions and confronts different participant perspectives" (Cotterrel 1996: 369–370).
2. I use the term *archive*, and not "written law" or "law-on-the-books," here because I seek to divorce this issue from accounts of the law that place its historical emergence within an oral/literacy framework (e.g., Goody 1986). This kind of account generally suggests that law emerges once societies or cultures move from largely oral modes of communication to written modes of communication. After all, writing – according to this kind of account – is crucial in organizing not only the past but, in Levi-Strauss' words, "the present and the future":

> Once men know how to write, they are enormously more able to keep in being a large body of knowledge. Writing might, that is to say, be regarded as a form of artificial memory, whose development should be accompanied by a deeper knowledge of the past and, therefore, by a greater ability to organize the present and the future. Of all the criteria by which people habitually distinguish civilization from barbarism, this should be the one most worth retaining: that certain peoples write and others do not. (Levi-Strauss 1961: 292)

In contrast with this rather narrow concentration on writing I emphasize the archive itself, as the notion of the archive is (at least conceptually, if not empirically) not tied up with a specific medium of communication. While writing surely may introduce efficient ways to retrieve, from the past, decisions in a search for precedent, I am not convinced that this archival "memory work" is adequately captured by mapping it narrowly on to the medium of writing. Oral modes of transmission may ensure both the law's memory and archive function – see e.g., the Quran, which literally translates as "recitation" (see Messick 1993). The archive, conceived broadly as a technology of memory, storage, and order conveniently escapes the narrow confines of the orality/literacy framework. Moreover, it also carries with it the suggestion that the archive itself is always the product of archival *work*, subject to ordering and interpretation, and as an object related to the technologies of law and/or State (see e.g., Osborne 1999).

3. This interest in local, epistemic practices is to be distinguished from exercises that treat the law as a more or less homogenous "epistemic subject" (Teubner 1989) that orders and constructs reality in its own terms. While this Luhmannian vocabulary allows us to decenter the seeing subject (just like Haraway's insistence on perceptual systems does (1988)), it is important to stay with the practical robustness, as well as the specificity of concrete practices. Here, the contrast I make is between, on the one hand, a vocabulary that ties the capacity for systemic observation onto societal subsystems, and on the other a more pragmatic understanding of truth making allows for multiplicity within and between "subsystems." By tying observation so tightly to the various societal subsystems, this Luhmannian approach after all leaves little room to appreciate the instances of multiplicity, both within and between various subsystems: the fact, for instance, that atherosclerosis is something multiple, even within what we might call the medical-scientific subsystem (Mol 2002); or the fact that there is, empirically speaking, no one legal perspective or no one sociological perspective to begin with. A second difference to be kept in mind, here, is the one between a Luhmannian concentration on communication – in other words, on semiosis – and Haraway's (1988) material-semiotics, which includes both meaning and things (see, for Luhmann's treatment of materiality (or lack thereof), Philoppopoulos-Mihalopulos 2014; van Oorschot and Schinkel 2015). In so doing we may come to appreciate the case file not only as the surface of semiotic signs, but as a material entity shaping judicial case-making practices (see also van Oorschot 2014a, van Oorschot and Mascini 2018).

4. Mol (2002) draws distinctions between the notions of performance, performativity, and that of enactment. Notions of performance needlessly assume the existence of an actor "backstage," or a "doer behind the deed" (cf. Butler 1990). The notion of performativity, however, is also problematic to Mol (2002), and for two additional reasons. First, the word remains too much burdened by its implication in debates regarding (social) identities, while she wants to be able to speak not (only) of the constitution of subjects (e.g., women, observers) but of objects (disease). Second, the notion of performativity remains too much tied to the doing and making of the social, while her proposed notion of enactment would be able to justice to both material and semiotic practices of world-making. For that reason, she prefers the term enactment (see Mol 2002: 32–41). In this book, I however tend to use both notions interchangeably.

3 Dealing with Difference

1. I am aware that my formulations in the preceding paragraph are likely to inspire some confusion in the reader. Interestingly, part of the controversy surrounding this study had to do with its reliance on odds ratios as measures of likelihood. Where the initial NRC article reported that foreign-looking and non-Dutch-speaking defendants were twenty times more likely than Dutch-looking and Dutch-speaking defendants to receive an unconditional prison term, commentators of the NRC newspaper were quick to point out that the original study relied upon a logistic regression analysis, which produces not measures of relative chances, but odds ratios (in Dutch: *wedsverhoudingen*). But the NRC editors should have spotted the difference between measures of relative chances and odds ratios; indeed, if foreign-looking and non-Dutch-speaking defendants indeed are twenty times more likely than the Dutch to receive a prison term, a quick glance at the original publication in the Dutch Jurists' Magazine would have suggested that this group has the impossible probability of going to prison of 2.2 (or 220 percent). After all, the Dutch go to prison in 11 percent of the cases and as such have a 0.11 probability of receiving an unconditional prison term (Table 1 in Wermink et al. 2012a: 730). A more accurate way of stating the researchers' results is to say that the probability of going to prison as compared to the probability of *not* going to prison is five times larger for the group of foreign-looking defendants than the probability of going to prison as compared to the probability of not going to prison is to the Dutch defendants. The actual relative probabilities are, according to some commentators, more likely to be somewhere around 2.5 (or 0.25 percent), but this is a conclusion based on a table in the original study that does not yet control for other important variables (see te Grotenhuis cited in NRC 2012, 31 March).
2. Latour (1999) speaks of "black-boxing" in the context of scientific work in a slightly different way than I am using it here. For Latour, black-boxing is a way of speaking about the way scientific or technical work is rendered invisible precisely because of its success (1999: 304). In that sense, it is a notion akin to that of infrastructure, sunken into the background of expectations (see e.g., Bowker and Star 1999). I however am using it to speak about the effect of statistical analyses such as the one discussed here. Black-boxing, in that sense, is an artifact of an analysis that renders the "internal complexity" of judicial decision-making only intelligible in terms of its input and output.

4 Situating Remorse

1. Although the authors draw on Foucault's work on discourse, their reading disregards some of Foucault's later writings (see Dingwall 2000: 903), and furthermore presents a rather Marxist reading of Foucault. Suggesting that discourse reflects power structures in society (Conley and O'Barr 1997: 7) erects once again is a distinction between the two – a distinction denied of course, in Foucault's emphasis on power/knowledge. Their emphasis on a dominant discourse furthermore resonates much more with a Marxist conception of ideology than with Foucault's emphasis on multiple discourses.

6 Folding Times, Making Truths

1. The difference between Latour's account and mine is arguably rooted in the *specificity* of the two sites studied: while the "material truth" is very much a local concern in "my" lower court criminal justice practices, Latour's Counsel of State – the highest administrative appellate court – is arguably a setting emphasizing legal qualification over the making of (legally relevant) facts. All the more reason, I would argue, to not generalize too hastily.

7 Productive Fictions for the Study of the Law

1. It is important to note, here, that Kafka did not himself order the chapters of *The Trial* as it is currently in circulation. After his death, his friend Max Brod structured and published his writing (against Kafka's stated wish that his writing be burned), placing the chapter with this crucial passage at the end of the novel. Deleuze and Guattari (1986) point out that it is likely that Kafka had not thought of this chapter as the last chapter of the book, as Kafka had given this chapter the title "a dream." Their reading of *The Trial* resonates with mine, then, as they, too, treat *The Trial* as a "virtually interminable" novel.

WORKS CITED

Abramowitz, M. & Black, D. (2010) "How Law Behaves: An Interview with Donald Black". *International Journal of Law, Crime and Justice* 38(1): 37–47.

Agamben, G. (1995) *Homo Sacer: Sovereign Power and Bare Life*. Stanford: Stanford University Press.

Arendt, H. (1963) *Eichmann in Jerusalem: A Report on the Banality of Evil*. New York: Viking Press.

Atkinson, J. M. & Drew, P. (1979) *Order in Court*. London: Palgrave Macmillan.

Austin, J. (1995 [1832]) *The Province of Jurisprudence Determined*. Cambridge: Cambridge University Press.

Austin, J. L. (1955) *How to Do Things with Words: The William James Lectures Delivered at Harvard University in 1955*. Cambridge: Harvard University Press.

Bade, J. J. & Nat, M. M. van der (2012) "Discrimineert de Rechter?". *Nederlands Juristenblad* 87(17): 1189–1190.

Balibar, E. & Wallerstein, I. (1991) *Race, Nation, Class: Ambiguous Identities*. New York/London: Verso.

Banakar, R. (2002) "Sociological Jurisprudence". In: Banakar, R. & Travers, M. (eds.) *An Introduction to Law and Social Theory*. Oxford: Hart.

Bandes, S. A. (2015) "Remorse and Criminal Justice". *Emotion Review* 8(1): 14–19.

Barad, K. (2003) "Posthumanist Performativity: Toward an Understanding of How Matter Comes to Matter". *Signs: Journal of Women in Culture and Society* 28(3): 801–831.

(2007) *Meeting the Universe Halfway: Quantum Physics and the Entanglement of Matter and Meaning*. Durham: Duke University Press.

Becker, H. S. (1982) *Art Worlds*. Berkeley: University of California Press.

(1996) "The Epistemology of Qualitative Research". In: Jessor, R., Colby, A. & Schweder, R. A. (eds.) *Ethnography and Human Development: Context and Meaning in Social Inquiry*. Chicago: Chicago University Press.

Benjamin, W. (1978 [1921]) *Reflections. Essays, Aphorisms, Autobiographical Writings*. New York: Schocken Books.

Bennett, L. W. & Feldman, M. S. (1981) *Reconstructing Reality in the Courtroom: Justice and Judgment in American Culture*. New Brunswick: Rutgers University Press.

Bentham, J. (1988 [1776]) *A Fragment on Government*. Cambridge: Cambridge University Press.

Berg, M. (1996) "Practices of Reading and Writing: The Constitutive Role of the Patient Record in Medical Work". *Sociology of Health and Illness* 18(4): 499–524.

Berg, M. & Bowker, G. (1997) "The Multiple Bodies of the Medical Record: Towards a Sociology of an Artifact". *The Sociological Quarterly* 38(3): 513–537.

Berg, M. & Goorman, E. (1999) "The Contextual Nature of Medical Information". *International Journal of Medical Informatics* 56(1): 51–66.

Berger, J. (1972) *Ways of Seeing*. London: Penguin Books.

Black, D. (1976) *The Behavior of Law*. New York: Academic Press.

Blom, M., Oudhof, J., Bijl, R. V. & Bakker, B. F. M. (2005) *Verdacht van Criminaliteit. Allochtonen en Autochtonen nader Bekeken*. Den Haag/Voorburg: Wetenschappelijk Onderzoek- en Documentatiecentrum/Centraal Bureau voor de Statistiek (WODC-Cahier 2005–2).

Boersma, S. & Schinkel, W. (2015) "Imagining Society. Logics of Visualization in Images of Immigrant Integration". *Environment and Planning D: Society and Space* 33(6): 1043–1062.

Boltanksi, L. & Thevenot, L. (2006) *On Justification: Economies of Worth*. New Jersey: Princeton University Press.

Bos, R. ten (2015) *Bureaucratie is een Inktvis*. Amsterdam: Boom Filosofie.

Borges, J. L. (1972) "On Exactitude in Science". In: *A Universal History of Infamy*. New York: Viking.

Bourdieu, P. (1979) *Distinction: A Social Critique of the Judgement of Taste*. Cambridge: Harvard University Press.

(1987) "The Force of Law: A Sociology of the Juridical Field". *The Hastings Law Journal* 38: 805–853.

Bowker, G. (1994) *Science on the Run*. Cambridge: MIT Press.

Bowker, G. & Star, S. L. (1999) *Sorting Things Out: Classification and Its Consequences*. Cambridge: MIT Press.

Bridges, G. S. & Steen, S. (1998) "Racial Disparities in Official Assessments of Juvenile Offenders: Attributional Stereotypes as Mediating Mechanisms". *American Sociological Review* 63(4): 554–570.

Briet, S. (1951) *Qu'est-ce que la Documentation*. Paris: Editions Documentaires Industrielles et Techniques.

Buckland, M. K. (1997) "What Is a 'Document'?". *Journal of the Association of Information Science and Technology* 48(9): 804–809.

Butler, J. (1990) *Gender Trouble: Feminism and the Subversion of Identity*. London: Routledge.

Callon, M. (1986) "Some Elements of a Sociology of Translation; Domestication of the Scallops and the Fisherman of St. Brieuc Bay". In: Law, J. (ed.) *Power, Action and Belief: A New Sociology of Knowledge?* London: Routledge.

Chakrabarty, D. (2000) *Provincializing Europe: Postcolonial Thought and Historical Difference*. New Jersey: Princeton University Press.

Cleiren, C. P. M. (2001) "Waarheid in het Strafrecht: Niet tot Elke Prijs". In: Cleiren, C. P. M., Bock, R. H. de & Klaassen, C. J. M. (eds.) *Het Procesrecht en de Waarheidsvinding*. Den Haag: Boom Juridische Uitgevers.

Conley, J. M. & O'Barr, W. M. (1990) *Rules Versus Relationships: The Ethnography of Legal Discourse*. Chicago: University of Chicago Press.

Conley, J. M. & O'Barr, W. M. (1997) *Just Words: Law, Language, and Power*. Chicago: University of Chicago Press.

Cotterrell, R. (1996) *Law's Community: Legal Theory in Sociological Perspective*. Oxford: Clarendon Press.

Daston, L. & Gallison, P. (1992) "The Image of Objectivity". *Representations* 40: 81–128.

Deleuze, G. (1990) *Negotiations 1979–1990*. New York: Columbia University Press.

(1993) *The Fold: Leibniz and the Baroque*. Minnesota: University of Minnesota Press.

Deleuze, G. & Guattari, F. (1986) *Kafka: Towards a Minor Literature*. Minneapolis: University of Minnesota Press.

Derrida, J. (1967) *Of Grammatology*. Baltimore: Johns Hopkins University Press.

(1992) *Acts of Literature*. New York & London: Routledge.

(1995) "Archive Fever: A Freudian Impression". *Diacritics* 25(2): 9–63.

Desrosières, A. (1998) *The Politics of Large Numbers: A History of Statistical Reasoning*. Cambridge: Harvard University Press.

Dewey, J. (1929) *The Quest for Certainty: A Study of the Relation of Knowledge and Action*. London: Capricorn Books.

Didion,J. (2006) *We Tell Ourselves Stories in Order to Live: Collection Nonfiction*. New York: Random House.

Dingwall, G. (2000) "Language, Law, and Power: Ethnomethodology, Conversation Analysis, and the Politics of Law and Society Studies". *Law & Social Inquiry* 25(3): 885–911.

Duncan, M. G. (2002) "'So Young and so Untender': Remorseless Children and the Expectations of the Law". *Columbia Law Review* 102(6): 1469–1526.

Dupret, B. (2007) "What Is Islamic Law? A Praxiological Answer and an Egyptian Case Study". *Theory, Culture & Society* 24(2): 79–100.

(2011) *Adjudication in Action: An Ethnomethodology of Law, Morality and Justice*. London: Routledge.

Dupret, B. & Ferrie, J. (2015) "The Practical Grammar of Law and Its Relation to Time". In: Dupret, B., Lynch, M. & Berard, T. (eds.) *Law at Work: Studies in Ethnomethods*. Oxford: Oxford University Press.

Dupret, B., Lynch, M. & Berard, T. (eds.) (2015) *Law at Work: Studies in Legal Ethnomethods*. Oxford: Oxford University Press.

Eisenberg, T., Garvey, S. P. & Wells, M. T. (1997) "But Was He Sorry? The Role of Remorse in Capital Sentencing". *Cornell Law Review* 83(6): 1599–1637.

Emerson, R. M. (1969) *Judging Delinquents: Context and Process in Juvenile Court.* Chicago: Aldine Publishing Company.

Emerson, R. M. & Paley, B. (1992) "Organizational Horizons for Complaint-Filing". In: Hawkings, K. (ed.) *The Uses of Discretion.* Oxford: Oxford University Press.

Essed, P. & Nimako, K. (2006) "Designs and (Co)-incidents: Cultures of Scholarship and Public Policy on Immigrants/Minorities in the Netherlands". *International Journal of Comparative Sociology* 47: 281–312.

Everett, R. S. & Nienstedt, B. C. (1999) "Race, Remorse, and Sentence Reduction: Is Saying You're Sorry Enough?". *Justice Quarterly* 16: 99–122.

Ewenstein, B. & Whyte, J. (2009) "Knowledge Practices in Design: The Role of Visual Representations as 'Epistemic Objects'". *Organization Studies* 30(1): 7–30.

Ewick, P. & Silbey, S. S. (1995) "Subversive Stories and Hegemonic Tales: Toward a Sociology of Narrative". *Law & Society Review* 29(2): 197–226.

Fanon, F. (1956) *Racism and Culture.* Presence Africaine.

Fine, R. (2002) "Marxism and the Social Theory of Law". In: Banakar, R. & Travers, M. (eds.) *An Introduction to Law and Social Theory.* Oxford: Hart.

Fitzpatrick, P. (1992) *The Mythology of Modern Law.* London: Routledge.

Foucault, M. (1977) *Discipline and Punish: The Birth of the Prison.* New York: Pantheon Books.

(2004) *Security, Territory, Population: Lectures at the Collège de France, 1977–1978.* New York: Picador.

Fraenckel, B., Pontille, D., Collard, D. & Deharo, G. (2010) *Le Travail des Huissiers, Transformations d'un Métier de l'Ecrit.* Toulouse: Octarès editions.

Fuchs, S. & Ward, S. (1994) "What Is Deconstruction, and Where and When Does It Take Place? Making Facts in Science, Building Cases in Law". *American Sociological Review* 59: 481–500.

Garfinkel, H. (1956) "The Conditions of Successful Status Degradation Ceremonies". *American Journal of Sociology* 61(5): 420–424.

(1967) *Studies in Ethnomethodology.* Upper Saddle River: Prentice Hall.

(2002) *Ethnomethodology's Program: Working Out Durkheim's Aphorism.* Lanham: Rowman & Littlefield.

Geschiere, P. (2009) *The Perils of Belonging: Autochthony, Citizenship, and Exclusion in Africa and Europe.* Chicago: University of Chicago Press.

Geschiere, P. & Jackson, S. (2006) "Autochthony and the Crisis of Citizenship: Democratization, Decentralization, and the Politics of Belonging". *African Studies Review* 49(2): 1–14.

Gibson, J. J. (1979) *The Ecological Approach to Visual Perception.* Boston: Houghton Mifflin.

Gieryn, T. F. (1983) "Boundary-Work and the Demarcation of Science from Non-Science: Strains and Interests in Professional Ideologies of Scientists". *American Sociological Review* 48(6): 781–795.

Goffman, E. (1956) "Conditions of Successful Status Degradation Ceremonies" *American Journal of Sociology* 61(5): 420–424.

(1959) *The Presentation of Self in Everyday Life*. New York: Anchor Books.

Goodman, N. (1978) *Ways of Worldmaking*. Cambridge: Hackett Publishing Company.

Goodwin, C. (1994) "Professional Vision". *American Anthropologist* 96(3): 606–633.

Goody, J. (1986) *The Logic of Writing and the Organisation of Society*. Cambridge: Cambridge University Press.

Grabham, E. (2011) "Doing Things with Time: Flexibility, Adaptability, and Elasticity in UK Equality Cases". *Canadian Journal of Law and Society* 26 (3): 485–508.

(2014) "The Strange Temporalities of Work Life-Balance Law". *feminists@law* 4 (1): 1–11.

Graeber, D. (2015) *The Utopia of Rules: On Technology, Stupidity, and the Secret Joys of Bureaucracy*. Brooklyn and London: Melville House.

Haan, W. de & Hielkema, J. (2005) "Tekenen van Berouw". *Nederlands Juristenblad* 80(19): 982–984.

Halliday, S., Burns, N., Hutton, N., McNeil, F. & Tata, C. (2008) "Shadow Writing and Participant Observation: A Study of Criminal Justice Social Work Around Sentencing". *Journal of Law and Society* 35(2): 189–213.

Halpern, O. (2014) *Beautiful Data: A History of Vision and Reason since 1945*. Durham: Duke University Press.

Hannah-Moffat, K. & Maurutto, P. (2010) "Restructuring Pre-sentence Reports. Race, Risk, and the PSR". *Punishment and Society* 12(3): 262–286.

Haraway, D. (1988) "Situated Knowledges: The Science Question in Feminism and the Privilige of Partial Perspective". *Feminist Studies* 14(3): 575–599.

(2016) *Staying with the Trouble: Making Kin in the Chthulucene*. Durham: Duke University Press.

Harper, R. P. (1998) *Inside the IMF: An Ethnography of Documents, Technology and Organisational Action*. Orlando: Academic Press.

Hart, H. L. A. (1958) "Positivism and the Separation of Law and Morals". *Harvard Law Review* 71(4): 593–629.

(1994 [1961]) *The Concept of Law*. Oxford: Oxford University Press.

Hartendorp, R. C. & Wagenaar, H. (2004) "De Praktische Rechter. De Opmerkelijke Relevantie van Paul Scholten voor een Eigentijdse Rechtsvindingstheorie". *Netherlands Journal of Legal Philosophy* 1: 60–89.

Hasenfeld, Y. (1972) "People Processing Organizations: An Exchange Approach". *American Sociological Review* 37: 256–263.

Hawkins, K. (ed.) (1992) *The Uses of Discretion*. Oxford: Oxford University Press.

Heath, C., Knoblauch, H. & Luff, P. (2000) "Technology and Social Interaction: The Emergence of 'Workplace Studies'". *British Journal of Sociology* 51(2): 299–320.

Heidegger, M. (1962) *Being and Time*. New York: University of New York Press.

Heritage, J. (1985) "Analyzing News Interviews: Aspects of the Production of Talk for an Overhearing Audience". In: Dijk, T. A. (ed.) *Handbook of Discourse Analysis*. New York: Academic Press.

Hirschauer, S. (2006) "Putting Things into Words. Ethnographic Description and the Silence of the Social". *Human Studies* 29(4): 413–441.

Houtem, H. van. (2010) "Waiting Before the Law: Kafka on the Border". *Social and Legal Studies* 19(3): 285–297.

Hull, M. (2003) "The File: Agency, Authority, and Autography in a Pakistan Bureaucracy". *Language and Communication* 23(3–4): 287–314.

(2012) "Documents and Bureaucracy". *Annual Review of Anthropology* 41: 251–267.

Hunt, A. (1983) "Behavioral Sociology of Law: A Critique of Donald Black". *Journal of Law and Society* 10(1): 19–46.

(2002) "The Problematisation of Law in Classical Social Theory". In: Banakar, R. & Travers, M. (eds.) *Law and Social Theory*. Oxford: Hart Publishing.

Hutchins, E. (1995) *Cognition in the Wild*. Cambridge: MIT University Press.

Hutton, N. (2013) "From Intuition to Database: Translating Justice". *Theoretical Criminology* 17(1): 109–128.

Ingold, T. (2006) "Up, Across and Along". *Place and Location: Studies in Environmental Aesthetics and Semiotics* 5: 21–36.

(2007) *Being Alive: Essays on Movement, Knowledge and Description*. London: Routledge.

Ingold, T. & Vergunst, J. (eds.) (2008) *Ways of Walking: Ethnography and Practice on Foot*. London: Routledge.

Jackson, B. S. (1988) *Law, Fact and Narrative Coherence*. Liverpool: Deborah Charles Publications.

(1990) "Narrative Theories and Legal Discourse". In: Nash, C. (ed.) *Narrative in Culture*. London: Routledge.

(1996) "'Anchored Narratives' and the Interface of Law, Psychology and Semiotics". *Legal and Criminal Psychology* 1: 17–45.

James, W. (1995 [1907]) *Pragmatism*. Cambridge: Harvard University Press.

(1909) *The Meaning of Truth*. Cambridge: Harvard University Press.

(1911) *Some Problems of Philosophy*. Cambridge: Harvard University Press.

Jasanoff, S. (2007) "Making Order: Law and Science in Action". In: Hackett, E. J., Amsterdamska, O., Lynch, M. & Wajcman, J. (eds.) *The Handbook of Science and Technology Studies*. Cambridge: The MIT Press.

Kafka, F. (1924) *The Trial*. Berlin: Verlag Die Schmiede.

Kelsen, H. (1960) *The Pure Theory of Law*. Vienna: Deuticke.

(1981) "On the Basis of Legal Validity". *American Journal of Jurisprudence* 26: 178–189.

Kirsch, D. (1995) "The Intelligent Use of Space". *Artificial Intelligence* 73: 31–68.

Komter, M. (1994) "Accusations and Defenses in Courtroom Interaction". *Discourse & Society* 5(2): 165–187.

(2000) "The Power of Legal Language: The Significance of Small Activities for Large Problems". *Semiotica* 131(3/4): 415–428.

(2002) "The Suspect's Own Words: The Treatment of Written Statements in Dutch Courtrooms". *International Journal of Speech, Language, and the Law* 9 (2): 168–192.

(2003) "The Interactional Dynamics of Eliciting a Confession in a Dutch Police Interrogation". *Research on Language and Social Interaction* 36(4): 433–470.

(2006) "From Talk to Text: The Interactional Construction of a Police Record". *Research on Language and Social Interaction* 39(3): 201–228.

(2019) *The Suspect's Statement: Talk and Text in The Criminal Process*. Cambridge: Cambridge University Press.

Kozin, A. (2007) "The Legal File: Folding Law, Folded Law". *International Journal for the Semiotics of Law* 20(1): 191–216.

Krebbeckx, W., Spronk, R. & M'charek, A. (2016) "Ethnicizing Sexuality: An Analysis of Research Practices in the Netherlands". *Ethnic and Racial Studies* 40(4): 636–655.

Lanzara, G. F. (2009) "Reshaping Practice Across Media: Material Mediation, Medium Specificity and Practical Knowledge in Judicial Work". *Organization Studies* 30(12): 1369–1390.

Latour, B. (1986) "Visualization and Cognition: Thinking with Eyes and Hands". In: Lynch, M. & Woolgar, S. (eds.) *Knowledge and Society: Studies in the Sociology of Culture Past and Present*, Vol. 6, Greenwich: JAI Press.

(1999) *Pandora's Hope: Essays on the Reality of Science Studies*. Cambridge: Harvard University Press.

(2005) *Reassembling the Social*. Oxford: Oxford University Press.

(2010) *The Making of Law: An Ethnography of the Conseil d'État*. Cambridge: Polity Press.

(2013) *An Inquiry into Modes of Existence*. Cambridge: Harvard University Press.

Latour, B. & Serres, M. (1995) *Conversations on Science, Culture, and Time*. Ann Arbor: University of Michigan Press.

Latour, B. & Woolgar, S. (1979) *Laboratory Life: The Construction of Scientific Facts*. New Jersey: Princeton University Press.

Law, J. (2009) "Collateral Realities". December 2009 edition. Retrieved from www.heterogeneities.net/publications/Law2009CollateralRealities.pdf.

Lehn, D. vom, Heath, C. & Hindmarsh, J. (2001) "Exhibiting Interaction: Conduct and Collaboration in Museums and Galleries". *Symbolic Interaction* 24(2): 189–216.

Levi-Strauss, C. (1961) *Sad Tropics*. New York: Criterion Books.

Lipsky, M. (1980) *Street-Level Bureaucracy: Dilemmas of the Individual in Public Services*. New York: Russell Sage.

Luff, P., Heath, C. & Greatbatch, D. (1992) "Tasks-in-Interaction: Paper and Screen-based Documentation in Collaborative Activity". *Proceedings of the Conference on Computer Supported Collaborative Work*. Toronto, ON, 163–170.

Luhmann, N. (1994) "'What Is the Case?' and 'What Lies Behind it?' The Two Sociologies and the Theory of Society". *Sociological Theory* 12(2): 126–139.

(2004) *Law As a Social System*. Oxford: Oxford University Press.

Lynch, M. (1993) *Scientific Practice and Ordinary Action*. Cambridge: Cambridge University Press.

(1997) "Review: Theorizing Practice". *Human Studies* 20(3): 335–344.

(1998) "Waste Managers? The New Penology, Crime Fighting, and Parole Agent Identity". *Law & Society Review* 32(4): 839–870.

Lynch, M. & Bogen, D. (1996) *The Spectacle of History: Speech, Text, and Memory at the Iran Contra Hearings*. Durham: Duke University Press.

Lynch, M. & McNally, R. (2005) "Chains of Custody: Representation, Visualization and Accountability in the Processing of DNA Evidence". *Communication & Cognition* 38(3/4): 297–318.

Lynch, M., Cole, S. A., McNally, R. & Jordan, K. (2008) *Truth Machine: The Contentious History of DNA Fingerprinting*. Chicago: University of Chicago Press.

Malinowski, B. (1922) *Argonauts of the Western Pacific*. London: Routledge & Sons.

Marx, K. (1887) *Capital: A Critique of Political Economy*. New York: International Publishers.

Martell, J. (2010) "Remorse and the Production of Truth". *Punishment and Society* 12(4): 414–437.

Mascini, P. & Houtman, D. (2002) "Resocialisatie als Tegenpool van Repressie: Een Springlevend Criminologisch Misverstand". *Tijdschrift voor Criminologie* 44 (1): 25–45.

Mascini, P., van Oorschot, I., Weenink, D., and Schippers, G. (2016) "Understanding Judges Sentencing Choice as Interpretative Work: An Exploratory Study in a Dutch Police Court." *Recht der Werkelijkheid* 37(1): 32–49.

Matoesian, G. (1993) *Reproducing Rape: Domination Through Talk in the Courtroom*. Cambridge: Polity Press.

Maurutto, P. & Hannah-Moffat, K. (2006) "Assembling Risk and the Restructuring of Penal Control". *The British Journal of Criminology* 46(3): 438–454.

Mazzarella, W. (2006) "Internet X-Ray: E-governance, Transparency, and the Politics of Immediation in India". *Public Culture* 18(3): 473–505.

M'charek, A. (2013) "Beyond Fact or Fiction: On the Materiality of Race in Practice". *Cultural Anthropology* 28(3): 420–442.

(2014) "Race, Time, and Folded Objects: The HeLa Error". *Theory, Culture and Society* 31(6): 29–56.

M'charek, A., Hagendijk, R. & Prainsack, B. (2013) "Equal Before the Law: on the Machinery of Sameness in Forensic DNA Practice". *Science, Technology & Human Values* 38(4): 542–565.

M'charek, A and van Oorschot, I. (2019) "What About Race?". In: Blok, A., Faris, I. and Roberts, C. (eds.) *The Routledge Companion to Actor Network-Theory*. London: Routledge.

M'charek, A. & Skinner, D. (2014) "Topologies of Race: Doing Territory, Population and Identity in Europe". *Science, Technology & Human Values* 39(4): 468–487.

M'charek, A., Schramm, K. & Skinner, D. (2014) "Technologies of Belonging: The Absent Presence of Race in Europe". *Science, Technology & Human Values* 39 (4): 459–467.

Mears, P. D. (1998) "The Sociology of Sentencing: Reconceptualizing Decisionmaking Processes and Outcomes". *Law & Society Review* 32(3): 667–724.

Messick, B. (1989) "Just Writing: Paradox and Political Economy in Yemeni Legal Documents". *Cultural Anthropology* 4(1): 26–50.

(1993) *The Calligraphic State. Textual Domination and History in a Muslim Society*. Los Angeles: University of California Press.

Mills, C. W. (1959) *The Sociological Imagination*. Oxford: Oxford University Press.

Millers, W. B. (1958) "Lower Class Culture as Generating Milieu of Gang Delinquency". *Journal of Social Issues* 14(3): 5–19.

Mirzoeff, N. (2015) *How to See the World*. New York: Pelican.

Mitchell, W. J. T. (2012) *Seeing Through Race*. Cambridge: Harvard University Press.

Mnookin, J. L. (1998) "The Image of Truth: Photographic Evidence and the Power of Analogy". *Yale Journal of Law & the Humanities* 10(1): 1–74.

Mol, A. (1999) "Ontological Politics. A Word and Some Questions". *The Sociological Review* 47(1): 74–89.

(2002) *The Body Multiple: Ontology in Medical Practice*. Durham: Duke University Press.

Morton, T. (2013) *Hyper-Objects: Philosophy and Ecology After the End of the World*. Minneapolis: University of Minnesota Press.

Mundy, M. & Pottage, R. A. (eds.) (2004) *Law, Anthropology, and the Constitution of the Social: Making Persons and Things*. Cambridge: Cambridge University Press.

Nietzsche, F. (1974 [1882]) *The Gay Science*. New York: Vintage Books.

Oorschot, I. van (2014a) "Seeing the Case Clearly: File-Work, Material Mediation, and Visualizing Practices in a Dutch Criminal Court". *Symbolic Interaction* 37 (4): 439–457.

(2014b) "Het Dossier-in-Actie: Vouw- en Ontvouwpraktijken in Juridische Waarheidsvinding". *Sociologie* 10(3/4): 301–318.

(2018) "Doing Times, Doing Truths". In Grabham, E. & Beynon Jones, S. (eds.) *Regulating Time*. London: Routledge Social Justice Series.

(2020) "Culture, Milieu, Phenotype: Articulating Race in Judicial Sense-Making Practice" in *Social & Legal Studies*, first published online, March 11, 2020, see https://journals.sagepub.com/doi/full/10.1177/0964663920907992.

Oorschot, I. van & Schinkel, W. (2015) "The Legal Case File as Border Object: On Self-Reference and Other-Reference in Criminal Law". *Journal of Law and Society* 42(4): 499–527.

Oorschot, I. van & Mascini, P. (2018) "Cases under Construction" in Van Boom, W. H., Desmet, P. & Mascini, P. (eds.) *Empirical Legal Research in Action: Reflections on Methods and Their Consequences*. Cheltenham: Edward Elgar Publishing.

Oorschot, I. van, Mascini, P. & Weenink, D. (2017) "Remorse in Context(s): A Qualitative Exploration of Remorse and Its Consequences". *Social & Legal Studies* 26(3): 359–377.

Orlikowski, W. J. (2006) "Material Knowing: The Scaffolding of Human Knowledgeability". *European Journal of Information Systems* 15(5): 460–466.

Osborne, T. (1999) "The Ordinariness of the Archive". *History of the Human Sciences* 12(2): 51–64.

Otte, R. (2015) *Het Proces. Strafrecht in de Praktijk*. Amsterdam: Boom.

Özdil, Z. (2014) "'Racism Is an American Problem': Dutch Exceptionalism and Its Politics of Denial". *Frame* 27(2): 49–64.

Philoppopoulos-Mihalopulos, A. (2014) "Critical Autopoiesis and the Materiality of Law". *International Journal of Semiotics of Law* 27(2): 165–177.

Possner, R. A. (2008) *How Judges Think*. Cambridge: Harvard University Press.

Pottage, A. (2012) "The Materiality of What?". *Journal of Law and Society* 39(1): 167–183.

(2014) "Law After Anthropology: Object and Technique in Roman Law". *Theory, Culture & Society* 31(2–3): 147–166.

Pound, R. (1910) "Law in Books and Law in Action". *American Law Review* 44(1): 12–36.

Pratt, M. L. (1986) "Fieldwork in Common Places". In: Clifford, J. & Marcus, G. E. (eds.) *Writing Culture. The Poetics and Politics of Ethnography*. Los Angeles: University of California Press.

Priel, D. (2013) "The Scientific Model of Jurisprudence". In: Beltrán, J. F., Moreso, J. J. & Papayannis, D. M. (eds.) *Neutrality and Theory of Law*. Dordrecht: Springer International Publishing.

Prior, L. (2008) "Repositioning Documents in Social Research". *Sociology* 42(5): 821–836.

Proeve, M. & Tudor, S. (2010) *Remorse. Psychological and Jurisprudential Perspectives*. London: Routledge.

Reekum, R. van (2014) *Out of Character: Debating Dutchness, Narrating Citizenship*. PhD-thesis. University of Amsterdam.

Ricoeur, P. (1992) *Oneself as Another*. Chicago: University of Chicago Press.

Riles, A. (2005) "A New Agenda for the Cultural Study of law: Taking on the Technicalities". *Buffalo Law Review* 53: 973–1033.

(2008) *Documents: Artifacts of Modern Knowledge*. Ann Arbor: University of Michigan Press

Rudzinski, A. W. (1976) "Petrażycki's Significance for Contemporary Legal and Moral Theory". *American Journal of Jurisprudence* 21: 107–130.

Schatzki, T. R., Cetina, K. K. & Savigny, E. von (2001) *The Practice Turn in Contemporary Theory*. New York: Routledge.

Scheffer, T. (2004) "Materialities of Legal Proceedings". *International Journal for Semiotics of Law* 17(4): 356–389.

(2005) "Courses of Mobilisation. Writing Systematic Micro-histories on Legal Discourse". In: Travers, M & Banakar, R. (eds.) *Theory and Method in Socio-Legal Research*. Oxford: Hart Publishing, 75–89.

(2006) "The Microformation of Criminal Defense: on the Lawyer's Notes, Speech Production, and the Field of Presence". *Research on Language and Social Interaction* 39(3): 303–342.

(2007) "File Work, Legal Care, and Professional Habitus: An Ethnographic Reflection on Different Styles of Advocacy". *International Journal of the Legal Profession* 14(1): 57–81.

(2010) *Adversarial Case-Making. An Ethnography of English Crown Court Procedure*. Leiden: Brill.

Schegloff, E. A. (1997) "Whose Text? Whose Context?". *Discourse & Society* 8(2): 165–187.

Schinkel, W. (2015) "The Sociologist and the State. An Assessment of Pierre Bourdieu's Sociology". *British Journal of Sociology* 66(2): 215–235.

(2014) *Over Nut en Nadeel van een Sociologie voor het Leven*. Amsterdam: Uitgeverij Boom.

Scholten, P. (2010) *Dorsten naar Gerechtigheid*. Deventer: Wolters Kluwer.

Scott, J. C. (1998) *Seeing Like a State: How Certain Schemes to Improve the Human Condition Have Failed*. New Haven: Yale University Press.

Sellen, A. J. & Harper, R. H. R. (2003) *The Myth of the Paperless Office*. Cambridge: MIT University Press.

Shapiro, S. J. (2006) "What Is the Internal Point of View?". *Yale Law School Faculty Scholarship Series*. Paper 1336.

Smith, D. E. (1984) "Textually Mediated Social Organization". *International Social Science Journal* 36(1): 59–75.

Spaak, T. (2005) "Kelsen and Hart on the Normativity of Law". In: Wahlgren, P. (ed.) *Perspectives on Jurisprudence: Essays in Honour of Jes Bjarup*. Stockholm: Institute for Scandinavian Law.

Spivak, G. C. (1988) "Can the Subaltern Speak?". In: Nelson, C. & Grossberg, L. (eds.) *Marxism and the Interpretation of Culture*. Urbana: University of Illinois Press.

Spohn, C. C. (2000) "Thirty Years of Sentencing Reform: The Quest for a Racially Neutral Sentencing Process". *Policies, Processes, and Decisions of the Criminal Justice System* 3: 427–501.

Star S. L. (1999) "An Ethnography of Infrastructure". *American Behavioral Scientist* 43(3): 377–391.

Steffensmeier, D., Ulmer, J. & Kramer, J. (1998) "The Interaction of Race, Gender, and Age in Criminal Sentencing: The Punishment Cost of being Young, Black, and Male". *Criminology* 36(4): 763–798.

Stein, Gertrude. (1937). *Everybody's Autobiography*. New York: Random House.

Stengers, I. (2005) "Introductory Notes on an Ecology of Practices". *Cultural Studies Review* 11(1): 183–196.

(2015) *In Catastrophic Times: Resisting the Coming Barbarism*. London: Open Humanities Press.

Suchman, L. (2002) "Located Accountabilities in Technology Production". *Scandinavian Journal of Information Systems* 14(2): 91–105.

Sudnow, D. (1965) "Normal Crimes: Sociological Features of the Penal Code in a Public Defender Office". *Social Problems* 12(3): 255–276.

Sundby, S. E. (1998) "The Capital Jury and Absolution: The Intersection of Trial Strategy, Remorse and the Death Penalty". *Cornell Law Review* 83(4): 1557–1598.

Tamanaha, B. Z. (2006) "A Socio-Legal Methodology for the Internal/External Distinction: Jurisprudential Implications". *Fordham Law Review* 75(3): 1255–1274.

Tata, C. (1997) "Conceptions and Representations of the Sentencing Decision Process". *Journal of Law and Society* 24(3): 395–420.

(2007) "Sentencing as Craftwork and the Binary Epistemologies of the Discretionary Decision Process". *Social and Legal Studies* 16: 1–24.

(2020) *Sentencing: A Social Process. Rethinking Research and Policy*. London: Palgrave MacMillan.

Tata, C., Burns, N., Halliday, S., Hutton, N. & McNeill, F. (2008) "Assisting and Advising the Sentencing Decision Process: The Pursuit of 'Quality' in Pre-Sentence Reports". *British Journal of Criminology* 48(6): 835–855.

Teubner, G. (1989) "How the Law Thinks: Towards a Constructivist Epistemology of Law". *Law & Society Review* 23(5): 727–758.

Thomas, W. I. & Thomas, D. S. (1928) *The Child in America: Behavior Problems and Programs*. New York: Knopf.

Thomas, Y. (1977) "Acte, Agent, Societe: Sur l'Homme Coupable dans la Pensée Juridique Romaine". *Archives de la Philosophie du Droit* 22: 67–85.

Tombs, J. & Jagger, E. (2006) "Denying Responsibility". *British Journal of Criminology* 46(5): 803–821.

Toom, V. (2010) *Dragers van Waarheid: Normatieve Aspecten van 20 Jaar Forensisch DNA Onderzoek in Nederland* (PhD Thesis). FMG: Amsterdam Institute for Social Science Research.

Travers, M. (1997) *The Reality of Law: Work and Talk in a Firm of Criminal Lawyers*. Brookfield: Ashgate.

Travers, M. & Manzo, J. E. (1997) *Law in Action: Ethnomethodological and Conversation Analytical Approaches to Law*. Aldershot: Ashgate.

Tuori, K. (2006) "Self-Description and External Description of the Law". *No Foundations: Journal of Extreme Legal Positivism* 2: 27–43.

Valverde, M. (2008) *Law's Dream of a Common Knowledge*. Princeton: Princeton University Press.

Vinx, L. (2012) "Austin, Kelsen, and the Model of Sovereignty: Notes of the History of Modern Legal Positivism". In: Freeman, M. & Mindus, P. (eds.) *The Legacy of John Austin's Jurisprudence*. Dordrecht: Springer International Publishing.

Vismann, C. (2008) *Files: Law and Media Technology*. Stanford: Stanford University Press.

Waldron, J. (1996) "Can There Be a Democratic Jurisprudence?". *New York University Public Law and Legal Theory Working Papers* 97.

Ward, G. H. (2006) "Sentencing Without Remorse". *Loyola University Chicago Law Journal* 38(1): 131–167.

Weber, M. (1978 [1922]) *Economy and Society*. Berkeley: University of California Press.

Weisman, R. (2004) "Showing Remorse: Reflections on the Gap Between Expression and Attribution in Cases of Wrongful Conviction". *Canadian Journal of Criminology and Criminal Justice* 46(2): 121–138.

(2009) "Being and Doing: The Judicial Use of Remorse to Construct Character and Community". *Social and Legal Studies* 18(1): 47–69.

(2014) *Showing Remorse. Law and the Social Control of Emotion*. London: Routledge.

Wekker, G. (2016) *White Innocence*. Durham: Duke University Press.

Wermink, G., Keijser, J. de & Schuyt, P. (2012a) "Verschillen in Straftoemeting in Soortgelijke Zaken: Een Kwalitatief Onderzoek naar de Rol van Specifieke Kenmerken van de Dader". *Nederlands Juristenblad* 87(11): 726–733.

Wermink, G., Keijser, J. de & Schuyt, P. (2012b) "Naschrift". *Nederlands Juristenblad* 87(17): 1193.

Whitehead, A. N. (1953) *Science in the Modern World*. Cambridge: Cambridge University Press.

Wittgenstein, L. (2001 [1958]) *Philosophical Investigations*. Oxford: Wiley-Blackwell.

Wood, L. A. & MacMartin, C. (2007) "Constructing Remorse. Judges' Sentencing Decisions in Child Sexual Assault Cases". *Journal of Language and Social Psychology* 26(4): 343–362.

Yanow, D. (2003) *Constructing "Race" and "Ethnicity" in America. Category-Making in Public Policy and Administration*. New York: Sharpe.

Zatz, M. (1987) "The Changing Forms of Racial/Ethnic Biases in Sentencing". *Journal of Research in Crime and Delinquency* 24: 69–92.

Newspaper Articles / Blogs

Algemeen Dagblad (2012, March 14) "Onderzoek: Met Buitenlands Uiterlijk eerder de Cel in". Retrieved from www.ad.nl/binnenland/onderzoek-met-buitenlands-uiterlijk-eerder-de-cel-in~a36ad6f6/.

FHJ Factcheck (2012, April 17) "Eerder de Cel in met Buitenlands Uiterlijk?". Retrieved from https://fhjfactcheck.wordpress.com/2012/04/17/eerder-de-cel-in-metbuitenlands-uiterlijk/.

NRC Handelsblad (2012, March 14) "Verdachte met een Buitenlands Uiterlijk krijgt eerder Celstraf". Retrieved from www.nrc.nl/nieuws/2012/03/14/verdachte-met-buitenlands-uiterlijk-krijgt-eerder-celstraf-a1446837.

NRC Handelsblad (2012, March 15) "De Intuïtieve Rechter Betrapt" Retrieved from www.nrc.nl/nieuws/2012/03/15/de-intuitieve-rechter-betrapt-1081541-a276449.

NRC Handelsblad (2012, March 31) "Statistiek in de Krant: Kansen zijn iets Anders dan Kansverhoudingen". Retrieved from www.nrc.nl/nieuws/2012/03/30/statistiek-in-de-krant-kansen-zijn-iets-anders-dan-kansverhoudingen-a1480848.

Reports / Policy Documents

De Rechtspraak (2014) Evaluatie Pilot 'Forensische Ondersteuning' bij gerechtshoven. Een Vraagbaak en Ondersteuning bij Forensische Dossiers in het Strafrechtelijk Proces. Den Haag.

De Rechtspraak (2015) Etnisch Gerelateerde Verschillen in Straftoemeting. Research Memoranda 10(1). Wermink, H, Wingerden, S. van, Wilsem, J. van & Nieuwbeerta, P. Den Haag.

De Rechtspraak (2016) Orientatiepunten voor Straftoemeting en LOVS Afspraken. Den Haag.

Kamerstukken II 2011/12 Vragen van het lid [...] aan de Minister van Veiligheid en Justitie over Verschillen in Straftoemeting in Soortgelijke Zaken.

Ingezonden 16 en 20 maart 2012.Vraagnummers 2012Z05320, 2012Z05321 en 2012Z05598.

Ministerie van Veiligheid en Justitie (2010) Wetenschappelijk Onderzoeks- en Documentatie Centrum (WODC). De Competentie van Enkelvoudige Kamers in Strafzaken Verruimd: Cijfermatige Gegevens en Ervaringen van de Rechtspraktijk. WODC-2010-Cahier 3.

Ministerie van Veiligheid en Justitie (2012) Beantwoording 3 Sets Kamervragen over het Bericht dat Verdachten met een Buitenlands Uiterlijk Strenger worden Gestraft. Brief van 3 april aan de Voorzitter van de Tweede Kamer. Kenmerk 246252: 1–6.

Other

Wermink, H. (2016, June 27) Personal Correspondence with the Author.

INDEX

CAMBRIDGE STUDIES IN LAW AND SOCIETY

Books in the Series

Diseases of the Will: Alcohol and the Dilemmas of Freedom
Mariana Valverde

The Politics of Truth and Reconciliation in South Africa: Legitimizing the Post-Apartheid State Richard A. Wilson

Modernism and the Grounds of Law
Peter Fitzpatrick

Unemployment and Government: Genealogies of the Social
William Walters

Autonomy and Ethnicity: Negotiating Competing Claims in Multi-Ethnic States
Yash Ghai

Constituting Democracy: Law, Globalism and South Africa's Political Reconstruction
Heinz Klug

The Ritual of Rights in Japan: Law, Society, and Health Policy
Eric A. Feldman

Governing Morals: A Social History of Moral Regulation Alan Hunt

The Colonies of Law: Colonialism, Zionism and Law in Early Mandate Palestine
Ronen Shamir

Law and Nature
David Delaney

Social Citizenship and Workfare in the United States and Western Europe: The Paradox of Inclusion
Joel F. Handler

Law, Anthropology, and the Constitution of the Social: Making Persons and Things
Edited by Alain Pottage and Martha Mundy

Judicial Review and Bureaucratic Impact: International and Interdisciplinary Perspectives
Edited by Marc Hertogh and Simon Halliday

Immigrants at the Margins: Law, Race, and Exclusion in Southern Europe
Kitty Calavita

Lawyers and Regulation: The Politics of the Administrative Process
Patrick Schmidt

Law and Globalization from Below: Toward a Cosmopolitan Legality
Edited by Boaventura de Sousa Santos and Cesar A. Rodriguez-Garavito

Public Accountability: Designs, Dilemmas and Experiences
Edited by Michael W. Dowdle

Law, Violence and Sovereignty Among West Bank Palestinians
Tobias Kelly

Legal Reform and Administrative Detention Powers in China
Sarah Biddulph

The Practice of Human Rights: Tracking Law Between the Global and the Local
Edited by Mark Goodale and Sally Engle Merry

Judges beyond Politics in Democracy and Dictatorship: Lessons from Chile
Lisa Hilbink

Paths to International Justice: Social and Legal Perspectives
Edited by Marie-Bénédicte Dembour and Tobias Kelly

Law and Society in Vietnam: The Transition from Socialism in Comparative Perspective
Mark Sidel

Constitutionalizing Economic Globalization: Investment Rules and Democracy's Promise
David Schneiderman

The New World Trade Organization Knowledge Agreements: 2nd Edition
Christopher Arup

Justice and Reconciliation in Post-Apartheid South Africa
Edited by François du Bois and Antje du Bois-Pedain

Militarization and Violence Against Women in Conflict Zones in the Middle East: A Palestinian Case-Study
Nadera Shalhoub-Kevorkian

Child Pornography and Sexual Grooming: Legal and Societal Responses
Suzanne Ost

Darfur and the Crime of Genocide
John Hagan and Wenona Rymond-Richmond

Fictions of Justice: The International Criminal Court and the Challenge of Legal Pluralism in Sub-Saharan Africa
Kamari Maxine Clarke

Conducting Law and Society Research: Reflections on Methods and Practices
Simon Halliday and Patrick Schmidt

Planted Flags: Trees, Land, and Law in Israel/Palestine
Irus Braverman

Culture Under Cross-Examination: International Justice and the Special Court for Sierra Leone
Tim Kelsall

Cultures of Legality: Judicialization and Political Activism in Latin America
Javier Couso, Alexandra Huneeus, and Rachel Sieder

Courting Democracy in Bosnia and Herzegovina: The Hague Tribunal's Impact in a Postwar State
Lara J. Nettelfield

The Gacaca Courts, Post-Genocide Justice and Reconciliation in Rwanda: Justice Without Lawyers
Phil Clark

Law, Society, and History: Themes in the Legal Sociology and Legal History of Lawrence M. Friedman
Edited by Robert W. Gordon and Morton J. Horwitz

After Abu Ghraib: Exploring Human Rights in America and the Middle East
Shadi Mokhtari

Adjudication in Religious Family Laws: Cultural Accommodation, Legal Pluralism, and Gender Equality in India
Gopika Solanki

Water on Tap: Rights and Regulation in the Transnational Governance of Urban Water Services
Bronwen Morgan

Elements of Moral Cognition: Rawls' Linguistic Analogy and the Cognitive Science of Moral and Legal Judgment
John Mikhail

Mitigation and Aggravation at Sentencing
Edited by Julian V. Roberts

Institutional Inequality and the Mobilization of the Family and Medical Leave Act: Rights on Leave
Catherine R. Albiston

Authoritarian Rule of Law: Legislation, Discourse and Legitimacy in Singapore
Jothie Rajah

Law and Development and the Global Discourses of Legal Transfers
Edited by John Gillespie and Pip Nicholson

Law Against the State: Ethnographic Forays into Law's Transformations
Edited by Julia Eckert, Brian Donahoe, Christian Strümpell and Zerrin Özlem Biner

Transnational Legal Ordering and State Change
Edited by Gregory C. Shaffer

Legal Mobilization Under Authoritarianism: The Case of Post-Colonial Hong Kong
Waikeung Tam

Complementarity in the Line of Fire: The Catalysing Effect of the International Criminal Court in Uganda and Sudan
Sarah M. H. Nouwen

Political and Legal Transformations of an Indonesian Polity: The Nagari from Colonisation to Decentralisation
Franz von Benda-Beckmann and Keebet von Benda-Beckmann

Pakistan's Experience with Formal Law: An Alien Justice
Osama Siddique

Human Rights Under State-Enforced Religious Family Laws in Israel, Egypt, and India
Yüksel Sezgin

Why Prison?
Edited by David Scott

Law's Fragile State: Colonial, Authoritarian, and Humanitarian Legacies in Sudan
Mark Fathi Massoud

Rights for Others: The Slow Home-Coming of Human Rights in the Netherlands
Barbara Oomen

European States and Their Muslim Citizens: The Impact of Institutions on Perceptions and Boundaries
Edited by John R. Bowen, Christophe Bertossi, Jan Willem Duyvendak, and Mona Lena Krook

Environmental Litigation in China: A Study in Political Ambivalence
Rachel E. Stern

Indigeneity and Legal Pluralism in India: Claims, Histories, Meanings
Pooja Parmar

Paper Tiger: Law, Bureaucracy and the Developmental State in Himalayan India
Nayanika Mathur

Religion, Law and Society Russell Sandberg

The Experiences of Face Veil Wearers in Europe and the Law
Edited by Eva Brems

The Contentious History of the International Bill of Human Rights
Christopher N. J. Roberts

Transnational Legal Orders
Edited by Terence C. Halliday and Gregory Shaffer

Lost in China? Law, Culture and Society in Post-1997 Hong Kong
Carol A. G. Jones

Security Theology, Surveillance and the Politics of Fear
Nadera Shalhoub-Kevorkian

Opposing the Rule of Law: How Myanmar's Courts Make Law and Order
Nick Cheesman

The Ironies of Colonial Governance: Law, Custom and Justice in Colonial India
James Jaffe

The Clinic and the Court: Law, Medicine and Anthropology
Edited by Ian Harper, Tobias Kelly, and Akshay Khanna

A World of Indicators: The Making of Government Knowledge Through Quantification
Edited by Richard Rottenburg, Sally Engle Merry, Sung-Joon Park, and Johanna Mugler

Contesting Immigration Policy in Court: Legal Activism and Its Radiating Effects in the United States and France
Leila Kawar

The Quiet Power of Indicators: Measuring Governance, Corruption, and Rule of Law
Edited by Sally Engle Merry, Kevin Davis, and Benedict Kingsbury

Investing in Authoritarian Rule: Punishment and Patronage in Rwanda's Gacaca Courts for Genocide Crimes
Anuradha Chakravarty

Contractual Knowledge: One Hundred Years of Legal Experimentation in Global Markets
Edited by Grégoire Mallard and Jérôme Sgard

Iraq and the Crimes of Aggressive War: The Legal Cynicism of Criminal Militarism
John Hagan, Joshua Kaiser, and Anna Hanson

Culture in the Domains of Law
Edited by René Provost

China and Islam: The Prophet, the Party, and Law
Matthew S. Erie

Diversity in Practice: Race, Gender, and Class in Legal and Professional Careers
Edited by Spencer Headworth and Robert Nelson

A Sociology of Constitutions: Constitutions and State Legitimacy in Historical-Sociological Perspective
Chris Thornhill

A Sociology of Transnational Constitutions: Social Foundations of the Post-National Legal Structure
Chris Thornhill

Shifting Legal Visions: Judicial Change and Human Rights Trials in Latin America
Ezequiel A. González Ocantos

The Demographic Transformations of Citizenship
Heli Askola

Criminal Defense in China: The Politics of Lawyers at Work
Sida Liu and Terence C. Halliday

Contesting Economic and Social Rights in Ireland: Constitution, State and Society, 1848–2016
Thomas Murray

Buried in the Heart: Women, Complex Victimhood and the War in Northern Uganda
Erin Baines

Palaces of Hope: The Anthropology of Global Organizations
Edited by Ronald Niezen and Maria Sapignoli

The Politics of Bureaucratic Corruption in Post-Transitional Eastern Europe
Marina Zaloznaya

Revisiting the Law and Governance of Trafficking, Forced Labor and Modern Slavery
Edited by Prabha Kotiswaran

Incitement on Trial: Prosecuting International Speech Crimes
Richard Ashby Wilson

Criminalizing Children: Welfare and the State in Australia
David McCallum

Global Lawmakers: International Organizations in the Crafting of World Markets
Susan Block-Lieb and Terence C. Halliday

Duties to Care: Dementia, Relationality and Law
Rosie Harding

Insiders, Outsiders, Injuries, and Law: Revisiting "The Oven Bird's Song"
Edited by Mary Nell Trautner

Hunting Justice: Displacement, Law, and Activism in the Kalahari
Maria Sapignoli

Injury and Injustice: The Cultural Politics of Harm and Redress
Edited by Anne Bloom, David M. Engel, and Michael McCann

Ruling Before the Law: The Politics of Legal Regimes in China and Indonesia
William Hurst

The Powers of Law: A Comparative Analysis of Sociopolitical Legal Studies
Mauricio García-Villegas

A Sociology of Justice in Russia
Edited by Marina Kurkchiyan and Agnieszka Kubal

Constituting Religion: Islam, Liberal Rights, and the Malaysian State
Tamir Moustafa

The Invention of the Passport: Surveillance, Citizenship and the State, Second Edition
John C. Torpey

Law's Trials: The Performance of Legal Institutions in the US "War on Terror"
Richard L. Abel

Law's Wars: The Fate of the Rule of Law in the US "War on Terror"
Richard L. Abel

Transforming Gender Citizenship: The Irresistible Rise of Gender Quotas in Europe
Edited by Eléonore Lépinard and Ruth Rubio-Marín

Muslim Women's Quest for Justice: Gender, Law and Activism in India
Mengia Hong Tschalaer

Children as 'Risk': Sexual Exploitation and Abuse by Children and Young People
Anne-Marie McAlinden

The Legal Process and the Promise of Justice: Studies Inspired by the Work of Malcolm Feeley
Jonathan Simon, Rosann Greenspan, Hadar Aviram

Sovereign Exchanges: Gifts, Trusts, Reparations, and Other Fetishes of International Solidarity
Grégoire Mallard

Measuring Justice: Quantitative Accountability and the National Prosecuting Authority in South Africa
Johanna Mugler

Negotiating the Power of NGOs: Women's Legal Rights in South Africa
Reem Wael

Indigenous Water Rights in Law and Regulation: Lessons from Comparative Experience
Elizabeth Jane Macpherson

The Edge of Law: Legal Geographies of a War Crimes Court
Alex Jeffrey

Everyday Justice: Law, Ethnography, and Injustice
Sandra Brunnegger

The Uncounted: Politics of Data in Global Health
Sara L. M. Davis

Transnational Legal Ordering of Criminal Justice
Gregory Shaffer and Ely Aaronson

CPSIA information can be obtained
at www.ICGtesting.com
Printed in the USA
LVHW081715260721
693678LV00002B/94

9 781108 494809